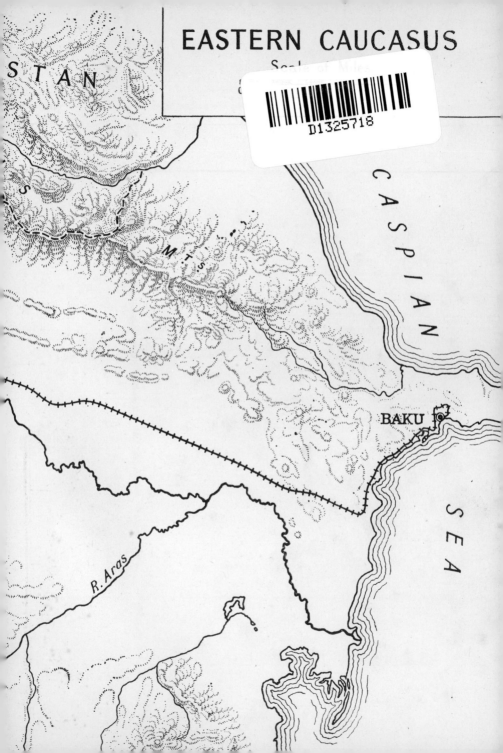

EASTERN CAUCASUS

Scale of Miles

STAN

MTS.

CASPIAN

BAKU

SEA

R. Aras

TRAVELLING NATURALIST

By the Same Author

SPORT IN PEACE AND WAR (1920)
SPORTING INTERLUDES AT GENEVA (1932)
FISHERMAN NATURALIST (1946)

Chapter Six

1. First snow on upper slopes, Caucasus.

TRAVELLING NATURALIST

by

ANTHONY BUXTON

COLLINS
ST. JAMES'S PLACE LONDON
1948

To

My Family

COPYRIGHT
PRINTED IN GREAT BRITAIN
COLLINS CLEAR-TYPE PRESS : LONDON AND GLASGOW
1948

CONTENTS

ILLUSTRATIONS
PHOTOGRAPHS

DRAWINGS

TRACKS

MAPS

PREFACE

WHY AM I, so soon after writing one book, sitting down to write another? The reason may sound inadequate but it is the best that I can give. My eldest daughter, who had not, I think, then read *Fisherman Naturalist*, said to me, while I was in pain, "With your arthritis, Daddy, why don't you sit still and write another book instead of rushing about all over the place?"

So here I sit, ransacking old diaries to see if there is anything in them that I have not said before, which can possibly interest any one else.

Perhaps it is good at these times of unpleasant news, of famine, disease, manufactured hatred and a spate of propaganda, mainly products of war, to cleanse our minds with a dose of fresh air.

Here on the Broads I can see the thirst of young people for something utterly unlike any of their war experiences. A party of young cockneys, the boys in short white ducks, and the girls in two or three coloured blobs (and so far as I could see nothing else), taking the trouble to pull a plank out of their boat to bridge a dyke. Why? To go and stroke some Suffolk Punches grazing in a marsh. A newspaper correspondent bicycling forty-four miles on a hot day in the hope of seeing something he had never seen before—a marsh harrier's nest. That's the stuff, and it will do them good—much more good than anything I can say to them. All I have done is to set down some of the things that have made and still make me happy. They are a mixed lot, picked anyhow—just stories of happy days spent some here, some far away.

This book is really a sort of sequel to *Fisherman Naturalist*, but it wanders, as its title implies, further afield. I have been told by her mother that a child of nine read *Fisherman Naturalist* from cover to cover—the nicest compliment which that book has received. Perhaps the last chapter of the present book may appeal to children. All the chapters, except the last, have geographical titles and are arranged more or less chronologically,

9

the expeditions to foreign countries coming in the order in which I made them, but the reader, who by the way is not in the least bound to stick to that order, will find himself going abroad for a spell and then coming back to England before he sets off again on his travels. On all my trips two things have accompanied me. A telescope given me by my father when I was about 12 years old and even then an old glass, and a greatcoat, covered with what once was a check strong enough to shock my family when I bought it in about 1904. Age has diminished the shock of the check but not the wear of the coat, which still withstands all weathers and has travelled thousands of miles. It has for long been entitled ' the old gal.'

There is a good deal of natural history mixed up with various forms of sport, such as fishing, hunting, shooting, stalking, tracking, etc., in different parts of this country and abroad. In this book a certain number, not very many, animals and birds get shot and not merely photographed, and it is no use pretending that I am not a predatory animal. Most people are, and to expect them to change their habits is like expecting a baboon to stop raiding gardens, or an otter to stop catching fish. I have certain principles in the matter; they are (1) that sport depends on the odds being on the side of the quarry, and the heavier the odds the better the sport, (2) that nothing should be done to interfere with creatures while they have a family in attendance too young to look after themselves. It is no use pretending that those principles fly very high, but perhaps they are better than no principles at all. Anyhow it is true that I am very fond of animals, by no means least those animals that I like hunting.

I have not included a chapter on Switzerland, not from any lack of affection or respect for one of the most charming and best-run countries, but because it would be second-hand writing: my experiences in natural history and sport in that country have been related in *Sporting Interludes at Geneva*.

My excuse for including some of my own drawings is that it is not much use talking about an animal without giving an indication of its appearance and alas I have no photographs of them taken in life, but I have where possible used photographs to check my drawings. They are nearly all copied from sketches made at the time, with the live animals in front of me. That is their only merit, if they have one, but at least it is true that there is no better way of learning an animal than by trying to draw it. I have been encouraged to put in the accounts of sporting expeditions abroad by the pleasure derived from the books written by my father the late Edward North Buxton, *Short Stalks* (two series), which to my mind give the best account of wild stalking I ever read.

My best thanks are due to the people who have provided me with photographs; their names are given under the illustrations: those without names were taken either by me or by members of my household. Special praise is due to Mr. A. A. Francis of Martham for his care and skill in producing prints from old photographs in albums and frames, whose negatives have been lost. I wish it had been possible to fit all illustrations in exactly their proper places in the text. I have tried to help readers by giving a plate or page reference to them in the text and a chapter reference on the illustrations themselves.

One

ESSEX

BOTH MY parents came from Norfolk, but settled down soon
after their marriage at Knighton, Buckhurst Hill, Essex, between
Epping and London. As much the youngest of a large family,
that was my home until I went to Geneva in 1919, and thence
to Horsey in Norfolk in 1930.

Essex is a county with two very distinct parts, the suburban,
with cockney as its language and the country districts further
North with the true Essex dialect allied to, but not the same as,
the language spoken in Norfolk and Suffolk. The fact that the
northern part of Essex has managed to keep its language is
perhaps partly due to the geography and the small number of
main roads or railways. There is a wide stretch of country
between the Liverpool Street—Cambridge railway and the
Liverpool Street—Colchester railway, in which there are no
main roads and no main railways, in which in fact nearly all
the roads were made after the fields, and conform to the ditches
bounding them: they twist about in all directions. That makes
for real country despite the proximity to London.

I mean to deal first, however, with the cockney part of the
county in which was my home, and as cockney is a favourite
language of mine, I shall say something about it. It has become
much the commonest of all the British languages and it is
spreading. The cockneys are a quick-witted people and they
show it in their language: they miss a lot out and leave it to be
inferred, and that makes it difficult for people unfamiliar with
their sense of humour to see the point of some of their stories.
Here is an illustration in a story told me by a lighterman.
"There was two coves goin' to 'ave a fight in a pub, and one of
'em never turned up. 'Orl right,' says Bill the publican, 'I'll
put on the gloves and show a bit of sport.' So 'e puts on the
gloves. 'Time,' says the referee. 'What! Not arf-past twelve,'

13

says the publican, looking round at the clock, but the other cove 'e knew what to do, 'e done it on him while 'e was a lookin' at the clock. So the publican goes artside to git a bref of air, is eye ole bein' bunged up. There he meets 'Enry Williams. ' 'Ullo, Bill,' says 'Enry, ' been fightin'?' ' No,' he says, ' I ain't. Ain't 'ad time. There's a cove in there wot as though.'"

Lightermen are very full of stories and I suppose that repartee is safe and pleasant from boat to boat. Here is another of their tales of fights. "There was two coves 'avin' a fight, and one of 'em 'it the other, didn't seem to 'it 'im very 'ard, but it cut nearly 'arf his face off. ' That's a vurry narsty crack you 'it 'im,' says the referee. ' Let's just 'ave a look inside your glove.' So 'e opens up 'is 'and and feels somefink vurry 'ard inside his glove. ' 'Ullo,' says the referee, ' what's that?' ' Oh, that,' he says, ' that's an 'orse shoe: I always carries that for *luck*.'"

My home was on the edge of Epping Forest and our wood, in which I spent much of my time, had been part of The Forest many years before it was opened to the public. It was a very beautiful wood, constantly made more beautiful by my father, who was an expert at the job, and it contained two ponds, the larger (Plate 3) near the house and the smaller one in the centre of the wood. All the wood and the ponds were bought after the death of my parents by the Forest and District Council jointly and are now again part of Epping Forest, and a very ornamental part of it, for great care is taken to preserve the rhododendrons, azaleas and daffodils planted by my father. It is the happiest possible solution—exactly what my parents and their family would have wished.

But in my home days it was private, and between the age of 8 and 18 it was there that I began to acquire a knowledge of the notes of birds. Learning the notes of birds is, in the initial stages, very hard work and I had to learn them for myself without being told—much the best way to learn anything. I can still remember the beginnings of the business, when I managed to separate a blackbird's notes from those of a song thrush and a missel thrush. Then there were the warblers: I had to stalk individual birds that were singing or making other noises, and obtain a good enough view of them to be able to recognise them in Dresser's Birds of Europe, to distinguish the song of a black-cap from that of a garden warbler, the song of a common white-throat from that of a lesser whitethroat. Finally there were the tits with about ten separate noises to learn from each tit. The tits took a long time to get themselves sorted out in my ear, but the fact that each successful definition of a particular note of a particular bird involved a personal stalk fixed the sound in my memory, and once a note is learnt in that way it is not easily forgotten. Personal discovery is much more effective than just being told, and when the commoner notes are grasped and fixed in the memory, anything fresh is caught by the ear.

When I was about eight years old a pair of kingfishers came to breed in a bank by a small pond near the large one. Rabbits however burrowed in the same place and the next year the birds moved to the island on the main pond. Since then I believe that they have never failed to breed there in any year and are a delight to the public, who can constantly see them. One spring there were three kingfishers and much excitement: I presume that the third was an extra cock. At any rate I found his corpse floating on the pond for he had been speared clean through the neck by his rival.

There were fish in the pond, and when in my very early days I began to take an interest in fish, I peered over the bank into the water, and leant forward too far. I fell straight in head first and was fished out by my nurse. The water tasted very nasty, as it does in a stagnant pond. The pond originally con-tained roach, perch and gudgeon, and I caught some of all of them and found the gudgeon much the best to eat. Then the pond was cleaned out and all the fish removed. Not long after it had again been filled with water vast quantities of small carp appeared, which had never been there before, together with perch, but the roach and the gudgeon when I left home had not returned. We never could understand where those large numbers of carp came from so suddenly. They gave amusing fishing for on a hot day they were visible swimming about near the surface in large herds, but they were difficult to catch whatever bait was used. I have never met anything quite so disgusting to eat.

The big pond near the house was the most sporting and difficult place in which to catch a rat. There was a long island covered with trees, which ran down the centre and all its banks and those round the rest of the pond were overgrown with thick vegetation. Moreover, the width of water from island to shore was in most places less than twenty yards, so that a rat could make the passage in one dive and until he was beat did not have to come up to breathe in open water. This meant that it was almost impossible to get a view at any rate until the very end of a hunt. I remember a particular hunt, when a brilliant terrier called Fram hit off the stale line of a rat at the end of the pond nearest the house, ran slowly up the left bank, put up the rat on the water's edge, cast herself on to the island, screamed from one end to the other of it, cast herself again across to the right bank, came up with her rat in a thicket of bamboo from which he again dived into the water and there caught him as he raised his nose to breathe. I saw the whole hunt from a boat, but I never once saw the rat until just before she caught him. Unlike most terriers she would speak on a stale line and had the knack, which my present terrier Jane also possesses, of hunting a diving rat by the scent from the bubbles it gives off when under water. A dog winding the water as it swims is an exciting form of hunting to see and it is a rare art. At one time we were rather short of rats, and I caught and brought home from Norfolk two doe rats in a cage and turned them out to produce fresh blood. The manœuvre was quite successful.

The pond in the middle of the wood contained golden tench, which are I think rather a rarity, but I have no recollection of hearing where they came from. We caught some of them in a kind of lobster pot without any bait like the pike trap recently introduced from France, and sent them away to someone who had asked for them, packed in damp moss after they had spent a night in a bath. They were beautiful fish and averaged well over 1 lb. They travelled quite happily in the moss and were none the worse for their journey. The ponds were kept as a

sanctuary and we never shot the duck, but it is strange that there
was so little variety—nothing but mallard on the big pond, and
occasional teal on the small one.

It was in Knighton wood that I first became acquainted with
hawfinches, of which there were a number, as there are throughout Epping Forest and in neighbouring woods containing hornbeam. In one season I found five nests in a comparatively small
area and sometimes they were difficult to find, for the altitude
and the sort of tree chosen varied greatly. I remember one at
the top of a large hornbeam, another high up in a holly and a
third on a thick oak bough, but the commonest site was a thin
thornbush and that sort were easy. I never found one in our
orchard, in fact they restricted their garden visits to the time
when the peas were ripe. They and the jays, of which there
were great numbers, used to get nearly all the peas. The greatest
excitement I remember in the matter of nests was the finding
of a corncrake's in a hayfield. That only happened once, I suppose
about 1890, and unfortunately the nest was destroyed by a
machine. The whole of one Easter holiday was spent in trying
to find a golden-crested wren's nest. It was found on the last
day of the holidays hung under the topmost branch of a tall fir.

I was soon introduced to Epping Forest proper by my father,
who had been foremost in the fight to secure it for the public.
At one time we had a couple of elk hounds and I used to go out
alone with one of these dogs on a lead in search of deer.
It was fine fun watching the dog tilt his nose to feel the wind
and then to see his whole body stiffen as the scent of deer reached
him. With a gentle movement of the head up and down he
would get the exact direction and then start off, pulling on the
cord, dragging me after him straight towards his quarry. I was
very small in those days, not much bigger than the elk hound,
and I was once dragged along the ground for some distance
clean off my feet. I carried no weapon but I learnt a lot about
the vagaries of wind, silent movement and the ways of deer.

Fallow, and remarkably dark ones, were the only deer left
in the Forest, for the last red deer had been killed some years
before I was born, but my father reintroduced roe from Dorset-

shire. They did not thrive and always confined themselves for
some unknown reason, possibly the presence of some fungus, to
a few comparatively small areas of the Forest and to certain
coverts outside it. I liked them better than fallow and still do
so, spending much time in watching them. I had a strange
experience with a roe in the Forest. In a small open space with
a little bracken and other low covert I saw a roe doe, who had
either heard or seen me, press her fawn down to the ground with
her chin. She was not a hundred yards off and I went straight
to the place, but despite a very careful search the fawn was never
found. The doe kept moving round me in a small circle calling
all the time to her fawn, and I finally gave it up in deference to
her feelings and went away. The drawing of a roe fawn by
Eberhardt—the best drawing of a wild animal that I know—
reminds me of that incident. Colonel Peter Barclay, commanding
a battalion of the Norfolk Regiment in Germany, tells me that
he saw there outside a wood a full-grown fox and a full-grown
roe obviously playing together. He reported the incident to the
German forester, who said that he had never known of a similar
case. They are certainly strange playmates for I imagine that a
fox would be considered a real danger by a roe doe with a fawn.

There were foxes and badgers in the forest, which excited me
immensely, and I used to sit up sometimes in the evening to
watch them. Often nothing much happened but there was one
red letter night at an earth (Plate 2) about fourteen miles from
the Bank of England. It was nearly the longest day of the year
and my sister and I climbed about 1½ hours before dark into the
crutches of two pollard hornbeams overlooking the earth. It
was a dead still evening and there was nobody about.

We had not been in position long before rabbits began to
appear and shortly afterwards foxcubs. There were ten foxcubs,
and one vixen, who was lame: we saw no other fox, so that she
was presumably the mother of that large family. They began
to play at once all over an open space a few yards away from
the trees in which we sat. The cubs made ineffective stalks at
the rabbits, who paid little attention to them, and there were
perpetual romps and games between the cubs, all visible to us

in a perfect light. The vixen sat about enjoying the scene as much as we did, but it was interrupted.

A fallow doe moved up from the valley below calling to her fawn, presumably hidden in the bracken behind us. The vixen at once became nervous, probably because she thought quite wrongly that the doe had been frightened by something else. Anyhow the vixen thought it advisable to get the cubs to ground: it was easier said than done. She did her best to round them up and get them into the holes, but they popped out again in a moment, for the mincing steps of the doe were very attractive and all the cubs started rushing after her. They raced right up to her hind legs and spat at her in the most ridiculous way. When she stopped, looked round and stared at them, they fled back to their mother and the doe carried straight on in search of her fawn.

When that scene in the play was over, the next began. From a large hole at the foot of my tree an old boar badger slowly emerged and sat himself down on the mound of earth at the entrance to the hole with a steep slope below him. After a long period of inaction and a careful survey of his surroundings, he began to search himself for fleas. All went according to plan until he discovered a flea low down on his stomach under his hind leg. It was a difficult place to reach and he overbalanced, rolled down the hill and picked himself up again, obviously hoping that no one had seen. We repressed our feelings and he remained quite unconscious of the fact that two people were sitting within five yards above him. Then two more old badgers emerged, followed by four bouncing, uproarious cubs.

Imagine the scene. We had now below us—none of them more than twenty yards away—seven badgers, ten foxcubs and a vixen, not to mention rabbits, and the light was still good. The badgers at once began to play in a ring of their own, paying not the smallest attention to the foxcubs, who were engaged in every imaginable game a few yards away. The badgers gave out grunts and squeaks which rather reminded me of ferrets in a bag, and their main form of sport was to let their next-door neighbour get half out of a hole and then jerk him backwards with a tweak of his hind leg from underground. They were very clumsy and absolutely ludicrous. In the middle of their performance one of the foxcubs left his playmates, strolled across to the badgers and sat down in the middle of their play-ring with his tongue lolling out, obviously laughing. The badger cubs paid not the smallest attention to him and just went on with their ridiculous games, squeaking, grunting, bumping and jostling.

The light began to go and at last we could see little below us, and I felt that the show as far as we were concerned was over. One of the old badgers was exactly below me, standing there thinking of nothing. I leant over and dropped a lighted pipe, which just missed his nose. There was a snort of horror and he dived backwards down the hole, followed by the rest of the players.

Some learned professor stated not long ago in an article that he did not believe that animals played. I could not help wondering whether he had ever seen an animal, and should like to hear his explanation of what we saw that night. I cannot think of any animal or bird that does not play, often when they are quite grown up.

On another occasion three of us, including a lady, were in trees above a badger earth. Nothing had appeared and presently we heard voices. Two Cockneys came walking up to the earth and suddenly spotted a lady sitting in the tree and then the other two of us. One of them turned first to my friend. "What the 'ell are ye doin'? What's the gime?" My friend promptly replied, "Watching for crocodiles coming out of their holes." This answer was ignored and the Cockney looked up again at the lady sitting in her tree and she was neither small nor young. "An 'er," he said, "settin' up there like a bloody bird on a perk. What's she? A balmy tart, or what?" There was nothing more to say and in any case we were past speech: we came down and went away, leaving the Cockneys completely puzzled.

My father was always having glades cut in the Forest to give a pleasant view from road or ride. One day I saw a pair of Londoners sitting at the far end of one of these glades looking towards the road, and overheard the following conversation. "D'yer see that 'ole in the trees?" "Yuss." "D'yer know what they done that for?" "No." "They done that so we can see the road." When I told my father of that conversation he felt that his forestry had achieved an additional result, which he had never thought of.

In my young days chasing rabbits with terriers soon evoked an interest in the science of hunting. At a very early age I began to show promise by reporting to an older companion that "I *saw* the scent go round the corner." When I went up to Cambridge this love of hunting drew me to the Trinity Beagles, and in my last year I was master, and in the Xmas vacation took the hounds home to Essex and had some fine sport there. Subsequently the 'beagle week' at my home became an institution and we crowded into it two days of fox-hunting and four days of beagling. On one occasion the week started by one of the company confessing that he had tipped the porter at the station with a golden ten-shilling piece in mistake for a sixpence, had asked for twopence change—and got it. I always hoped that the lucky porter derived as much fun with his friends out of that tip as we did.

During the beagle week I once made an appalling fool of myself and have no hope of ever being forgiven by the master of the beagles, Maurice Barclay, now master of the Puckeridge. Hounds came by train from Cambridge to Broxbourne, and the meet being about two miles away, we met the hounds at the station and walked across the fields towards the meet, drawing for a hare on the way—a foolish thing to do in itself and not fair on the field, who were waiting for us at the meet. We found a hare which ran in the right direction towards the meet, but before hounds had crossed the third field a fox jumped up in the middle of them and off they went in view. There was a scream-ing scent and for the next forty minutes they were generally in sound but never in sight of us. At the end of that time we heard them turn and begin to come back towards us, and Maurice Barclay and I ran to the top of a grass hill and the fox crossed the field just in front of us. He was not dead beat but his brush was down, his mouth was open, his tongue was back, he had had

nearly enough and the pack were screaming up at no distance
behind him. I knew the Essex hounds were meeting in that bit
of country the next day and I had a fit of idiotic conscience. I
said to Maurice Barclay, "We must stop them." "All right," he
said and sat down and I think cried. Unfortunately we succeeded in stopping them, heaven knows how: if we had not done
so, nothing could have saved that fox but an open earth. The
field at the meet were naturally furious at being kept waiting,
and when I told the Master of the Foxhounds next day what had
happened, he said, "Why on earth did you stop them?" Why,
indeed? The comment of James Bailey, huntsman to the Essex,
was, "Catch 'em if you can, sir. Catch 'em if you can."

The hunt with the beagles that stands out freshest in my
memory was on a day during the beagle week, a few years after
I had gone down from Cambridge. The master of the year had
run a thorn into his leg the week before, and being too lame to
hunt hounds himself very kindly invited me to do so. I did
not know more than a few of the hounds, mainly puppies which
I had walked, but had hunted with most of their forebears and
remembered their form. For the benefit of those who know
Epping Forest I give the details of the hunt. The meet was near
Chigwell Lane, East of Loughton, in a bit of country well
poached from that place and only supporting just the correct
number of hares. Local knowledge directed us to draw a rough
grass field close to Loughton, and to my astonishment up jumped
three hares, probably the only ones in the parish. Hounds
selected the hare which made straight for Loughton, and the
pack crossed the main road at the bottom of Goldings Hill and
in no time were into the Forest. The first thing that entered
my head was the certain presence of deer. The Trinity Foot
Beagles were not used to deer at Cambridge, and some of the
puppies that I had walked had occasionally hunted them in the
playful days of their youth. What was going to happen now,
would they disgrace me in front of every one?

It was obvious that there was a capital scent, and after entering
the Forest and running to Loughton Camp, hounds turned
south and crossed the road that runs from the Roebuck Inn to

Loughton and reached the edge of Fairmead, then an open grass plain. Then they turned and I could hear them screaming back straight towards us. Colonel Seymour Gosling, Master of the Foxhounds, and I stood on the road watching, and the whole pack crashed out of the covert, swung themselves over the road, hit the line on the far side, crashed into a thicket of holly and went chiming away to the north. "They *can* hunt," said the M.F.H., and I felt very happy, as we plugged along a ride which luckily ran parallel with the line they were taking. They kept very straight on past Monk Wood, and in an open bit of heather near that fine bit of beech forest a herd of deer stood at gaze. Hounds ran straight on through the middle of the parting herd, while not a hound paid the smallest attention to the deer bounding away on either side of them, and from that time on my mind on that score was at rest.

We had been running for nearly an hour when they reached the pond at the top of Goldings Hill, and for the first time in the hunt I saw our hare slipping out of long grass ahead of them and crossing the road near the edge of the Forest, with open grass fields sloping down towards the railway between Chigwell Lane and Theydon Bois stations. Would she go away? I thought so and spurted to be near hounds if she did, but it was not to be. She kept along the edge of the Forest and then turned west towards the Wake Arms, recrossing the road towards Monk Wood to the south. I was getting pretty blown and was glad of the loan of a farmer's pony for the next mile or so to Loughton Camp, but hereabouts the hare began to twist and turn and I felt I could be more use to hounds on my feet. There was not much for me to do, but at one point where they checked for a moment, one of the puppies that I had walked made a glorious hit. She was a stuffy little bitch called Jollity—a name that suited her. I hope that the personal cheer I gave her, made it one of the proudest moments of her life. She made many hits that day, and it was a sight to see her driving at the head of the pack through the heather.

Then on through the pollard hornbeams of Loughton Camp to the long ride that runs north and south through the Forest

at the back of Loughton, and here there was a holloa—about the
first that I had heard throughout the hunt. As I reached the
place my sister, who had seen the hare, told me that she thought
it was a fresh one, and in any case clean. I hesitated: there were,
I knew, very few hares in the Forest; only one other had been
reported in the course of the hunt: even if the hare had been
muddy at some stage, she would quickly have cleaned up on the
leaves and heather, and in any event, if they had changed it was
quite impossible to say where. Then a hound spoke confidently
forrard and I made up my mind to leave them alone, cheered
and doubled on my horn.

They were running slowly now but very steadily, and I felt
that the slackening of the pace might be due to failing scent
from a beaten hare. They kept along the bottom of a little
valley and then climbed up a slope bare of trees facing me.
Suddenly out of the grass in the middle of the opening up jumped
the hare. I screamed the word that should only be used when
there is a chance to get them a view, and one hound at least got
it and with all heads up to the 'Tallyho,' they flew through the
grass and into her before she reached the trees. It was a great
finish to the finest woodland hunt I ever saw.

Then we went home to lunch, and in the afternoon had
another good hunt, this time in the open, and lost a beaten hare
at the last moment in the thick laurels of a garden. In the middle
of this second hunt I became so utterly beat that I squatted in a
plough to get my wind. It was indeed a gruelling day, particularly for me for I had not been running with the beagles
four days a week like the undergraduates, and had been kept
going entirely by the love of hunting hounds.

So much for the Cockney end of Essex, and now for the
northern half of the county, which I know best from hunting
with the Essex Foxhounds. Since earlier in this chapter I told
some Cockney stories, I must relate one from the other end of
the county which was given me by a master of the Essex language,
Colonel Deacon, a beloved colonel of the Yeomanry. Two farmers
at market were discussing a sick horse, and one of them pre-
scribed a dose. "Troy tew point of hair oil and a bit of garlic.

Fox stalking mole. Chapter. 1.

Asia Minor Wild Sheep. Chapter 2

That'll dew it; Oi hed a horse sick just loike that." They met again the following week and the prescriber of the drug asked, "Well heow's your ould horse?" "Ah, that doid." "Ow did ut, sow d'd moine."

In order to preserve foxes I used to rent the shooting of a wood in the north of the county, in the Friday country of the Essex Hunt. I was always very nervous when hounds were drawing my covert that by some misadventure they would not find, but it was a great thrill to go on to a corner and tuck myself into the hedge to watch for what I felt was my own fox going away. I shall always be grateful to Masters of the Essex hounds for granting me this privilege—not only at coverts for which I was responsible. If a fox came out I used to sit hunched up trying to look as if I had seen nothing, terrified that my horse might move. Luckily a horse that knows the job does nothing but quiver and cock its ears. Then there is the added thrill of deciding how long to wait before letting the world know the secret. The choice of the safe moment to holloa without danger of the fox doubling back into covert should, I think, depend on the manner of the fox. If he moves off boldly there is not much danger of his turning back when he has gone a hundred yards, but if he looks doubtful it is best to let him get clear of the first field before moving or making any sound.

In one season we had an extraordinary run of lucky Fridays, and to make it all the pleasanter for me, my wood was responsible for several of the best hunts. A fortnight before the day I propose to describe, the first whip and I had been badly left when hounds had turned from our end of the wood, and it was only thanks to the one check in the hunt caused by a plough team that we ever caught them up and saw them run to a cutting on the Great Eastern Railway by Audley End, where they were stopped through fear of trains, after making an eight-mile point.

The second day in this bit of country was perhaps even better. We had had a long circular hunt in the morning in thick fog, and when it was over the Master decided to go straight to my wood as the next draw. I went to my usual corner on the edge of a grass field that divided the woodland into two portions, and the first whipper in, Harry Speke, was opposite me at the next corner. I heard them find and come, thank heavens, straight in my direction, while I sat there quivering like my horse with excitement. About fifty yards from me out came a long grey fox with a lot of dark hair in his brush and a large white tag at the end of it. I let him cross the meadow before I holloaed, and directly hounds were out on the line, galloped parallel with them and up a ride in the second wood to its further side. I arrived there just in time: the fox was leaving the second wood as I peeped out, and crossing a ploughed field with a long easy stride.

Hounds came streaming away from the covert and flung themselves out on the line in the open, and we were away with a glorious start heading for about where Suffolk, Essex and Cambridgeshire meet. The fox kept on a remarkably straight course, paying no attention to fences and running the middle of the fields as though he knew exactly where he was going. I remember one nasty blind place at the top of a hill at which Harry Speke turned in his saddle and yelled at me, "Look out, sir, it's a big un," but all was well and for the most part it was easy country. When we had been running for about twenty minutes without the semblance of a check or even a falter, the country became more and more open and the fields larger. I wondered where we could be going, and the Huntsman, James Bailey, said as we galloped alongside, "He must be coming back to us now, sir." I looked ahead in the hope of getting a view but it was not to be. A circular chalk pit appeared in front of us, hounds swept in an avalanche through its opening and up the steep side and clustered, baying at an open hole under the lip of the pit. We were out of our country and into, I think, the New-market and Thurlow's and there we left him, but there was still time for one more hunt.

We jogged to the nearest covert and found at once, I suspect, a fox that had been moved earlier in the day. In any event scent was as good as ever, and hounds screamed across the open to a wood belonging to the Puckeridge Hunt. The second whipper in and I galloped along the side of it to a road that bordered the further end. As I jumped into the road I looked to my left and saw something galloping down the road, but for a moment was uncertain of its identity. Then it turned, waved a brush and jumped back into the wood. I galloped to another corner, where I and Harry Speke watched in opposite directions with hounds chiming through the wood behind us. It was very exciting and I felt sure that we were about to get another view. We did. Out came the fox, very beat, not thirty yards off, and started across the next field obliquely towards a fence that ran out from the wood. I thought he might turn back into the wood on the other side of this fence and nipped through it to prevent such a move, while Harry Speke holloaed the hounds on to the line. Then seeing no more of the fox, I felt that he must have hugged the fence, and so galloped on to try and get another view. Presently I saw him well out in a field and obviously wondering what to do next.

The fox sat down on his haunches listening, and I put up my hat and waited silent, looking round for the pack. The Huntsman, James Bailey, had seen my hat and was galloping hounds up to me. I wondered if they would arrive in time to get a view before the fox reached the next fence, and in fact only one or two hounds saw him, but that was enough. There was a rush and a scramble through the fence, and into a dell with a pond in it, and climbing up the bank on the far side of the pond was the fox clear for every hound to see. They all rolled into the pond together and we rode home content. This sounds rather bloodthirsty and I am reminded of a remark by James Bailey, concerning foxes. "I love 'em in the summer, sir. They *are* such pretty things. But I hate 'em in the winter. I'll catch every fox I can." Anyhow if the vote were put to the foxes, ' Shall hunting cease? ' they would all vote No, and rightly. There is nothing worse than gin and poison.

Short, who at one time whipped in to the Essex, used to rehearse his holloa in his boots.

goorn awaay '

goorn away,

' Gorn away,

and then the long-drawn hooting holloa. He could make a
glorious noise. I remember an exciting occasion when a fox was
discovered lying on the bough of a tree well over forty feet
above the ground in Screens Park. Hounds were kept back at
least a hundred yards, a ladder was fetched and a man climbed
up towards the fox, which ran along the bough and jumped.
The hounds saw him move, broke away and raced for the spot,
so that when he landed they had covered much of the distance.
The fox landed on his feet but seemed a little winded or at any
rate shaken, as well he might have been on landing from such
a height. He collected himself, however, and got into his stride
when hounds were almost on him, and skirting the pack broad-
side on to the leading hounds, he fairly raced across their front
with a nasty look on his face as though to say, "Come on, one
of you." My impression was that some at least of the leading
hounds said, "Your's" to their neighbours; at any rate, the fox
just cleared them with a twist: a five-yards' lead was soon twenty,
and twenty turned to fifty. Then he just walked away over the
park, leaving them standing. With such a fox and such a start
it looked as if we were in for a great hunt over the open country
of the Roothings, but it was not a good hunting day, and at
the end of twenty minutes he had run us out of scent. That
was a great fox.

I started one day from Poplar in the East End of London to
hunt in the north of Essex. No cab appeared to take me to
Stratford station to catch the train and I hailed a passing brick
cart. A man in a top hat, pink coat and hunting boots standing
up in an open cart is not common in that part of London, and
as my driver whipped up his horse into a gallop in order that
I might catch the train we were the centre of interest. At Stratford station a party of factory girls were awaiting their train
on the opposite platform to me, and of course spotted me. "Gawd
love a duck, look at that!" and other comments followed. Then
came the question, "Where are ye goin', Guvnor?" "To Dunmow." "To Dunmow! What d'yer want to go there for? Lots
of rabbits in Stratford."

In addition to hunting I occasionally made up a party to

shoot the woods I had rented, and generally did so the week after
hounds had drawn them—never before, for foxes were always
the first consideration. James Bailey often used to come out and
was a very keen shooter. The best fun, however, was provided
by the beaters, produced mainly by a Church Army training
college for agricultural workers. These beaters were ignorant
of the country but very keen. I remember one who had just
seen a fellow-beater wringing a rabbit's neck, picking up a hen
pheasant and performing the same operation across his knee:
the pheasant naturally came in half. The local farmers, who
came to shoot, all had their pet corners which I had to try and
remember, for nothing gave greater offence than putting the
wrong farmer at the right place. We used to end the day with
a partridge drive over a valley, and as there was generally not
much time left for partridges, we divided the beaters into two
and drove over the valley from both directions simultaneously.
I can recommend the practice: it is exciting but not as a rule
very murderous.

There has been a good deal about hunting in this chapter
and it is not specifically mentioned elsewhere in this book, so
that here if anywhere seems the place to give a few general
thoughts on the subject. They are given with diffidence and the
knowledge that they will produce argument. It is common to
speak of a fox's point being some particular wood. I am convinced from experience not only with foxes but also with other
animals, such as deer and hares, that this is not strictly correct.
The point of a fox or of any other hunted animal is not a place:
it is a substitute fox to take over the job. The other fox may be
in a wood or a field of kale or indeed anywhere. It is difficult, of
course, to see the transfer of responsibility with a fox, but I have
often seen it both with hares and deer, and the substitute seems
to take over the job voluntarily.

I believe that much too little attention is paid by huntsmen
to the direction of the wind. A hound or any sort of animal
that hunts by scent must be perpetually conscious of where the
wind is. I have often seen a huntsman gallop his hounds to a
holloa at *right angles* to the line of the fox. If the fox has run

down-wind this is likely to result in hounds running heel, for their first indication of the scent will come from up-wind of them and they will turn towards it. The proper course is so to manœuvre the pack before they reach the spot where the fox has been seen, that they reach it at an oblique angle and can be laid on the line with their heads pointing in the right direction —the way their quarry has gone.

Checks are, I think, more often caused by a fox turning down rather than up-wind. If he turns up-wind the fact would, I think, generally be notified to the noses of the hounds, and they would turn with him or at least would probably make their first swing up-wind, in obedience to their noses. Unless, therefore, some fairly obvious cause for the check is visible, such as manure, a road, a man in sight, etc., the proper first cast seems to me to be one which brings hounds across the line of a possible, indeed probable, sharp *down* wind turn of the fox, and the more they are brought across the line *into* the wind the better, for it will help them in picking up the line, if their noses face more or less up-wind.

I believe also that coverts ought to be drawn up-wind and that if they are drawn in the opposite direction foxes may either slip away too soon on a hint from their ears or their noses, or they may be passed over and not found at all. In thick covert a fox will sometimes sit very tight, and hounds ought to be given every chance to wind him, which they can sometimes do at a great distance if drawing up-wind. I remember riding down a path behind a huntsman drawing a covert full of holly: some hounds were at his heels and I saw a fox jump across the path out of a holly bush just behind them. Not a single hound received any indication that a fox had moved no doubt because the wind was wrong for them.

On a really first-class scenting day I have often seen hounds, particularly when running up-wind, cease to hunt the actual line of the fox, when they reach the middle of a field, and race with heads up straight for the place in the next fence through which the fox has passed. They can under such conditions wind from a great distance the scent left on the fence where the fox has brushed through it. That, of course, only happens on a very good scenting day.

My two terriers, Jane and Ginger (Plate 9), recently gave an example of the distance at which they can smell game up-wind of them. I was walking with them along a farm road from east to west, the wind being at right angles from the north, and on the up-wind side of the road was a deep wide dyke full of water. Both dogs put their heads up and obviously winded something, but they kept with me until we reached a bridge over the dyke. Then both of them shot off perfectly straight and at full gallop but on two diverging lines, one north and the other north-east. After both had galloped over three hundred yards, one put up a pheasant and the other a hare. Wind is everything to a dog, but it is difficult for a human being with his degenerate nose to understand how all important it is.

One afternoon while coming home early from hunting, I met a fox that had obviously done some work. He crossed the road without noticing me and cast himself along the fence with his nose down. He was, I suspect, trying for the line of another fox, who might take over his responsibilities. In Scotland a big stag that I was trying to photograph had soiled in a peat hag and then gone to sleep. His hinds, which were lying about fifty yards to our side of him, spotted us and bolted without the stag seeing them go. Suddenly he woke up and realised that the hinds were no longer there. He put his head down, picked up the line and hunted them just like a hound until he caught them up about a mile away. Stags are nasty-tempered animals in October, and he no doubt told them what he thought of them for giving him the slip.

I believe that in most places the main prey of a fox is mole. I have twice had good views of foxes stalking moles, once in Switzerland and once in Belgium. The best view was in Belgium for there was deep snow which in bright sunlight made a perfect background so that every detail could be seen. I was on the edge of a wide clearing in a wood in the middle of the day, when I saw a fox come out from the trees and carefully quarter the open ground. I kept my telescope on him and he was not two hundred yards away, so that I could even see his eyes. Some fresh mole-hills showed black against the snow, and the fox worked his way to a position down-wind of the mole-hills and then made a perfect point—brush stiff and straight and one foreleg up, just like a pointer. He paused for a few moments, and then slowly advanced; at first he crouched, but then, presumably because he realised that his body would make a scrunching sound against the frosted snow, he again raised his body clear of the snow and stepped gingerly and silently forward, raising and putting down each foot with great care. When he reached a point within a long jump of the occupied mole-hill, he stopped, cocked his ears, turned his head left and right to catch the smallest sound of the mole at his work, and lay right back on his haunches ready to spring. The spring, when it came, was a magnificent bound, followed by a quick sharp dig with his ears back and a nasty look on his face. He had missed, and realised that if the mole were not grabbed at once digging was useless, and he at once proceeded to quarter the ground again until he got another point. I watched nine points, nine stalks, and nine springs, but they all ended in failure, probably because owing to the frost the mole always heard the fox, and no doubt he was out at that time of day, because silent stalking had been quite impossible during the hard frost at night. I have reproduced some sketches of this incident done at the time which will be found facing page 24.

I saw with the Essex a good instance of the folly of paying too much attention to looks in preference to working qualities of hounds. Two hounds from the Essex Hunt won first prizes at Peterboro' for unentered bitches. Both of them were absolutely useless out hunting, and one of the two used to spend the whole day at the huntsman's heels, dragging listlessly about as though she absolutely loathed hunting. I am sure she did. Why breed from such hounds and ignore those which possess the best noses and the best hunting qualities? Fashion or the taste of the moment plays, I think, too big a part. We and the French have exactly opposite ideas on the question of what hounds' legs and feet ought to be like. Our fashion is in cat's feet and a leg rather

 [*Photo : E. Bernard Cook*

2. Fox-badger playground, Epping Forest.

[*Photo : E. Bernard Cook*

3. Knighton Pond showing island on left.

over than back at the knee. The French always go for hares'
feet and have no objection to a hound being rather back at the
knee. Possibly both are wrong, and I cannot think of a better
leg and foot than those of a fox. His leg is if anything slightly
back at the knee and his foot is nearly as round as a cat's, but
his claws project far in front of it.

Two

ASIA MINOR

THE PRIMARY OBJECT of a journey made by Peter Haig Thomas, referred to hereinafter as P. H. T., and myself to Asia Minor, now many years ago, was to stalk wild sheep on the northern slopes of the Taurus mountains, but we made a preliminary excursion at the end of September to the Mourad Dagh, which was subsequently, after the 1914-18 war, the scene of the decisive defeat of the Greeks by the Turks.

We finally left the train from Smyrna at a place called Oturak, but on the way there we spent one night at Ushak, and were shown a bedroom in the local hotel which contained a large bell rope hanging down the wall. The bell did not ring, but, poised just below it on the wall as the only mural decoration, was the largest bug I ever saw. Asia Minor is famous for these animals, but this was the father of all the bugs, and we left him to it and tried to sleep on a heap of coal outside in the station yard. The night got colder and colder, and finally we gave it up returned to our room and slept undisturbed, probably because the bug had got tired of waiting.

The Mourad Dagh and certain other wooded mountains in Asia Minor, like the Ak Dagh, are inhabited by red deer, the same type and size of deer as those described in later chapters on the Caucasus. We found, and indeed we had been told beforehand, that for some extraordinary reason the stags on the Mourad Dagh never roar. Whether they have learnt by experience that it is a dangerous thing to do or whether they are descended from individuals which have lost the use of their voices, I do not know. Anyhow it is a fact that they do not and that stags on the Ak Dagh, which is at no very great distance, do roar.

This silence made it extraordinarily difficult to locate them or to do anything with them. We had to rely almost entirely on tracking and tracking generally on dry pine needles. We took with us, however, a Norwegian elkhound and he did nearly get me a chance or two. The nearest approach I attained to a shot was when I was accompanied by a Pyrenean chasseur and a native Turk. We had followed tracks of a stag that the dog could just wind for about two miles, and once the dog got or seemed to get the scent of the animal direct. We were moving through comparatively thin pine forest and, while the Pyrenean accompanied by the Turk held the cord attached to the dog, I kept a few yards to one side. Suddenly the two men saw the stag, which was invisible to me, and the Turk gesticulated: this was fatal, and by the time I had reached them the stag was gone. He was described as enormous but I was doubtful. The Pyrenean, who was accustomed to izzard, a very small animal, expressed himself forcibly. "Mais quel animal! Jamais je n'ai vu le pareil. Il avait quatre cornes entre les yeux." That sounds to me more like a two- or three-year-old, and even such a beast would look enormous to a chasseur of izzard.

The elkhound was sometimes rather an embarrassment. In the train he was tied up in the guard's van, and once at a station he spied some pariah dogs on the platform. He broke his collar, leapt from the train and laid hold of one of the pariahs just as the train was about to start. He was seized with great difficulty, the pariah rescued, and the train allowed to depart.

P. H. T. had, I think, two very difficult chances at stags and missed them, and the whole expedition was a failure in the matter of stags, but it was interesting if not beautiful country and we had plenty of excitement. The birds of the country were typical of fir forest. There were plenty of woodpeckers, including the great black, various eagles which I found difficult to identify, lammergeiers, and griffon vultures. Smaller birds had a distinct British flavour, blackbirds, robins, wrens, etc.

One day, when I was out in the forest alone, I was mystified by a perfectly straight narrow white path descending from a rounded top through scrub to level ground. With difficulty, for it was very steep and extremely slippery, I climbed straight up the path to the top, where I came suddenly upon an old Turk chipping away at a millstone and smoking a very dirty white pipe. I also was smoking a pipe, and the polite old gentleman immediately offered to swop pipes, which is apparently the right thing to do in Turkey when you meet a new acquaintance. Being all in favour of good manners, I had to agree and hope he enjoyed the taste of my pipe better than I enjoyed his. The object of the path was now of course obvious: when he finished a millstone, he simply started it on its way at the top of the path, and it rolled fast and straight down the path to the bottom. The particular millstone on which he was engaged was almost finished, and if I had struggled up that path a little later I might have met it hurtling down.

We were puzzled and rather annoyed by the burrowings of some mysterious animals, which would often in the night tunnel under our tent and even upset its balance by weakening the soil under a pole or under a camp-bed—in fact they were always liable to let us down. The burrows, which were very common in clearings in the forest, looked like oversized rat-holes with large mole-hills intervening between them. We were determined to catch one of these burrowers and consulted the natives of the country. They said that the name of the animal was ' Kustebek,' and one aged and particularly lazy Turk volunteered to catch one, if we would give him some onions. His method of hunting was at any rate comfortable, and involved no movement and no exertion: that is, I think, why he volunteered. He selected a mole-hill and then dug down into the loose earth with a tent peg until he came to the animal's tunnel underneath it, and left the earth in and over the tunnel loose. In this loose earth he placed slices of onion, and drove two tent pegs into the ground so that their points rested exactly on the roof of the tunnel on either side of the loose earth containing the onions. He then sat himself Turkish fashion on his hunkers in front of the two pegs, armed with a wooden mallet. The theory of the business was that, when Kustebek arrived by underground attracted by the onions, his presence in the loose earth would be obvious from the fact that the earth would move; then all the Turk had to do was to make a clean right and left on the

tent pegs with his mallet, which would drive
the pegs into the tunnels and so block Kustebek's escape forwards or backwards.

This sounded all right in theory, but
during the first day of practice the old Turk
never did make a right and left: he always
missed one and sometimes both of the pegs
with his mallet, so that Kustebek invariably
escaped either backwards or forwards by
underground. Practice, however, makes
perfect, and on the second day a real right
and left was brought off, the Turk drove his
fingers into the loose earth and firmly implanted on one of them out came Kustebek.
He was well worth all the trouble. Shaped

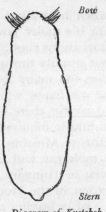

Bow

Stern

Diagram of Kustebek

like a barge, except that it was practically impossible to
determine which was his bow and which was his stern, he was
about the size of a young rabbit when it is first allowed out.
The difficulty of determining which was bow and which was
stern was accentuated by the fact that he went backwards quite
as often and quite as readily as forwards. After careful examination we found one feature (it was about the only one) which
gave the tip about bow and stern. He had a formidable and long
array of whiskers sticking out on either side, fairly near his
front end. Otherwise what are usually known as features were
simply not there, or at least not visible. To the amateur artist
he was an absolute godsend; one could have drawn with a ruler
almost everything about him but his whiskers. A diagram of
him is shown here. He had no eyes, at least no visible eyes, no
ears, at least no external ears. He was very flat, as though he had
been squashed by a perpetual weight of soil, and wore a pretty
coat of grey moleskin. If you looked carefully you discovered
that he had a small pink nose and stumpy tail that looked just
like it, but you had to turn him upside down to find his mouth,
which was placed in the same position as that of a shark or a
dogfish—underneath and some way back from the bow.

We discovered his mouth by putting him down on a biscuit,

when he walked some way across it before beginning to eat. On his under jaw were two enormous teeth, which seemed to start in his chest. He was absolutely tame at once and ate slowly but steadily through any biscuit we gave him. Probably we gave him too many for after a few days, alas, he died. I hope that he was happy while he was with us, but it was really impossible to say for there was nothing to go by. When we got home we naturally inquired all about him and his relations at the Natural History Museum, and the authorities there told us that he was a mole rat, and that either he or a cousin of his existed as far west as Hungary. Personally I have never met him anywhere except in the Mourad Dagh: I should love to meet him again.

After leaving the country of red deer and mole rats (Kuştebek was the one and only item in the bag), we moved west via Afium-Kara-Hissar (Black Castle of Opium) to Eregli, which was then railhead on the Baghdad railway, since the tunnel had not yet been made to continue the line through the Taurus Mountains or Bulgar Dagh, down to the coastal plain. We were now in a totally different country and a little geography lesson is rather essential: the relevant endpaper map will help. Asia Minor consists of a high plateau shaped like a saucer, with steep slopes on the outer edge down to the sea, particularly steep in the region of the Taurus, and inhabited by wild goat (*Capra aegagrus*), and gentle slopes to the interior of the saucer. The most remarkable feature of the country, or that part of it in which we now were, was that there was no escape for the water descending to the inland plateau from the mountains that formed the edge of the saucer. All the streams (there were not many of them) simply ended in salt lakes or got lost in the sand. We never visited the only stream which runs for any distance. It issues quite suddenly from the mountains at a place called Divle and is said to contain trout.

We moved south-west from Eregli and camped on the northern slopes of the Taurus, which are here rolling bare pink-coloured hills overlooking what is now to all intents and purposes practically desert. It was not so once, for the plain was dotted in all directions with the ruins of villages and the remains of walls and aqueducts. It had obviously once been a thickly populated country, and I imagine that the reason for the change was the Turks' habit of destroying their forests and so diminishing the rainfall.

It was, as we saw it, an arid land, and our camping sites were mainly determined by the presence of springs, which were by no means frequent. The lakes were all on the plain itself, and in any case they were useless for camping since the water was far too salt. Moreover, they and their thick reed-beds were the haunt of myriads of mosquitoes, which we carefully avoided for fear of malaria. Much the most attractive local food we obtained was Yoghurt, a form of sour milk, which was generally brought to camp in a dirty old sack. A good deal of barley was grown on the plateau in the saucer. It was a strange country, but in October it had its attractions for the weather was delightful, and the temperature just right for the long days of spying and stalking that extremely intelligent animal the wild sheep of Asia Minor. A drawing of this sheep will be found facing page 25.

This sheep is a large pale-coloured edition of the moufflon of Sardinia, but the old rams had the points of their horns turned back and inwards over their withers, in contrast to the horns of Sardinian sheep, which curl forwards and upwards on either side of their cheeks. The shape of the horns of the sheep of Asia Minor and their nearest relations is peculiar. The sheep of Cyprus are merely a small island form of the sheep of Asia Minor, but further east again in Persia is a very similar animal, but with horns that curl forward. To make the matter still more complicated the wild sheep of India, the Urial, again turns his horns backwards. So does the wild sheep of North Africa who provides, in the opinion of a French experienced chasseur, "la plus, plus plus jolie chasse qu'il y a." I can think of no satisfactory explanation for these strange vagaries of fashion in horns. The old rams of the Asia Minor sheep are very beautiful animals; their faces are grey, in fact almost white, the body colour is dark pinkish brown, but with a pronounced white saddle mark bordered with dark hair half-way along the body, of the same pattern as a Sardinian ram's, and their fronts are decorated with a fine black line which descends from the top of the throat to the chest, and broadens at the base into a large black bull's eye.

The ewes are nothing much to look at compared to the rams, for they carry no horns and none of the other adornments such as saddle marks or black line down the front, and are generally lighter coloured. They are not striking in appearance as the rams certainly are. Moreover, it seemed to us that the rams were far more intelligent than the ewes and took elaborate precautions to ensure their safety. Sheep are not great climbers, and nowhere in their country was there any ground that could be called steep. Their idea of suitable ground on which to spend the day is a place where a really long view can be obtained, either a flat plateau on the top of a mountain or a flat plain at the bottom of it.

We discovered that good sheep ground always had a pink tint to it, but whether the sheep selected their ground mainly to match their colour or because it contained the food they sought, I am not certain. The hills were extraordinarily bare of vegetation and very dry, but there grew on them a little creeping plant with oblong leaves, which slightly resembled clover. The leaves were grey outside, but if cut open the interior showed green and had the property of retaining moisture. This plant, whose name I do not know, was the main food of the sheep. It did not grow very thick anywhere and the result was that the animals, when on the feed, moved fast and long distances. That added to the difficulty of a stalk.

We saw many instances of the care the old rams took over their personal safety. The following account of what I witnessed, so to speak from behind the scenes, is a good instance of the steps they take to make all secure. From the top of a low ridge I saw five rams (three big ones and two small) which had not been disturbed, walking slowly away over a plain below me. Beyond the plain was another low ridge, with one large rock on the top of it—the only real feature which broke a monotonous skyline. The sheep ascended this ridge at a slow walk and all stopped about one hundred yards short of the skyline. One of the old rams then dug his horns into the ribs of one of the youngsters ('fags' is a better word), who clearly understood what was expected of him. This young gentleman moved quietly forward to the rocks on the skyline and very carefully peeped round it over the top, while the rest of the herd stood still watching him. They allowed him a good five minutes to examine the country beyond the ridge and then one of the old rams gave a little toss to his head, meaning no doubt " that's good enough," and at the signal they all moved up to the scout and over the top. I never saw a bit of reconnoitring better done, and we were placed to watch the whole manœuvre in the position of a general inspecting a field day.

I had a strange experience with a party of rams and have never understood exactly what happened or why. Not far from camp we saw four rams coming along a ridge towards us, and by a running stalk got within one hundred yards of them just as they were preparing to lie down. One of the party was the biggest ram I ever saw and none of them were small. I was making absolutely sure with my telescope which was the patriarch, when they all sat down and practically the whole of his precious body was covered by a rock. They seemed, however, perfectly happy and we were content to wait until they got up, when I felt that with patience an easy shot was a certainty. Then in the distance a Yuruk shepherd started yelling at his dog; after listening for some time, this sound got on their nerves, and without a moment's warning they bolted at full gallop. I felt that they would settle down again and did not take the running shot.

In fact we refound them without much difficulty lower down the slope. The three smaller sheep fed slowly out of sight, but the old gentleman remained lying all alone, and behaved as though he was sick of the company of his companions and pre-ferred to be on his own. There was one slight hollow, which passed within shot of his position, and it looked deep enough to cover me if I crawled flat, but there were two hundred yards of open ground to cross in full view before I could get into this little hollow. Presently the ram got up, looked at a small isolated bush near him, curved his neck, charged the bush and proceeded to smash it with his horns from every angle. That was my chance and with my eyes on him I slithered forward whenever he was most heavily engaged with the bush, but before I could reach the hollow he had tired of his game and walked quietly off downhill and round a corner of rocks out of sight. It took me no time to reach the corner and the ground beyond it was not particularly complicated, sloping for a short distance to a little valley with the opposite slope in full view. I examined every inch of that ground but I never saw the ram again. He had not rejoined his recent companions for we refound them later and he was not with them. What happened to him? Did he squat and allow me to pass him or did he suddenly determine to seek different country and gallop off out of sight on his own? We never solved the mystery and I never saw his like again.

All the stalking was interesting and generally involved very flat crawling. I had an exciting crawl after a herd of twelve sheep on a flat plateau. A Pyrenean and a Turk were with me when we found these sheep, but it was obvious that the best hope of getting within shot was to crawl alone and make use of a few thuya bushes scattered about on the plateau. We crawled slowly to a bush and all lay down behind it, but my main dread and that of the Pyrenean was that the Turk would lose his patience and move. While I crawled on alone, the Pyrenean lay by the Turk's side, threatening him with dire consequences if he budged an inch.

It was capital sport trying to put an inadequate thuya bush between me and at least the most wakeful sheep. The stalk was slightly downhill and I squirmed along on my back so as to keep my eyes on the sheep, feet foremost, dead flat from bush to bush, but always in danger of being spotted by one of them. Finally the bushes gave out, and I tried to get a little nearer with nothing left to cover me, when at last one of the biggest rams spotted something raised his head and stared. It was no good attempting further progress, and as he stood facing me his black throat line and black patch on his chest gave a good mark. I sat up and shot him in the centre of the bull's-eye and he collapsed stone dead. None of the others had seen me and after a scamper of a few yards they stopped and another big ram gave a perfect chance. For some reason, probably because in my hurry and excitement I had not closed the bolt right home, the rifle refused to go off, and I failed to get a right and left. Anyhow we had secured a beautiful old ram and, as I refused to allow the Turk to cut his throat from ear to ear in Mohammedan fashion and spoil the skin, he in turn refused to touch the sheep, so that the Pyrenean and I had a tiring job in getting his heavy body back to camp.

While stalking alone on another day I was carefully and silently rounding a corner of rocks, when I came plump on to a Turk within ten yards with a very long gun, doing exactly the same thing from the opposite direction. We were both properly taken aback; I certainly felt as if I was poaching, as indeed I suppose I was, and the Turk looked as if he considered that he was poaching too, which was probably also true, although what constituted poaching in that country was never very clear to me. Anyhow we were both quite obviously after wild sheep, and we parted and went our different ways without argument or any show of ill feeling.

Our main trouble was caused by the wandering shepherds, the Yuruks, and still more by their dogs. These dogs, the only privately owned dogs in the country, where normally a dog is a pariah and nobody's property, were a menace. They considered it, no doubt correctly, to be their business to protect the flocks under their charge against all possible assailants and that apparently included human beings as well as wolves. They were fine specimens like mastiffs, creamy white with black muzzles, and they would come full gallop at any human being other than their masters so that we learnt to give any flock of sheep or goats a wide berth. They were no doubt valuable dogs, for there were quite a number of wolves in the country and effective protection of the flocks was essential. We were on several occasions charged by these dogs and it was an alarming experience. When the Yuruks and their dogs were about, the wild sheep left and we never discovered where they went, probably to the summit of the Taurus range. Our best chance came when, owing to a religious festival, the Yuruks descended from the mountains for a short spell and left the country quiet.

On one occasion when a dog demonstrated against me its owner was present and he swore at it and made it come to heel. The danger, and it is a real one, was due to the fact that the dogs were often alone with their flocks, and their owners were absent or out of sight. I do not think that the dogs wore collars, certainly not collars with spikes. In the Pyrenees, when I was there in 1909, we saw the same type of sheepdog, creamy white with black muzzles, and the enemies to their flocks were bears, for I do not think that there were any wolves. These Pyrenean dogs wore collars with spikes on them, which were no doubt intended to prevent the bears hugging them. It is an interesting fact that this same type of sheepdog should be used in the Pyrenees, the Balkans, Asia Minor, and for all I know in many other places.

Although we were constantly seeing foxes (our foxes apparently but desert coloured) we seldom saw wolves. I once disturbed a party of four wolves, who disappeared at full gallop, and did not look very large or formidable. I also saw a wolf by a prairie dog's hole. He was sitting on his haunches with his ears cocked and his head on one side, looking just like a dog marking a rat. The occupants of the holes, rodents which I have called prairie dogs, inhabited the plains rather than the mountains and seemed to favour caravan routes, no doubt because they gave a chance of extra food in the shape of corn and other things dropped by travellers.

There were quite a number of sand grouse which flighted long distances to the salt lakes on the plain to drink, and on some of the lower hills there were quantities of chukor, the Eastern form of a French partridge. We were also surprised to find rock pigeons in a country that did not appear to suit them. Their roosting places were in old deep disused wells, the relics of a former civilisation often situated far from any present human habitation. There was an attractive mountain nuthatch in the bare hills, which were quite treeless, and these birds ran about on the rocks in exactly the same way as our nuthatches run about on the bark of trees. There was also a desert nightjar, very like our own but coloured to suit his surroundings.

The salt lakes had large thick reed-beds growing on their margins and were full of wild geese, swans and duck of various kinds. We tried to get flying geese with a .350 rifle, but oddly enough we missed them. There were also, judging by the tracks, a number of wild pig inhabiting the reed-beds, and a troop of them were seen one day at dawn returning over the bare slopes to their home. Our best view of a pig, however, was from the carriage window of the train. When just outside Eregli we suddenly saw a little cloud of dust blow past the window, and there within a few yards of the train was a fine old boar spurting across some bare fields, having no doubt been disturbed from his siesta on the railway bank.

It is a rule in the Near East (and no doubt elsewhere) that you must not disappoint foreigners. We had much evidence of the strict way in which this rule is observed by the Turks. Whenever we asked, as we constantly did, whether a particular bit of country contained wild sheep, or other game, the answer given with a wave of the hand round most of the horizon was invariably, "Boudah chok, chok chok" ("Heaps of them over there"), varied occasionally, to give a suggestion of veracity, by a point to a particular spot, and the remark, "Boudah yok" ("None there").

The general impression given was that there was so much game that you had to push them aside to get about at all. We never actually had to do this, and in fact the sheep took a lot of finding. We came to the conclusion that native information on game was not worth bothering about and that we must go entirely by our own eyes and glasses. We got heartily sick of those two words ' chok ' and ' yok,' but at least they were easy to remember and sounded easy to spell: whether they are as easy as they sound, I have no idea.

On the plain were vast numbers of lesser kestrel, each bird hovering over its particular bit of territory, apparently watching for gecko or some other lizard. There were also numbers of grey shrikes and wheatears.

On the advice of a Turk, who I imagine wanted to let us out camels for the purpose, we made a futile expedition north across the plain to a low range of hills called the Karadja Dagh. He said that these hills were full of sheep and so they were, but the sheep were tame, and the country was totally unsuitable for the wild variety: it was, however, the home of enormous numbers of chukor, and we asked our Turkish guide, who had a very long single-barrelled shotgun, if he would shoot some for us to eat. He agreed, but in the evening, when no partridges materialised, he confessed that powder and shot were so expensive that he had refrained from letting off his gun.

When our guide met a lady outside a village, said to be his sister-in-law, a violent altercation started apparently about pay-ment for the camels, which the lady insisted, probably with truth, belonged to her. The old rascal raised his long stick to beat her, and I intervened only just in time, wrapped my arms round the Turk and his stick and hurled him aside. Naturally, after this, relations between us deteriorated and we had a tiring and un-comfortable march back across the plain, with the Turk con-stantly trying to make us camp in impossible places. We kept him going until dark by bagging his water-bottle and carrying it at the head of the column, and refusing to give him a drink until he had done a full day's march. Our one reliable man, an Albanian called Bekir, tried to soothe the Turk by stroking his beard, but it was not very successful and I see no reason why it should have been. The march ended abruptly by the Turk cutting the ropes binding the loads on the camels, and on the morrow we were glad to be rid of him, when we hired fresh transport from a neighbouring village.

When back on our old ground I stalked one day entirely alone, meaning to rejoin the rest of the party in the evening at a given spot by the railway to which camp was to be moved. I failed to find camp (which, owing to camels not turning up, had never moved at all), and as dark was coming on my prospects of food and shelter were distinctly poor. The best thing to do seemed to be to follow the railway in the hope of reaching some sort of shelter. I had not gone far when I came upon a wooden hut and on knocking at the door found the hut full of Turks, who were working on the line. There were good beds in the hut but there was a man to each bed, and I naturally expected to have to make the best of it on the floor. I was, however, in accordance with the strict laws of hospitality in the East at once welcomed and made the guest of the evening. None of these charming people had apparently heard of my existence, and they were astonished at an Englishman being out alone in the mountains after wild sheep, but I was accepted at my face value, given a hearty meal of pilaf (rice and meat), and despite all remonstrances put to bed. My telescope and rifle caused intense interest, and on the whole I suppose that I gave a good evening's entertainment to vary the monotony of their existence. They seemed delighted with my attempts at their language, but the thing which tickled them most was my inability to sit for dinner cross-legged on my hunkers in Turkish fashion, without having my back propped up from behind with a box.

When a day or two later we got another ram I tried to repay my hosts for their charming hospitality by hanging a haunch above their door. They were all out at work at the time, so that we never heard whether it was appreciated. This particular ram was spied on a slope the other side of a flat open plain, which we should never have been able to cross unseen but for the railway. Thanks to its embankment it was possible to cross the plain completely concealed and then come down on the sheep from above. That was the only easy stalk I ever had in the sheep country.

Much the finest stalking performance was brought off by P. H. T. The luck had been all my way and he had not had a chance at a good ram, when near the end of our time he found four rams, two of them exceptionally big. He was getting fairly close to them, when some ewes appeared exactly where they were not wanted. Rather than risk disturbing the ewes and so spoiling the stalk he retired unseen and left them quiet for the night. On the following day, owing to the presence of a band of about forty ewes and to the direction of the wind, he found it impossible to reach a spot from which he could spy the ground

where the rams had been the day before. Again he decided not
to risk it. On the third day the wind was right, he reached the
desired point for spying, found his four rams, and had a capital
stalk, which ended with a right and left of the two best; the
two best were about as big as they make them—a real reward
for patience and skill.

Our visit to Asia Minor took place just after the Young
Turks had instituted the New Constitution, and a venerable old
gentleman came from a village to our camp to discuss it. He
asked us whether under the New Constitution there would be
compulsory military service, whether he could have any non-
Mahommedan wives and whether he would have to pay taxes. We
made no attempt to answer the first two questions, but thought
that he would probably still be asked to pay taxes. "Then," he
replied, "what on earth is the good of the Constitution?"

After a month of roughing it, we stayed a night at Konia
on the way back and to celebrate the occasion asked for wine.
We were advised to try the white wine of Jerusalem and took
the advice to the tune of a bottle each. I cannot remember that
P. H. T. was affected, but personally I never drank anything that
so quickly went to my head. Konia is Iconium of the Bible, and
I can confirm St. Paul's vivid account of shaking the dust of it
off his feet: it is about the dustiest place I ever visited.

On our return to England I went to the Natural History
Museum at South Kensington and showed the authorities there
the skins of the sheep we had shot, all on the same range and in
a comparatively small area. One of the skins laid out on the
floor was that of an old grey-headed ram, and another was that
of a three-year-old with no grey on him. An old gentleman,
whose head was grey, pointed out the difference in colour and
said at once that the two skins must belong to two different
species. I touched my hair, which was then brown, and asked
him if he considered that he and I were different species. This
craze for finding new species was just as prevalent then as it is
now, and some people seem to spend their whole lives at it.

I have not heard any news of the sheep of Asia Minor for
many years, but to others who may go in search of them my

4. Worth a good spy. Catalonia, Pyrenees.

5, 6. Vallee d'Arazas, Pyrenees.

Chapter Three
[*Photos : Peter Haig Thomas*

advice would be to make the trip in October, when the weather is generally fine and not too hot, in fact perfect stalking weather, to look for bare rocky hills with a pink tint to them, and to try to find ground free from Yuruks and their noisy savage dogs.

Three

THE PYRENEES

A FRIEND younger than myself, Thurston Holland Hibbert, now Lord Knutsford, who shall be known as T., and I went to the Pyrenees in the autumn of 1909, our main object being to stalk izzard, as chamois are called in that country. We first travelled by train to St. Béat on the railway to Bagnères de Luchon and thence up the Garonne into Spain. We subsequently returned via Tarbes and Gavarnie to re-enter Spain south of the latter place. The relevant endpaper map shows the country we visited.

One of my most vivid recollections of the Pyrenees is the oaths—the most satisfying oaths I ever heard or used. There were two in particular: I have never seen them written, have no idea how to spell them and still less of what they mean. I once asked my French partner at a dance in Spain what they meant, and she blushed and made no answer, so we had better leave it at that. Anyhow here are the oaths as they sounded to me: "_Ooh_, ma gagnolle," and the second "_Mi_ caréo." If you pronounce them as they are pronounced on both sides of the Franco-Spanish frontier, they are gorgeous sounds and very satisfying. The _patois_ common to the mountain peoples on the two sides of the range is neither French nor Spanish and does not sound in the least like either. I never mastered it and imagine it would be extremely difficult to do so, for neither Spanish nor French would help much, if at all. Except for those lovely oaths, I thought it was an ugly language.

The inhabitants of the two sides of the frontier pretended not to like each other, and I gather still so pretend, but in fact they seemed to us very much akin, and to get on extremely well together, not least in the smuggling business, which was and I expect still is extensive, no doubt giving them a lot of fun and I dare say some profit.

We crossed the frontier not far from Marignac on the Garonne with rifles hidden under the seat of a ' diligence,' the driver on the box sitting facing us and talking the whole time without paying any regard to the road or the horses. Our French stalker, who came from Gavarnie, advised us to tip the douanier to prevent him from looking under the seat. "Il vaut mieux lui donner cinq francs. Ils aiment bien l'argent, ces Espagnolles." It seemed cheap to me, but the man never looked under the seat, and we got through with our rifles and followed the road up the Garonne. The Garonne rises in Spain and the Franco-Spanish frontier in this area is some way north of its source, at a spot where the river runs through a gorge between two high ridges north of the true watershed. The road ended quite suddenly and surprisingly in a flight of steps leading to the village of Salardu. From there onwards it was all mule work, and my advice to travellers in the high Pyrenees is to buy their mules at the start of their journey and re-sell them at the end: otherwise they will be continuously done in the eye, as we were every time we wanted to move camp and had to hire fresh mules; these incidentally never turned up at the time and seldom on the day they were ordered. At the time of year we were there, the end of September and the beginning of October, the quarry we sought lived high up on the bare rocky peaks, and we therefore camped as high as we conveniently could, usually four to six hours from any village. In fact, we hardly saw any inhabitants at all except a very occasional shepherd, and it was as wild a country as any one could wish for.

Before describing the animals of the country, I must introduce our companions. We were met at St. Béat by a first-class chasseur, Castagnez Germanne, and by François Salle, who acted as cook, both from Gavarnie. Castagnez was the son-in-law of Calestin Passet, who had previously accompanied my father on sporting expeditions to many countries, and Castagnez confessed to me, "Mon beau père m'a *commandé* pour être marié à sa fille, parce qu'il m'a trouvé bon *chasseur*." Celestin was right, for Castagnez followed in the footsteps of his father-in-law in the matter of spying, stalking and mountaineering, and had firmly implanted in his head Celestin's dictum, "C'est la *longue-vue* qui *fait* la chasse." Both of them were brilliant with a telescope, in fact I never met their equals.

It has always shocked me that the French, with their intensely vivid language, should have nothing better than 'faire l'approche' to express stalking, as opposed to 'faire la battue' to express driving. At the actual business of stalking, however, the phrases they use are very akin to their Scottish equivalents. "Vous voyez ce petit mamelon? Eh bien, il s'est couché un tout petit peu à gauche" is very close to "Are ye seein' yon wee knollie? Wull he's lyin' jist a buttie east (or west) o' that." A Scotsman deals in east and west (never in north and south) and not in lefts and rights, but that is about the only difference, and I could quote many such instances of similarity; for instance, the answer, when you refuse to fire at some beast that is obviously too small to shoot. "Ooh, il n'est pas mal, quand même." "Och, he's no' a bad beast, whatever." French is a capital language to stalk or fish in, and I find myself often thinking in it and using it in both those forms of sport.

François Salle was a fine broad-shouldered, much older man than Castagnez and a capital camp cook; he was particularly strong on soup, but I remember that one of our staple foods was quince jam in bars, looking like pink household soap. François was more than a cook, he was a real wit—a great boon in camp: he interlarded his many stories with "au bout d'un moment." One morning after a night of pouring rain, when we shouted from our camp beds, "De l'eau chaud, s'il vous plait, François," a rugged face appeared at the tent door and François surveyed the scene of a roaring burn traversing the tent between our two beds. "Ooh, ma gagnolle," he said, "il n'est pas l'eau qui manque." T. had put all his clothes neatly in a bundle on his side of the tent so that they were safe and sound to one side of the burn. My belongings having been left anywhere and anyhow, were swept to the tent door by the water.

François liked, sometimes too well, the rough red wine of the country and saw to it that the camp was always well supplied —not a bad thing at the end of a long day in that rugged country.

We also picked up a Spaniard, Jean, who was, I imagine, primarily the local poacher, and as we later discovered a few other things besides. He was not a bad stalker, knew the ground and kept us laughing.

So much for our party, and I must now describe the type of country we explored and the wild creatures it contained. Owing to the nature of the rocks and the frequency of thunderstorms, the peaks were jagged and extremely steep, and the valleys filled with masses of rock of every size and shape, split off by lightning and projected down the slopes. In most mountainous countries it is possible to find a reasonably easy route up the bottom of a valley. Not so in the Pyrenees, at least not in Catalonia. The "chaos de rochers," as they are so aptly called, turn the traveller out of the valleys on to the ridges, and the ridges themselves are seldom good going. Moreover, the rocks are "pas solides" and it was essential to test each piece of rock before applying your full weight to it. Grips had to be chosen with great care. "Accrochez vous bien." "Mettez la main par ici, par ici. Pas celui-la, il n'est pas solide," were the constant injunctions.

As can be imagined in such a country, a small animal like an izzard, which seldom weighs over sixty pounds (sketches of izzard are facing page 56), is a difficult thing to spot, and is always liable to be hidden by a rock far larger than itself. The ground was full of pockets, and the best way to find the quarry was to remember the golden rule for spying, "Pour bien regarder, il faut être toute à faite en face." Even so, animals visible at one moment might be behind a rock or hidden in a pocket the next, which made long, careful and repeated spying essential. Plate 4 shows typical izzard country in Catalonia. In the actual stalking there was seldom any difficulty in such a complicated country in keeping out of sight: the wind was the trouble, as it always is on steep ground. You never could tell for certain exactly the direction in which it would be blowing, on the particular ridge and still less in the particular couloir (corrie) in which the izzard were. Moreover, there was little grass on those rocky slopes to blow in the wind and so give away its direction. I remember one izzard who had placed himself near a high ridge, and looking through telescopes we could see by the waving grass that the wind came to him from all directions. He was unapproachable. The ground was distinctly difficult, but much to my surprise I found that I rather rejoiced in the passage of a ' mauvais pas.' This was obviously inherited from my father, who was a keen mountaineer in the days when Englishmen were first conquering the Alps.

An izzard, or chamois as it is called in the rest of Europe, constitutes the most remarkable case that I know of constancy of type in widely separated areas. It is an animal that is absolutely confined to mountain ranges and would never think of crossing a wide plain, and yet to-day the izzard of the Pyrenees is hardly distinguishable from the chamois of the Alps and the chamois of the Caucasus, all ranges widely separated from each other by country that no chamois would even look at. The same compact little body, set on the same solid legs, the same ' crinière ' of long hair on the withers and above the hips, that makes him look so much bigger than he is, and gives such a sporting outline to his back, the same cheeky little face with its black and white markings and the same sturdy pair of horns ' bien crochés ': the same sturdy merry mountaineer fit to survive on the steepest ground and the deepest snow—but he must have sun. There are no chamois in Norway, no doubt because there is no winter sun in that country. How is it that there has been practically no deviation in type, of animals that cannot have crossed from one range to the other of Europe during the time that this part of the world has been anything like its present form and shape? I know no greater mystery in the study of natural history, and the only similar case that I can think of is that of ptarmigan, a bird inhabiting only the tops in Scotland, Scandinavia, the Alps and the Pyrenees.

What is a chamois? Is he an antelope? In my opinion the klipspringer of a South African kopje is about his nearest relation, certainly in shape and habits, but there always seems to me some element of a goat about a chamois: to my mind he is worthy of a class all to himself. "On peut monter, ou montent les izzards" is true, although not always easy. It would not be true if you exchange the word 'monter' for 'déscendre,' for they seem to go downhill in one if necessary. There is a better climber than man or izzard in one part of the Pyrenees and in certain other ranges of Spain, and that is the 'bouquetin,' the Spanish ibex. I shall refer to him when I reach his part of the range, which was not in Catalonia, but it is worth pointing out here that, while izzard or chamois are practically identical in all the different ranges, this is not the case with ibex. The Spanish ibex is found nowhere but in Spain. Closest to him are the two types of 'turr' which inhabit the Western and Eastern Caucasus, but they have distinct features, and so does the ibex of the Alps; still more different is the ibex or wild goat of Crete, Asia Minor and Persia. All are goats with the smell and habits of goats, but they differ widely and there are others further east which are again distinct.

There are or were, when we were there, bears in the Pyrenees, and I gather a good many of them. We never happened to see one, but we often found their tracks and the sheepdogs were, as mentioned in the chapter on Asia Minor, furnished with collars studded with spikes expressly to protect them from bears. We heard some of the dogs barking at bears, and the shepherds told us next morning that these animals had been trying to get at their sheep all night. They asked us to organise a drive to rid them of these marauders, but for some reason it never came off and would probably have had no result in any case. We were told that bears also existed in considerable numbers in the forest about Luz on the French side of the Pyrenees and that most tame travelling bears were obtained from this district. I do not know if they have managed to hold out until to-day, but I should be surprised if they did not still exist in the wild country on the Spanish side.

Something must be said of the birds. We saw one or two capercailzie in the forest but were generally far above the ground they favoured. There were a few ptarmigan, but not so many as I should have expected and we never came across any black-game, nor do I remember hazel-hen but think that they must have existed in the forests of the Pyrenees, as they do in the

forests of the Alps and the Jura. The most attractive bird that
I met in the Pyrenees, and I met him there for the first time,
was the rock creeper. He reminded me most of a red admiral
butterfly flitting about precipices in crimson, grey and black.
He was not content with anything short of a real precipice
(there were plenty of them), and scorned a slope, however rocky,
that human beings could scale.

There were a number of crested tits in the fir forests and also
firecrests. I must confess that firecrests are much smarter birds
than our familiar goldcrests. The whitish cheeks, the black line
through the eye, and the more flashy crest, particularly when
erected and spread in display, give the tiny creatures an air of
minute distinction. The notes of the two birds are very alike
in tone but there is this difference. Lord Grey has given a
delightful description of a goldcrest's song in the *Charm of Birds*.
He says that it suggests to him ' a tiny stream trickling and
rippling over a small pebbly channel, and at the end going over
a miniature cascade.' In a firecrest's song there is no cascade:
it just ripples on. The small bird of the tops which remains in
my memory is the alpine accentor, which although he lives in
such a different type of country is a first cousin of our hedge
sparrow. He has a nice red-brown sheen on his plumage, but is,
like his cousin, a modest little creature.

The wag among Pyrenean birds is the chough: he is the
yellow-billed variety and lives in the same country as the izzard.
In fact his main job in life appears to be ragging izzard, a
pastime at which he never tires. One day we were sitting eating
lunch on a high ridge overlooking lower slopes, and beyond
them the plains of Spain. On a ledge below us was a herd of
izzard, does and kids. While I was watching them with a telescope a chough singled out for his attention an old doe lying
with a kid nestling against her side. The bird kept hopping and
fluttering nearer and nearer to the kid, which nestled closer and
closer towards its mother's foreleg. The kid was obviously
worried by the chough, but the old doe pretended to be fast asleep.
With a final bounce and flutter the chough almost touched the
kid, when instantly its mother lowered her head and made a

Cette diable de femelle, qui ne veut pas bouger.

Doe & Kid.

Le vieux soldat.

Izzard. Chapter 3.

East Caucasian Turr   Chapter 6.

violent and sudden sweep of her horns at the bully. She just, only just, missed the chough, and he fled terrified to seek a less dangerous subject for his attention.

It was a hot day, and suddenly with one accord the whole herd of izzard set off at full gallop to quench their thirst at a burn. While there they heard far below them, but hidden from sight, shepherds calling, and the sound worried them for they could not quite place it. Again they set off at full gallop to a point on the ridge below them from which they could actually see the shepherds, and having satisfied themselves that the men and their dogs were sufficiently far below them to be harmless, they returned at full gallop to their original position and settled down again to their siesta.

I was surprised at the number of vultures, in particular Egyptian vultures, which breed in the precipices, and we also saw lammergeier fairly often—nine of them on one day coming to a kill. I wondered how vultures found enough carrion in a country with such a small population of men and beasts, but no doubt they range far over the plain for food.

There would no doubt have been a great number of trout in the lakes and rivers, if they had not been so systematically netted by the Spaniards. In fact we did enjoy, on off days from stalking, some very interesting fishing, but it is best to look for trout in Spain far from the haunts of man. The most prolific place was a deep loch, called the Etang Gerebez, set in an amphi-theatre of peaks at least four hours from any village. There on a sunny day trout rose well, but the food supply must have been poor for their condition and colour were bad: some of them, however, weighed 1 lb. In the rivers they were smaller, but in one stream at least they were very pretty fish. The rocks in this stream, which ran through the Vallée d'Arazas mentioned later, were pale limestone and the trout were pale grey with brilliant pink spots. They were very shy and naturally so, for they had learnt that human beings are extremely dangerous creatures, but they were comparatively uninstructed in the matter of fine gut and a dry fly. During a hatch in this gin-clear stream they took a dry fly well, if the fisherman could stalk within shot of them, but I have never met trout who were so quick at going to ground under a rock when hooked. They had no doubt learnt that trick from heavy netting: underground was the only safe place to be when human beings were about.

One day when I explored a likely-looking stream and saw hardly any fish, I reached at last a bridge by the douane at Bouchéraut, and below it was a single trout poised near the surface. I do not know how he had managed to survive in such a dangerous spot, for douaniers with nothing to do were always hanging about the bridge. After a good deal of trouble I caught that trout on a dry fly, and the Spanish onlooker obviously considered that my methods were ludicrously troublesome and obsolete: no doubt he was very much annoyed that I caught it at all. Impressed by the general air of indolence of the inhabitants, I asked Castagnez, "Qu'est ce qu'ils font par ici, ces douaniers?" The answer was instantaneous and rather startling: "Beuh, ils ne font que les enfants et ils font beaucoup, quand même," 'Quand même' is the commonest end to any sentence in the Pyrenees, and corresponds exactly to the Scottish 'whativer.' One day T. lent the Spaniard Jean his father's best split-cane rod —a dangerous proceeding, for Jean, on hooking a fish, hurled everything backwards through the air over his head: he carried the fish in his cloth belly-band.

It is about time that I got down to the serious business of stalking. On our first day in camp we all climbed together, and while spying a large couloir I suddenly saw, in the middle of the field of my glass, my first izzard perched on a rock in a ' chaos de rochers.' In the excitement of telling the rest of the party of my success I lost the place and never refound him. No doubt he had jumped off his perch and become hidden by one of the many enormous boulders. Then the mist came down sudden and thick, and we descended, but into the wrong valley and had to reclimb to correct our direction. The rest of the way back to camp was a nightmare. It became quite dark and we were reduced on that steep ground to lighting matches, and with them toilet paper piece by piece, which gave us light enough to descend a few yards at a time. We reached camp at last very beat.

I will describe from the account in my diary a memorable day. It illustrates at least one of the main features of the trip —my capacity of missing time after time perfectly good chances at izzard. It may be urged in excuse that shots often had to be taken from uncomfortable positions, and I am reminded of one, when I rested one foot on Castagnez's head and the other on the air. It shows also that the country inhabited by izzard is not one in which to walk ' les mains dans les poches.' Castagnez and I worked round the base of a forbidding-looking mountain called the Pic de Bonaigue, when I spotted with my eyes a single beast that I thought was a buck. It was suspicious and I asked Castagnez if *he* thought it was a buck. He replied that he was quite sure, and I took the shot at about one hundred and fifty yards. The beast bolted with a kid that I had not seen beside it, and I have never missed with greater satisfaction. Later we jumped a real ' solitaire ' (the expression used in France for old male animals), and I had a pretty hopeless galloping shot and missed again. On the east of the Pic de Bonaigue, some way from the top, we saw many tracks, and after a careful spy found six bucks with does and kids scattered about all over the slope above them. It looked a fairly easy stalk, if we could keep out of sight of the does, but the ravine we were in was formed of absolutely rotten rocks, which came away in your hand whenever you touched them, and we had the greatest difficulty in scaling its sides. Thence we crawled into another ravine no better than the first, but it led us under cover the way we wanted to go, and after a scramble we reached a spot within long range.

The izzard were feeding and chasing each other all over the place, and generally behaving as izzard do, as if life was a glorious thing and full of fun. I tried at the height of their sports to crawl in closer but there was no covert, and while I was wriggling about among some small rocks some of the bucks came in towards me. I raised my glass to try to make out which was the biggest and was instantly spotted. The shot was rather hurried, but they were only about sixty yards off and the miss was quite inexcusable.

We had started at dawn, it was now 5 p.m., and I did not

like the idea of failing to reach camp on that ground before dark. We reckoned that we should have at least half an hour of walking in the dark, and decided not to risk it but to go down to the Hospice de Bonaigue, which we could see in the valley straight below us. So far as we could tell from where we were there was nothing impassable between us and the hospice, and we set off at a run down the slope. All went well until we were three-quarters of the way to the bottom and the light beginning to go. Then suddenly the ground fell away in an absolute precipice. We tried one or two places, but Castagnez, who had ventured further than I to peer below, called back, "Pour moi peutêtre: pour vous jamais."

There was no more light, there was nothing to do but sit it out for the night. We had just enough matches and paper to get a fire going out of some fir-stumps, but the ground was so steep that we had to brace our legs against a rock or a log and sleep was impossible. Moreover, we had had nothing but a light lunch and that early in the day, and had no food left. Worse still, we had had no water for many hours, and although we could hear a gurgling burn below us, the precipice intervened. We had run and got very hot, and now it was cold and we were aching with thirst, hunger and fatigue. How I cursed the sound of that burn. We licked the dew off the leaves, and huddled together to wait for dawn. "A present," said my guide and philosopher, "nous ne sommes pas trop heureux, mais je serai bien content de le raconter après." I felt a little doubtful about 3 a.m. whether we were ever going to get out again to a place where we could 'raconter' anything to anybody.

However, dawn came at last and we worked our way weakly and carefully along some awful ground on the lip of the precipice, tried one place that might lead to a crevasse in its surface, but that led to nothing possible, and so painfully remounted to the crest. Then, thank heavens, a little further on we found a trickle of water and soon afterwards some bilberries. That made all the difference—life and spirits returned and before long we came to a sort of fault in the rock wall. The rest was steep but comparatively easy, and by 8 a.m. we were in the hos-

pice, and after eating far too big a breakfast to follow such a
night, I turned the biggest flock of cats I ever saw off a bed and
curled up to cook myself against a sort of brazier inserted under
the bedclothes to the risk of my skin and, I imagine, to the
whole house.

I remember waking up to a terrific stomachache, cured
partly by the arrival of T., who had with great foresight and an
eye for country brought camp to search for us in the Bonaigue
valley, and partly by the spying of a magnificent 'solitaire'
from the doorstep of the hospice. T. went after him on the
morrow and only just failed to get a chance, while I took an
easier day than usual, but one full of interest.

We had seen a 'solitaire' near the head of the valley above
us, but he was very suspicious, and eventually joined another
buck with a doe and kid, to whom he imparted his suspicions.
They tried to get out of the top of the valley by a pass or
'brèche' as it is called in that country, but it was too difficult
for the kid, which had an attack of nerves. After our late
experience I sympathised, and so did the rest of the izzard party.
They would not go on without the kid, and all dashed back
downhill again and into a hollow in the rocks on our side of the
ridge. At this moment another highly suspicious doe appeared
on the skyline and refused to go away. "Cette diable de vieille
femelle, qui ne veut bas bouger," said Castagnez, and I thought
how like that was to "yon old deil of a hind, that wull no' move,"
in Scotland. But the old doe was worse than any hind, for when
I started to crawl in on the bucks hidden in this hollow, she
started whistling her soul out, and that was too much for anybody's nerves. Out came the whole party from the hollow at
full gallop and up the slope to the 'brèche.' This time, with fear
behind as well as before, they managed it, kid and all, and disappeared for ever over the top, and we trailed down the hill to the
hospice and its cats, none of them house-trained, jumping two
big 'solitaires' in the wood on the way down.

The next day we moved to the head of the Vallée d'Espot,
which leads down into Spain joining the valley from Esterri di
Anio, and camped facing a fantastic red peak of great beauty

rising from splendid fir forests, called Los Encantados (the enchanted hills). It was while we were at this camp that we were kept awake by sheepdogs barking all night at bears, and when I was stalking on Los Encantados with Castagnez we were extremely grateful to a bear, whose tracks showed us the way safely through ' un bien mauvais pas.' Castagnez told us that, when acting as guide to a French mountaineer, he had once climbed Los Encantados, and a very difficult climb it had proved. When nearing the peak they had seen two izzard above them. These two beasts tried to mount in front of them, but came to a place which defeated them and dashed back at full gallop along the only possible route, which the two mountaineers were taking. The men stood still and the izzards jumped on to their backs and off them again as they fled down the mountain. The name Encantados is derived from the following story, which I have told already in *Fisherman Naturalist* but which can hardly be omitted here. A chasseur from Espot, instead of joining the rest of the inhabitants on the Fête de St. Hubert to attend service at a chapel by a lake at the foot of the mountain, went off with his dog to hunt izzard on the peak. Strange rumblings were heard by the congregation, and man and dog were never seen again. Even St. Hubert, the patron saint of la chasse, was annoyed at such a breach of discipline and lack of manners. No doubt it was St. Hubert who directed the bear to show Castagnez and me the way down from the enchanted peak.

At this point in the tour T. had secured two good bucks, while I, owing to disgraceful shooting due partly to the sights of my rifle being out of the true, had not scored at all. We were then suddenly bereft of our Spanish stalker, Jean, who came to me one evening in camp to inform me "Ma merey est maladey " (I write it as he said it), and of course we told him to go at once to look after her in a distant village from which two messengers of the bad news had come. The following morning T. and I, who were both trained to the uppermost point of fitness, set off at a run to the village of Espot, followed by Castagnez at a more leisurely pace, in search of mules to move camp. We had not got far when we met two Spanish gendarmes armed and shod

in sandshoes, quite unsuitable for such rocky ground. We gave
them a cheery greeting and ran on, when there was a shout:
we stopped to see the gendarmes pointing their rifles at us and
saying in peremptory tones something we did not understand.
At this moment Castagnez luckily arrived and explained the
situation. They were bound for our camp for the purpose of
arresting Jean for a theft he was said to have committed at
Salardu in the previous year. We told them that the bird had
flown towards ' merey maladey ' and all had lunch together at
Espot, and thence, after much haggling, returned with mules,
hired as usual at exorbitant price.

The next morning, having sent off camp round to another
valley, T., Castagnez and I all started together, and after various
excitements saw three bucks gallop from rocks below us, whence
they had probably heard us, and finally take up a commanding
position below the south face of the great rugged Pic of Basièro.
One of the three was the biggest buck any of us had seen, and
none of them were to be sneezed at. This old warrior carried
one hind leg broken at the fetlock, and we named him ' le vieux
soldat ': despite this disability he was quite capable of tackling
bad ground. They lay down on a patch of snow in the centre
of the cirque below a precipice, and we all agreed that 'le vieux
soldat' knew his job. In that place they were quite unstalkable,
for any approach from above was ruled out by the precipice,
and it was equally barred from below by the wind which whistled
up the cirque towards the izzard from every angle. We made
a minute survey of the geography with our glasses, saw that
there were only two possible brèches leading out of the cirque
on its eastern side, and that where we lay on the western was
also a likely passage. A sketch of " le vieux soldat" faces page 56.

The upper brèche, which looked extremely difficult, led to
the skyline close to the top of Basièro. We doubted if ' le vieux
soldat ' would tackle it. The other, which though steep looked
possible, cut through the precipice wall lower down the cirque.
We therefore made the following plan. T. was to take up a
commanding position on the west of the cirque near where we
were. I was to try to work my way clean round the back of

Basièro and finally reach the top of the second brèche, which we thought the most likely of the two for the izzard to choose, if they moved east; while Castagnez, after giving me 1½ hours to get round to my post, was to move them from below. Old Basièro sat there frowning at me and I wondered what lay at the back of his head, but I was very fit and set off in a state of high excitement. It was going to be fun whatever happened, and ' le vieux soldat ' was a prize worth any amount of sweat and trouble. The ground I had to traverse was quite new to me and was hidden by the face of the mountain that I had to circumvent. As I look back on it now I can see that it was a pretty mad venture, but it did not strike me in that light then. •

For the first half of the journey there was nothing formidable and I made good pace, but soon after passing round the north face of the Pic a steep narrow gulley composed of absolutely rotten rocks crossed my path. Whatever I clutched came crumbling out in my hand, and the gulley took so long to negotiate that it was obvious that I should never reach my post by any time like the appointed hour. However, it was circumvented at last and a second gulley hardly less formidable intervened. I was debating whether it would not be better to give up and make my way down to Espot for the night, when from a ' chaos de rochers ' up jumped a fine buck. It was a very snap shot, but for once the bullet hit the izzard. Success at last but not ' le vieux soldat.' I whipped off his head, slung it on my back, and raced on to my post at the head of the chosen brèche.

My watch showed that I was about two hours late, and I felt that Castagnez must have given me up and the planned manœuvre be over. Exultant at having defeated Basièro and got my buck, I stood on the skyline and let out a ' whoop ' of triumph that echoed far and wide round the cirque. It was one of the maddest things I ever did. Down below me there was Castagnez, who had waited patiently for my arrival, trying to signal to me that the three izzards, including ' le vieux soldat,' were making for the second brèche. I failed to understand and stood like a fool where I was, instead of bolting to cut them off, as I might possibly have done. When after scrambling down the

brêche I rejoined them T. and Castagnez told me exactly what
they thought of the contents of my head, and we trudged down
the valley to reach camp at dark. That was a real day and we
dreamed of ' le vieux soldat,' a gentleman that we never saw
again, nor any other quite his like.

On our last day in Catalonia Castagnez and I, after a hard
but unsuccessful stalk, were on our way down to join the others
at Salardu, when we heard music in a village. "C'est la fête de
Tréedos," said Castagnez, "ça doit être amusant, il faut y aller."
The village of Tréedos was not much out of the way, and off we
went straight for the music. Neither of us had shaved for many
days, our clothes were torn to ribands and our boots were studded
with heavy nails; both of us carried telescopes and I a rifle. As
we reached the village M. le Maire advanced to meet us in all
his regalia, and offered with a bow a drink of wine in greeting.

I must explain that in the Pyrenees the universal method of
drinking is as follows: the wine is carried in a skin bag with
a neck to it, and this is held at arm's-length and the wine poured
in a thin stream through the air into the mouth, which must
never touch the gourd. This method of drinking takes a lot of
learning: it is not easy at first to hit the mouth at all, still less
easy to avoid choking. Despite much practice, I was still far
from expert and Castagnez knew it. As I took the proffered gift
with a bow and lifted the goatskin aloft in my hands there was
a titter from behind. Damn Castagnez, why could not he restrain
his feelings at such a solemn moment? I braced myself; this
time there was not going to be a miss: I made a perfect shot
and drank long, happily and accurately. I bowed again to the
Maire and turned to Castagnez. "Voilà mon vieux," I said with
pride and dignity. "Ça n'a pas marché trop mal."

M. le Maire informed me politely that he judged from my
accent that I came from Paris, which proved at least that he had
never visited that place. The Maire's remark was too much for
Castagnez, who split with laughter, and we moved together into
the merry circle of dancers in the square, formed of stone blocks
heavily coated with cow dung. There we danced in our strange
attire with the Spanish beauties of the place, to the music of a

rather drunken band of two—an entertaining finish to our journey in Catalonia. Years afterwards in Norway, Godfrey Phillimore and his wife, whom I then met for the first time, told me that on a journey up Haute Garonne on their way to the little independent republic of Andorra, they had heard strange tales of a weird Englishman by name Antonio Buxtoni, who was then hunting in the mountains.

From Catalonia we returned to the railway and travelled through France by train via Tarbes to Gavarnie, which lies below the famous cirque, on the northern slopes of Mont Perdu. Gavarnie is writ large in my family's history and we received a mighty welcome from Monsieur Bellou at the Hôtel des Voyageurs. Before I was born, my father had journeyed to the South of France in search of a place suitable for my mother, who had been ill and had been advised to seek mountain air and sun. He had come by chance to the Hôtel des Voyageurs at Gavarnie and from its doorstep had spied an izzard, borrowed a sort of blunderbuss from M. Bellou, stalked and shot the izzard. He at once telegraphed to my mother that he had found the very spot for her, and so began a series of pleasant holidays for my parents and their family at Gavarnie and in the neighbouring valleys on both sides of the frontier. Moreover, it was there that he found that famous chasseur, Celestin Passet, father-in-law of Castagnez. Celestin once came on my father's invitation to England and was shown the sights of London, including the Zoo and the Law Courts. When the judge entered court in his wig, Celestin, shaking his finger at him, was overheard to murmur, "Ah, le vieux cochon." Luckily the judge did not overhear the remark and might not have understood it. When we came to Gavarnie Celestin was an old man for the mountains, but not too old to accompany us, and never have I met a hunting companion with such a store of humour, or with such a flair for work with a telescope. He stands apart from all the spyers that I have met.

We found a great contrast between Catalonia and the country about Mont Perdu. In Catalonia the going was always hard, in fact a perpetual scramble but seldom impossible. In the country round Mont Perdu it was sometimes quite easy, but then suddenly the traveller was brought up short by ground that was quite impossible. Our main object in this part of the country was to visit the Vallée d'Arazas, a rift in the mountains which cuts a huge trench through the southern face of Mont Perdu, on the Spanish side, and issues into a valley that leads past the village of Torla in Spain. There is an easy but long way round to this village over the Port D'Espagne and past the Douane at Bouchéraut to the foot of the valley, but we took a more difficult route, via the Pic D'Escusan, and thence along a horribly narrow ledge overlooking the Vallée d'Arazas. T. was quite impervious and did not mind the ledge at all, but my boots had worn out and I was wearing a pair of Spanish *espadrilles* which gave me a poor grip, moreover they kept coming off and the laces broke. For the first time on that trip I had a bad attack of nerves, and it was not improved when Celestin seemed doubtful of the way off the ledge down a rocky scree that was supposed to lead us to the floor of the valley. I looked at it and was more than doubtful, but after a careful survey Celestin, who had investigated ahead, recognised some landmark and cheerily summoned us on to follow him. He was right and we got safely down, but did not reach the *Cabane*, which was to be our main home, until two hours after dark. On the steep ground of the Pyrenees the question is always being asked, "Est-ce qu'on peut déscendre par ici?" Celestin's cheery answer used to be, "Déscendre? Mais oui: bien vite!—C'est remonter après——" which I should translate by, "Get *down*? *Rather:* quick as you like—it's getting *up* again——"

I must try to describe the Vallée d'Arazas (Plates 5, 6), for T., who had recently complained that he was sick of beautiful views, was as astonished as I was at the wonders of the place. It was not like anything that either of us had ever seen, even in that world of beauty that constitutes the Pyrenees. Judging by coloured photographs, the nearest thing to it is the Grand Canyon in the Rocky Mountains. The valley (trough is a better word), which is about eight miles long, looks like an enormous trench cut by giants out of the rock, and cut in steps. In all that length of over sixteen miles round the lip of the valley there are, if my memory is correct, only three ways passable for man from the lip to the bottom of the valley, and one of those ways is artificial: at my father's instigation iron spikes had been driven into the rock at the worst spot to give a hold for hands and feet.

I have said that the trench is cut in steps, and one of the most astounding features was the colour of those steps. The upper precipices are pure white from the lip to the little narrow ledge, which runs all round the circuit of the valley and is called 'la plus haute corniche.' Below that is the second step, much deeper and coloured bright shades of orange and red: these red precipices terminate in 'la grande corniche,' which is much wider (averaging twenty to thirty yards) than the upper corniche. Below la grande corniche are more precipices and very steep but possible slopes down to the floor of the valley. These slopes are covered by a glorious forest of pine and beech and box, the home of the great black woodpecker, the firecrest and many other birds, with Egyptian vultures frequenting the precipices. The floor of the valley—and travellers are grateful for it—is comparatively flat. One visitor described the Vallée d'Arazas as "Not really very steep but all sloping the wrong way," and indeed the impression from the floor of the trench is that it is narrower at the top than at the bottom and that the sides slope inwards. The floor of the valley is a vivid green, and through it flows a lovely burn or ' gave,' as it is called in the Pyrenees, the home of the grey trout with pink spots already described.

There are, I am told, although I have never visited them, two other valleys of similar formation running out from the southern face of Mont Perdu. One of them is called the Vallée de Pinède. I forget the name of the other. These extraordinary clefts are the home of that best of all climbers, the Spanish ibex or ' bouquetin' which also inhabits the Sierra de Grêdos near Madrid and certain other Sierras in Spain.

We were soon to learn some of the feats of which the ' bouquetin ' is capable. Celestin spying from high up on the south side of the valley, spotted what he described as ' un bien joli papa! ' This old goat was lying on a minute ledge fairly

low down in the forest on the north side of the valley, and
Celestin assured us that there was no possible way off that ledge
for man or beast for a long distance. It was too late to do anything about it that evening, but Celestin believed that the
'bouquetin' would be there on the morrow, for the simple
reason that he could not get off the ledge. We scrambled up the
next morning by a possible place some distance from where the
animal had been seen, and followed in single file along the
narrow ledge, until we came to the place where he had been
spied the evening before. There were his tracks and we followed
them in great excitement along the ledge: the tracks ended
abruptly. Where had he gone? Where could he or where could
anything but a bird have gone? We peered down over the cliff
into the forest below us. Could anything take that jump and
live? We returned, descended from the ledge and examined the
ground below the place where the tracks had ended; there were
the marks where he had landed like an india-rubber ball, and
walked calmly off on his evening feed. On one or two occasions
our men, who had a dog, saw ibex, with this exception all ewes,
but neither T. nor I ever set eyes on one. Nevertheless, it was
delightful to sit about in that glorious place, with nerves aquiver
for something that might come but never came.

T. left for home before me, and after travelling with him to
Bouchéraut I went up to hunt izzard on the pics overlooking a
village with the delightful name of Panticosa. One incident is
worth recording. Just below the crest that runs between the
Pic de Fenez and the Pic d'Otal I spied a fine old solitaire. It was
a glorious day and he lay there basking in the sun, completely
unapproachable from above and with a perfect view of all the
country that lay below him and between us and his castle. By
a very careful stalk, we reached the end of a ravine which ran
up towards him, but we could get no further. While we watched
him through our telescopes a flock of choughs arrived and no
doubt thought him a capital object on which to vent their high
spirits and love of mischief. They whirled continually round his
head, shrieking and striking at him while he jerked his horns at
any bird that ventured too close.

We noticed that his gaze seemed concentrated in our direction and we wondered, although the distance seemed too great, whether he had seen something of us. He also kept looking down straight below him as though he were searching for a place for his evening meal, and as there was clearly no grazing near his rocky couch, we felt that he must eventually come down. At last he stood up, the choughs renewed their game with added zest and suddenly he descended at full gallop, but stopping occasionally to look always in our direction. Whenever he stopped, the choughs whistled round him, almost hitting him on the head and setting him off again on his downward journey. He seemed so bent on coming in our direction that Castagnez suggested, "Il nous croit d'être femelles! Il va nous faire une petite visite!"

Before long his descent took him behind a ridge that for the moment hid his view of our position, and we raced to the ridge to intercept him. I looked over but saw nothing. In fact, the izzard and I had passed each other with the ridge between us, he making for the exact spot where we had been sitting. Not seeing him, I raced back to look over the other side of the ridge. There was a snorting whistle and off he galloped down the hill. My first shot went anywhere, the second was nearer and the third crumpled him up. He was a grand old buck, blind in one eye, with a splendid 'crinière' and thick horns 'bien écartés' (well turned out at the tips).

At the back of the head of an izzard are two deep glands in folds of skin, one on each side behind the ears and below the horns. The function of these strangely situated glands is doubtful, but they swell and deepen every year, attaining their maximum development in the rutting season, and then dwindle again until they are hardly noticeable. In this particular buck they were far more pronounced than in any other we killed and they emitted a very strong smell. It was only October 7th and therefore very early in the season for a buck to pay much attention to does, for the normal time of the rut of chamois and izzard is November. I think that for some reason this old gentleman had got his dates wrong, and that Castagnez's ' Il nous croit d'être femelles ' was correct. He was bound for us and we should never have got him but for that strange freak of passion a month too early. Castagnez carried this heavy old 'solitaire' on his shoulders, holding all four legs in front of him all the way back to Bouchéraut. It always astonished us that the men could carry apparently with ease a whole izzard in this way over the roughest ground with no more comment than a cheery 'on est bien chargé!' We skinned this izzard hung up on a hook in the douanier's kitchen, and I shall never forget the smell with which he filled the room.

While in this part of the country I saw an excellent example of the gathering of vultures to a kill. I had shot a buck izzard on the top of a ridge overlooking Panticosa, and after skinning and cutting up the carcase for carrying, Castagnez and I were sitting to eat our lunch among some rocks one hundred yards away from the discarded remains of the izzard. We had only been sitting there about a quarter of an hour, when there was a swish and a single vulture alighted by the carcase, after flying low along the ridge. At intervals of about five minutes other single vultures kept arriving, not apparently from high up in the sky, but all taking exactly the same line, low along the ridge. I suppose that the vulture watching our part of the country from high up in the sky had spotted the carcase and made his last turn before alighting along the ridge. Other vultures miles away had seen that swoop and that last turn, and followed exactly the first bird's line of approach. It was all quite different from what I had expected: no assembly in the air, no swoop visible from the blue, but an exact repetition by each single bird, arriving at distinct intervals, of the low glide along the ridge to the kill.

A Spaniard who had cut off my month's beard and trimmed my hair, invited me to a ball at Torla. I could hardly refuse, and apart from the ball I wanted to visit that dirty but picturesque village. It was well worth it. In addition to the people of the immediate neighbourhood, guests had crossed the frontier from France to attend the ceremony, and all the world, Spanish and French, were there. We started to dance by daylight in the village square but the performance was complicated by the arrival of all the cows, goats, sheep and pigs of the village being driven in through the square for the night.

After dark it was considered improper to dance in the square, and we moved to a fine old hall with an iron floor, and there continued the performance. My hair-cutter was an efficient master of ceremonies, but there was one custom which struck me as embarrassing, at least for some of the ladies. There were two rows of chairs arranged back to back in the middle of the hall, and at the end of each dance the gentlemen deposited their partners on these chairs. Before the next dance the gentlemen selected their partners from the two rows of chairs, but there were always just two or three ladies left seated out in the blue, and naturally they were not the best lookers. Our plan of sitting out round a ballroom or in separate rooms seems to be better than the Spanish one of depositing the leavings in the middle of the ballroom.

After the dance at Torla I returned with Castagnez to the Vallée d'Arazas, and finally left it by one of the three possible exits up the side—a cheminée which provided a sporting scramble up a very confined cleft in the rocks. On the edge of the plateau at the top was a shepherd living in an old stone hut, and guarding sheep and goats, which had had to be hauled by rope up the precipice on to the plateau for their summer grazing. The flocks belonged to a village called Fanlo, some six hours away in Spain, and the shepherd told us that once a week his daughter mounted alone up the cheminée with a sack of potatoes for him on her back.

He was living far from the world and his views about it were original. He asked, for instance, if it was true that we had to cross the sea from England in order to reach the Pyrenees; whether the South African war was over and if so who had won. News must travel slow at those levels for the date was eight years after the end of that war. He was extremely interesting about local matters and told us the following story. He had been sheltering from a terrific snowstorm in his hut and his flock was gathered in a tight ball—all heads down and together —in a little hollow just outside the hut, when down the mountain dashed three izzard, which charged into the middle of the flock of sheep and shared its warmth and protection until the storm was over. We dined and slept with him. He was not prepared for company and there was only one sardine tin to drink from and one wooden spoon, but his manners as host were perfect. At the end of each course he licked the spoon and then passed it to us.

On the following morning after a cold night in that infernally draughty stone hut, we stalked our way across the plateau, and after ending the season typically for me with another miss, we reached the Brèche de Roland from the south side. It is an astounding place. The great wall that divides Spain from France is cut as though with a chisel in this one place, leaving a narrow door through the wall of rock. The story goes that Roland, returning on his horse from Spain and seeing this great wall before him, drew his sword and charged it. It must have been a good horse and a good sword for the wall gave, the chunk of solid rock was cut clean out like a hunk of cheese and he landed safely at a spot about five miles away in the valley behind Gavarnie. Unbelievers are shown the tracks of his landing to this day. With my memories of our descent along the ledge that gave me the attack of nerves and of our scramble up the cheminée, I wondered how that horse ever reached the plateau and got into position for the charge. Having swallowed the earlier part of the story, any one seeing the Brèche de Roland will swallow the second part with ease, and in any case will find it difficult to suggest any other explanation of that clean cut door that gives passage between France and Spain. We sat on the Brèche and marvelled at the view, while Castagnez told me of how they set nets across the door to catch migrating pigeons rushing through. Then we walked down ' les mains dans les poches,' through the cirque to Gavarnie.

Celestin welcomed us and offered to drive me next morning down the valley to Luz St. Sauveur, of which he was Maire, and where he was going to preside at a meeting. I accepted with delight for to have such company on a beautiful drive was perfect, but I was quite unprepared for the appearance of Celestin, whom I had always seen clad for the mountains. He was dressed in a black frock-coat and long flappy patent leather boots, and looked like a Foreign Minister attending a Cabinet meeting. We trundled down the valley in a high dog-cart, while he regaled me with stories of the past and stories of the day. We talked, I remember, of politics and the Government. "Gouvernement! Mon dieu, qu'est que c'est le Gouvernement? Rien que les impôts." The Maires of France are a fine independent lot and the backbone of their country. I thought what fun those meetings at St. Sauveur must be, graced by a chairman with such a sparkling wit.

My last view of the Pyrenees was in the early morning from the terrace of a hotel in Pau. Lit by the morning sun, the long proud line of peaks gleamed to the south. I had penetrated deep and learnt to love them—both sides of them, the Spanish and the French.

Four

HAMPSHIRE

THERE ARE going to be a good many trout in this chapter, but it was not in Hampshire that I caught my first one. That event occurred, when I was about seven, in a small burn at Garrogie, near Loch Killin in Inverness-shire. Of course it was caught on a worm in a spate and was very small indeed, but it was a trout and that year I caught a good many of them, but only when the water was high and coloured. The next year I went up in the world as high as a fly, and since there were plenty of trout and they were not very well educated, they provided enough practice and success to feed my keenness.

My first English trout was caught in the brook at Warham, near Wells, on the North Norfolk coast, where I was staying with my uncle, Charlie Digby, rector of Warham. It was much the biggest fish I had then caught and weighed perhaps three-quarters of a pound and its capture was one of the biggest moments of my young life, but it was the only fish I caught there. My visits to Warham were more concerned with ratting than with fishing, and my uncle was one of the best shots at a rat with a stick I ever met: he was also a wonderful gardener and capital company.

The first chalk stream to which I was introduced was in Hertfordshire and very appropriately no fish were caught. My chief memory of the day is of a series of torpedoes racing off under water in all directions, scared by far too bold an approach. I knew nothing then about how to stalk a trout and my host, realising, I suppose, that there was no hope of my catching anything in the open and in full daylight, took me to try my hand under a mill-arch, where light hardly penetrated. There one fish did turn and look at my fly or at something where I believed my fly to be, but it did not take hold. It was a blank

day, but an exciting one for me; it must have been a maddening
one for my host.

My first introduction to the chalk streams of Hampshire
came many years later, when I was invited to fish on the Itchen
at St. Cross, downstream of Winchester. The surroundings were
beautiful, but the number of spectators was rather embarrassing
to me although not to the trout, who were used to them. The
fish were rather small for a river like the Itchen and not particularly difficult to catch, but my clearest memory is of a trout
further downstream which completely defeated me. He rose all
day and at frequent intervals within an inch of the far bank. It
was not a particularly difficult place, but he never paid the
smallest attention to anything I gave him and never resented
anything I did to him. He just went steadily on, rising very
quietly and refusing to be interrupted. Finally I waded across,
stalked him very carefully and lying flat on my stomach on the
bank just upstream of him discovered what he was taking.
A steady stream of green and other coloured smut was passing
over him and he was quietly sucking in these minute insects and
paid not the smallest attention to anything else. I might have
found this out sooner instead of wasting half the day on him.

My next visit to Hampshire, made when Driffield trout had
taught me most of the things I know, or think I know, about
chalk-stream fishing, was to Leckford on the Test. It was mid-
June, the weather was very hot and fine, and one member of the
party, who ought to have known better, propounded the theory
on the first night of my visit that no big trout ever put his head
up in the morning to take a fly until 11.30 a.m. I woke early
next morning to a glorious still day of brilliant sun, which drew
me to the river at 8 a.m. I reached it at the downstream end of
a wide winding stretch of deep water with an even flow and,
despite the sayings of the evening before, trout were putting up
their heads all over it, to take advantage of a hearty hatch of fly.
I wore no waders in those days and, taking off my coat and
tucking my fly-box into my shirt, I walked straight in up to
my middle and never came out again for about two hours.

It was a glorious experience; the sun was hot, the water was cool: all up the stretch of river in front of me, as far as I could see, trout were rising steadily and quietly and many of them were big. There was no hurry, every one else was in bed: I had the whole thing to myself. The trout were not difficult and I could and did select the biggest. Of course many of them were missed and lost, but when I got back heavily laden to the house the rest of the party were just setting out in time to meet the fish first putting up his head at 11.30 a.m. I showed them a few that would never put up their heads again, and in fact the rise was over for the day and nothing more happened until the late evening.

There is one arm of the river at Leckford which runs between banks so boggy and covered with such thick vegetation that the only way to fish it is to pole slowly up in a punt. On one evening on this delightful bit of water, as we reached a round pool at the top, a bubble was seen under the bank, which might have been made by a rat or by anything. We waited and watched and the bubble appeared again in the same place and was once more repeated. As the fly floated over the place there was again a bubble, nothing more, but he was there all right and racing round the pool in a circle. Presently he charged the punt in an attempt to escape downstream and we had some exciting moments before he was landed—a fish of well over 3 lbs. It is strange how small a commotion is made by the biggest fish in taking a fly quietly floating under a bank.

The Test fish struck me as easy to catch, compared with those in the Driffield beck, and that is the experience of others who have fished both rivers. At Leckford trout were artificially fed and turned into the river when they had reached a certain weight, but I doubt whether after a few weeks of freedom this made them much easier to catch. This was not done at Driffield, where they were all natural wild fish, but I believe that the difference between the two rivers and the greater difficulty of catching fish at Driffield is due mainly to the size of the natural fly. Except on rare occasions, when there is a hatch of big female dun, the fly at Driffield seems to me too small to imitate successfully and that is not generally the case on the Test or the Itchen.

I have fished higher up the Test at Longparish and higher still 'Where bright waters meet" and the Bourne joins the main river. Both are delightful stretches of water, but when I was there the upper Test contained many dark-coloured, ill-conditioned fish and I am told that this is still the case. My choice of places in this water was off the back of an island at Longparish. It was overgrown with trees and generally difficult to get at; moreover, it was a quiet place out of sight of everybody I cannot remember whether I caught anything there, but there were exciting struggles with boughs under water and above it, and fish almost impossible to get at, which perhaps looked bigger than they were.

Most of my fishing in Hampshire has been done on the Itchen, but I am not going to enter into a controversy concerning its relative merits compared with those of the Test; they are both too pleasant to argue about. One of my visits introduced me to Mr. Neville Chamberlain. When he arrived I had just found with some difficulty a chiff-chaff's nest at the base of a thick hedge in Sir Francis Lindley's garden, and we clicked over the chiff-chaff.

I was horrified at the size of the pouch sent down to him early in the morning from the Foreign Office; by the time he had got through all that the rise would be over. My fears were groundless; the contents of the pouch were demolished before breakfast, although it contained unpleasant news about Mussolini, and we started punctually for the river, both of us as keen as schoolboys. In fact we were in such good time that the trout were not yet out of bed, and while we sat on the bank discussing the international situation a snipe attracted our attention. We forgot politics, found the snipe's nest and then a yellow wagtail's, and so were in a proper mood for tackling anything.

Presently in the bright sunlight a fly or two appeared and we looked again at the river bisecting a large lush meadow below a wood with a lake in it. As usual in fine sunny weather, the hatched fly was off the water too quick to give a trout much of a chance to take it. In fact the trout, very sensibly, were not bothering themselves with these spluttering insects that took to the air before they could open their mouths. They were concentrating on the nymphs, which at least for the moment had no usable wings and therefore could not fly away out of danger. The trout were stationing themselves just below patches of weed and in hollows on the top of the weed, for nymphs concentrate in such places before they hatch. A very obvious fish took up his position opposite to us against the far bank, and Mr. Chamberlain, who had not had much experience of fishing with a nymph, asked me to have a shot at it. These things seldom come off, but that trout rose to the occasion, sucked in my nymph, and Mr. Chamberlain netted him for me. Then we each took a bank and moved upstream opposite each other.

All the best fish were out and busy and the river was full of them. I cannot remember what we caught but we were kept as busy as bees, and one of my main recollections is of the colour and condition of the fish. Fat, rich red-brown backs and yellow sides glistening in the sun; firm muscular bodies poised over bright green weeds, making sideways grabs and lunges at nymphs both on the surface at the moment of hatching and just below it a moment earlier. They were making the most of the occasion and so were we. I remember marking above me the swirl of a big fish in a little runnel between two patches of weed. So many nymphs were passing the spot, where this fish had taken his stand, that it took some time to induce him to select mine from all that company. When hooked he came squirting past me downstream, raced on, dived under a great bed of weed, and then charged upstream again along the other bank: that was too much for anything and the gut broke. He seemed at the time to be about the king fish of the meadow, but between us we caught enough and big enough to make a few disasters seem of small account. It was a wonderful day with the Itchen trout at their best.

Further downstream than this meadow is a road bridge under which the water pours through a number of narrow brick arches, about the width of a two-pound trout laid at right angles to the stream. I went there one day with my daughter Elizabeth, and while I walked up to the railway bridge just above it, she attended to the road bridge. On previous occasions a down-stream suck had made it impossible to float a fly without drag over fish stationed at the downstream end of the arches except by dangling a fly down through the air off the bridge itself, but on this occasion a change for the better had taken place. Whether the improvement was due to a different growth of weed or to a change in the bed of the river I do not know. Anyhow on this occasion it was possible, by a careful approach from mid-stream below, to get within easy shot and make a fly come down the stream from the arches naturally and without drag.

There were four good trout, each occupying an exit from one of these narrow arches with their heads just under the brick-work and their tails generally in full view in the open below. To get them to see the fly it had to be flicked up inside the narrow arch. That was the fun of the thing, and you could make as many bad shots as you liked without doing any harm or dis-turbing the fish. On the few occasions when a really good shot was made, the fly was whisked right up the arch into the dark out of sight, and the fisherman had to spot his fly as it emerged again from the darkness and determine whether the next fly the trout took was his or one of the natural flies which were emerging from under the bridge all the time.

Elizabeth's eyes are better than mine, and as I was wading under the railway arch above I heard a yell from downstream. When I had scrambled out, and run down to her, she was just slipping the net under the best of the four trout and before long she had done the same to a second. I then took on the other two, while she stood by my side. With one of them I had lost sight of my fly and was not certain whether in fact it had gone where it was meant to go, up the arch, when the trout rose, dipped down again and returned to his station. Without Elizabeth's shout, "He has got it," I should probably never have struck at all. I was just in time and soon afterwards got No. 4 as well. In fact we fairly cleared those arches, and the keeper, whom we met next day, asked if we knew what had happened to the trout of the road bridge which had all disappeared. We were able to answer "that this was hardly odd, because we had eaten every one." It was one of those rare occasions when the fishing looked difficult and was in fact perfectly easy.

Several streams enter the lake at Alresford, and if it were not for the fact that they are almost choked with mud so that little weed can grow, they would be ideal fishing water. As it is they provide sport, although fish have to be looked for and are not to be found round every bend. The few that exist are abnormally fat and of a lovely colour. These streams traverse an absolute jungle of marsh vegetation, in fact the place looks as if it ought to contain hippopotamus or elephant, whereas in fact there is nothing bigger than an otter and a host of warblers. Tough reeds grow in the streams, there are innumerable bushes always placed in exactly the correct position to catch the fly behind your back, when you cast at the only trout you see. If that is not the case the trout sits just upstream of the bush, so that you cannot get at him at all, or else places himself between two tall upright reeds, one of which is certain to intercept the fly, which was otherwise going to land exactly on his nose.

It is a capital place in which to lose your temper, but just occasionally either the trout or the bushes or the reeds sort themselves out into better positions and a fish somehow or other gets himself caught. It is no use in such a place thinking of giving a hooked trout any law. The teeth must be clenched and the trout held as in a vice, for if given the smallest chance the fish is certain to reach some perfectly hopeless obstruction. It is wonderful, if you make up your mind and hold firm, what gut will sometimes stand on such occasions. If by some unholy fluke you do catch anything, it will be worth looking at and worth eating. Fly is scarce, few people bother to fish the place, and a trout that has taken its station near the surface is almost certain to have a go at any fly real or artificial that floats past it. They do not get many chances at fly and they make the most of them, but I never can understand how they manage to be so indecently fat.

An owner of fishing on the Itchen always informed his guests that there was no evening rise on his stretch of the river. None of them apparently ever had the pluck to test the truth of

T.N.   F this assertion, which in fact was made because the host disliked any change in his dining arrangements or turning out in the evening. I have attended this function of the evening rise on a good many occasions on the Itchen, and cannot imagine that any stretch of the river can be free of evening rises, but the Itchen flows the wrong way to enable the fisherman to get the best of the evening light. For the evening rise a river ought to flow from west to east, and the Itchen (it is the only fault I have to find with it) flows for most of its length in exactly the opposite direction.

I can only remember one occasion when I did full justice to an evening rise on the Itchen, and that was on the water which Edward Grey used to fish. There have, however, been many evenings when trout boiled and excitement was intense. People often complain nowadays of the lack of fly on our rivers. On the Itchen the trouble seems to me to consist of the reverse condition—far too much of it, giving one's own poor little insect only one chance in a thousand of getting eaten. In the evenings, moreover, there is often not only too much fly but too many sorts of fly, with the trout only eating one sort and that never the one you happen to be fishing with. I used to be quick at changing my fly even in the bad evening light, but those days are gone, and although I still keep in my head a certain tooth with a razor edge that will snip clean through any gut in a second, I cannot see well enough to get the gut to go through the eye. When at last by some fluke it does so, my fingers in the excitement all become thumbs, and the knot refuses to be tied. I am no longer really fit for the evening rise, but that does not prevent my attendance; it merely prevents me catching fish.

There was an evening two years ago when three of us went down to the Itchen by the village of Stoke. We arrived at the river just as the fish were beginning to perform, and by the time we had all entered the water at three different spots there were rises enough all round each of us to make any one lose their heads. We all lost ours, and the trout did not. We flogged and we flogged, while the trout rose gaily on; the harder we cast, the faster they rose. At last one took my fly by mistake

and in my fury I dealt him such a strike as would have parted
any gut. The same thing happened five minutes later, and then
at last one was hooked and landed. That was the only fish I
caught and the other two did equally well or equally badly. It
was one of those occasions when enormous bags seem certain,
but nothing happens, except complete loss of temper. At any
rate it was very exciting and no doubt it is good for a fisherman
to be made to look an utter fool by a trout.

A tip was given me some years ago by Sir Francis Lindley
about dealing with a trout caught when you are wading in
midstream far from the bank and are in a frantic hurry to catch
another. You do not want to waste a moment in wading to
the bank, which, moreover, would cause a wave and might put
down other fish. There is not of course really all that hurry;
you are probably not going to catch another trout all day, but
you think you are and anyhow here is the tip. The trout that
you have by some fluke actually caught is in the net, which is
held in your left hand: the rod is in your right hand. Pull out
a good long length of slack line off the reel (that is the most
important point of all, for it will prevent you breaking your
rod). Drop the rod, butt downwards, inside your waders; you
can do it without even looking at the rod or at your waders,
unless they are very tight or you are very fat, and can keep your
eye on the fish in the net all the time. Having dropped the rod
into your waders, your right hand is free again: grip the trout
with your right hand, and grip him firmly; whack him on the
head with the landing-net handle or any other hard weapon (that
is the moment when you would have broken the point of your
rod, if you had not pulled out the length of slack).

Now hitch the basket on your back round to your front with
a violent sideways shrug, and slip the trout through the opening
in the lid of the basket. He won't go in: so much the better.
With my basket, if he won't go in, the trout is $1\frac{1}{2}$ lbs. If he
would just squeeze in, he would be just over $1\frac{1}{4}$ lbs., but he won't
so he is a most satisfactory fish. If he is so big that you have to
open the lid of the basket, never mind; open it, chuck him in,
ram him down and, remember, shut up the lid of the basket

again. Give another violent sideways hitch to get the basket round again behind you. Don't drop the net, it will take you ages to find it in all that weed and make you very wet diving for it. Now you are all ready again, rod intact, gut trailing anywhere, fly caught in something—probably the back of your waders. Untangle, pick your rod up again from inside your waders, dry your fly and up and at them. The tip has taken a long time to give, but all that business should be done quickly with a little practice, particularly when another trout is rising with a resounding ' glok ' all the time you are fumbling with the net, the trout, the basket, and all the other ingredients, including yourself.

If I hook a trout above me and he comes, as he often does, downstream towards me, I cannot reel quick enough to keep the line tight on him. Wherefore I pull in slack line as fast as I can with my hand and so keep in touch with the fish. This of course results in coils of line lying about anywhere in the water or on the bank. That is a nuisance and may be dangerous, but it is worth anything not to let the line go slack on the trout, or so it seems to me. The important thing to remember is not to move your feet during the process. If you do, a coil of line will certainly loop itself round your leg and land you in a proper pickle. That has happened to me with a big sea trout; my companion laughed so much that he was utterly helpless and did nothing whatever to help me, as I floundered and leapt about, while the line screamed and the trout nearly twisted my leg off. If you like you need not pull in slack you can reel up instead, which is admittedly safer in the matter of major accidents to yourself and more dignified, but not safer *vis-à-vis* the trout and the hook in his mouth. You can do whichever you like so far as I am concerned. I shall haul in slack; I do it without even thinking, for there is never time to think on these few occasions when a trout is actually hooked. After that it is mainly instinct which directs a fisherman's actions, and so it is even before he has hooked a fish.

Some trout are not hooked when they ought to be. Last summer a big fish used to cruise in a weir pool sucking in flies quietly as they came sailing round a backwater. I stalked him successfully and reached a position just above him with a bush as background, from where I could dangle a fly over his nose without letting the line lie on the surface and get caught in a backwater. I stood waiting until the trout slowly swam into just the position most convenient to me, and then softly dropped the fly on to his nose. He tilted up, opened his mouth and sucked. I was just going to strike, when he opened his mouth again and blew a bubble into the air with the fly in it. Somebody must have been there before me to educate that trout: I never got him.

It is not a matter for boasting (rather for eternal regret) but I did once put back a trout of over 2 lbs. from the Itchen. It happened thus: I was loosed on a stretch of water by a laundry, where trout being handy for the house are particularly welcome to fishermen who have not too much time at their disposal to wander far from home. It happened to be a morning when the fish on that stretch, and there were plenty of them, were at the top of their form. They were nymphing their heads off, they had lost their senses and they were stupid as owls. I had caught eleven of them and one weighed 2 lbs. I began to feel guilty, but near the top of the stretch the biggest fish of all was still gorging nymphs. He was irresistible and he was just as stupid as his brothers. He ate my nymph and got himself caught. Then my conscience woke right up: I admired him, patted his fat sides and slipped him back, and went home, feeling foolish but very righteous. Later I was told that something went wrong on that bit of water, some of the survivors disappeared and the rest went off in condition. We might just as well have eaten that fat trout, while we were in a position to do so.

On two or three occasions I have fished for salmon in Hampshire, on the Avon some miles below Salisbury, and I have been very successful at catching kelts but not at catching fresh fish. I once caught four kelts in one day, which is good going or would be, if they were not kelts. There is a very attractive stone bridge with three arches close to the main road between Ringwood and Fordingbridge. I looked down into the river one day off the top of this bridge, and there exactly below me was a great big fresh salmon scratching lice off his tummy against the pier of the bridge. He was in a perfect place to get himself caught and a large yellow fly was dangled down to him and swayed in the current. He took not the faintest notice of it and went on scratching his stomach, but the yellow fly was too much for a long lean kelt, who floundered on to it and hooked himself.

At this moment there happened to pass a young airman and his girl, and they saw the rod bend and became very excited—still more so when I ran off the bridge and down the bank. It was sad having to explain to them that there was nothing to be excited about and that, whatever the length of the fish, it would have to be put back into the river. The kelt was hauled out in a very few minutes and released again and the two spectators continued on their way, wiser but sadder people. I got two more kelts from under that bridge and lost another, but never a touch from a fresh fish. Anyhow a kelt is exciting enough as long as you are not sure whether it is a kelt or not, and it was impossible to be sure for a moment or two what had taken the fly under the arches of that bridge. There would be a smacking flummox, with a good sound to it, a hearty jerk, an equally hearty strike from me, a moment or two of pulling and excitement, and then the long lean grey form of a useless kelt.

I left the bridge and went upstream over flat dry marshes by the great big overgrown chalk stream with firm banks and no particular indication of where to fish for a salmon, for there were no pools in the ordinary sense of the word and the whole length of the river looked deep enough to hold a salmon anywhere. However, I was told where to fish by my host, who knew, and obeyed orders and on one occasion the real thing happened. There was a sort of gleam of pale yellow under the surface in midstream, a good heavy thump followed by a splash with the indistinct form of a large fish in the middle of it. I was still not quite sure and was afraid to summon my companion for possibly another kelt from several hundred yards away, where he was baling out a punt. I pulled at the fish as hard as I could and, instead of tamely submitting, he pulled back and began to jerk his head. Then he made a good strong run out across and turned upstream. That was no kelt and I let out a proper holloa.

Soon after my companion had joined me, rather blown after his run, the fish set sail downstream and took out a good length of line, as he forced his way below the far bank. My companion said ' Look out,' but the going was ludicrously easy and I was soon level with the fish and then below him again. That turned him and he did a foolish thing. He breasted the current and struggled straight upstream again, while I lay back and made him fight for every inch. At length he stopped, too blown to breast the current further, and I walked away inland, the fish following me right across to my side of the river. I ran in towards him reeling, repeated the manœuvre, and presently he was on a short line close by us and in full view. It was all over very quickly and he proved to be a beautifully shaped cock fish of 30 lbs.

At lunch I tested the nylon cast and it seemed to be sound and not to object to any of the hearty pulls I gave it, before going back to the pool where I had caught the salmon. There was a nasty wind and where I began to cast a dead tree stood in an awkward position behind me. I caught the tree (I always do) but the fly came away quite easily in response to a flick, and I went on fishing and reached the spot where success had come in the morning. Exactly as the fly reached the place where it had been taken before, a large pale yellow form showed under water, then just broke the surface, and again came that satisfying ' thump,' and a violent response from me. The hook went right home, and, as I knew, with no fear of its ever coming out again; the nylon cast broke at the fly and flew into the air, and I cursed myself for not having looked at it after it had hit the tree. But for that nylon cast and the tree and my carelessness, there might, I believe, have been two thirty-pounders to lug home instead of only one, and I have never caught another thirty-pounder before or since.

So far this chapter has given hardly any indication that Hampshire contains anything but fish and large fish at that.

That is not quite true: there is also the New Forest, which holds hardly any fish and they quite small, but a lot of other things of importance—for instance, woodlarks, which, although extremely small, are very important indeed.

Many years ago, my friend Capt. W. S. Medlicott and I took the train to Salisbury and thence bicycled in the evening to Downton near the northern edge of the forest. We had made no plans of where we were going to stay, no plans at all except that we were going to look for woodlarks, but it was late by the time we reached Downton and we stopped at the first inn, which was very small, and asked if we could stay there for the night. The man and his wife who kept the inn looked surprised at our request, but accepted us, gave us a good cold supper, clean beds and a satisfying early breakfast. We asked for the bill and were told three shillings. "Three shillings each?" "No, three shillings altogether." "How do you make that out?" "Sixpence each for supper, sixpence for bed, sixpence for breakfast." That was many years ago but even in those days it was not excessive. I doubt if it can be done now, even at Downton. I forget the name of the pub.

Then to the woodlarks. We looked for open plains covered with very short heather and stunted thin growth of bracken with trees not too far off, for the legs of a woodlark are very short and he dislikes thick cover and enjoys a few trees on which to perch. In one of such places we heard a woodlark singing. Skylarks are responsible for some of the worst poetry in the British language, but the little woodlark remains ignored in verse, although to my ears his song is worth ten times the price of any skylark's. Moreover, he has not copied the silly habit of soaring clean out of sight, while you crick your neck and strain your eyes to see him. A woodlark goes up to a reasonable height and then flies round in circles, where you can watch and hear him comfortably. Moreover, he is very pleasant to hear: his performance shows real quality and is not just a loud outpouring of over-exuberant song. All the same, skylarks admittedly liven up country that might otherwise be dull.

Our particular woodlark descended to earth and was presently joined by his hen, and we walked up to look at them as they ran about on a bit of bare ground, trilling softly to each other and to us. Woodlarks look demure and innocent little things, but, despite this appearance of lack of knowledge of the world, they are the very devil, when it is a question of finding their nests and that is what we were determined to do. We sat down to watch and the woodlarks did not seem to object to our presence, but in fact I have no doubt that they kept an extremely suspicious and watchful eye on us. I forget how many hours we spent on them, but little by little we collected evidence pointing to the fact that they had a nest, and that it was somewhere in a certain portion of the open plain.

Then at long last we got a definite bit of information. A bird went down to a spot we could mark almost to an inch, and though we watched and watched that bird did not rise again. One of us walked to the place, while the other sat still watching and ready to give detailed directions. When both of us were satisfied that we had really got the right spot, we joined forces there and looked carefully at the ground just round our feet. There she was, tucked up tight in the sparse cover in a little hollow on a bank, sitting like a stone with her stumpy little tail cocked behind her and her sparkling black eye looking at us, set off by the clear white eyestreak above it. We had beaten them and we left her sitting safely on her eggs, while the cock sang us off his property, which, now I come to look again at the map, may have been just over the Wiltshire border and not in Hampshire at all.

Five

YORKSHIRE

THERE IS no more varied county than Yorkshire, for it contains, apart from its industrial districts, which I shall leave out, wide expanses of moor covered with heather, chalk wolds and chalk streams starting suddenly from wide valleys at their feet, flat plains round York and Hull, and to the west a variegated country of moor, grass hills, deep valleys and streams, which run fast and clear at their source and degenerate into muddy rivers as they flow east towards the sea.

I shall go first to the chalk streams that come from the Wolds for it was on one of them, the Driffield Beck, that I had my first real introduction to fishing with a dry fly. It was a hard school for I have never fished on a more difficult river, but it was a good school for there was always plenty to fish for. There was no lack of practice or of subjects to practise on: moreover, there was every type of water, a wide river meandering through open meadows, narrow streams with their banks covered with trees, mill pools, hatch holes, clear ponds with springs in them, narrow ditches full of watercress and with thick growth on their boggy banks—indeed all sorts of queer places where a trout might be found apart from the main river, and where he might feed at different times from the rest of his brethren. Once for instance two of us wandering up a small ditch came to a clear pond whose existence I had never even suspected. It was full of trout cruising about and easy to see but nothing like so easy to catch. All this meant for me at least long days, for there was always something to do.

I remember many days on that river, but naturally those of the greatest success remain clearer in the mind. There was a stretch of water held up at a mill by Dawson's Dam. As it neared the dam the current got slower and slower, and the fishing more and more difficult. In all that water in fine weather the trout seldom took floating duns in daytime and were almost invariably engaged in eating nymphs or small black smut. There was much weed and the fly had to be placed accurately between patches of it that broke the surface. It was about as difficult a place as any I have met, but it was very attractive and hard to get away from, for fish were constantly to be seen on it busily feeding. I only once got really square with Dawson's Dam and that was on a wet day.

The wind was south-east—very pleasant for I was on the south bank—and this meant that the breeze was behind me and up and across the stream. It was pouring with rain when I got there and there was no sign of fly or fish. Should I move and see if conditions were different elsewhere, or should I sit it out and watch what happened? I had never been at Dawson's Dam on a really wet day before and decided to sit it out. The rain continued in a steady downpour, and about midday a young under-keeper turned up who was rather inexperienced but good company and mad keen. We stood there watching, and at about 12.30 trout were seen moving very quietly up into their stations and a few fly began to hatch which were battered by the rain and floated down the river, but it was not until about 1.15 that the show really began. When it did begin, it began in earnest and all the best fish took part. The dun were of a respectable size, not horrid little insects too small to imitate. There was no nymphing and the fly that hatched were so battered by the rain, which was now coming down harder than ever, that they could not get off the water and floated quietly down on the surface— a constant procession and an easy prey for the fish. The difficulty was to keep the eye on the right fly—the artificial—among a host of real ones, and it was best to choose a moment when there was a pause in the procession of natural fly and then try to cover the fish. I do not for a moment suppose that I stuck to this excellent advice, for I was much too excited and cast fast and often, trying by violent whipping in the air to keep the fly dry.

The under-keeper was in a frenzy and kept up a running commentary on the fish, my casting and everything else. He

had never seen trout so mad before and he expected me to hook
a fish at every cast. His eyes were good and he was useful in
spotting the heaviest fish, but I expect that he prevented me
from keeping cool—not that I should have done so in any case.
He was capital company. "Yon's a champion fish. Bar gom ees
taaken 'em. Aye, yon's 'im. Cliver now, cliver!" (as I was trying
to put the fly just right). "Bar gom yon's cliver. 'Ees gotten
it." There was much weed but success prevents any nervousness
with a hooked fish, and although I lost some through being too
hard, I lost none through being too soft and no time in playing
them. From 1.30 till 4 p.m. the rain and the rise continued, and
the harder it rained the better they rose. Somewhere in that
stretch of water there must have been a fish of 2 lbs., but we did
not find him, and there was so many good fish rising within
reach that it was difficult to tear oneself away and look for a
bigger. We caught and we lost several of 1¾ lbs. and when the
rain and the rise stopped together at 4 p.m. there were six brace
in my basket. "Yon's a champion day," said my friend as we
parted to get some tea and indeed it was, but that was not all.

After tea the sky cleared, the wind dropped, and there was
every sign of a perfect evening. I went back to Dawson's Dam,
this time alone, and waited wondering whether those trout,
which had had such a feast, would be ready for more and whether
indeed there would be any more. There was plenty more;
spinners began to fall and later duns again began to hatch. It
was not such a savage business as in the morning, but fish again
rose confidently and more confidently as the light began to go.
I was allowed ten brace in the day and therefore still had four
brace to get in the evening to reach the limit. After catching a
particularly good trout (which made nine brace) there were
still two to get, but the next fish was only just about the limit
and, being greedy for something better, I put him back and the
light began to go. A fish that ought to have been caught was
missed, and there was no time left for missing. I got one more
trout big enough to keep, but then the light went altogether
and I stopped, short of one fish. It was the biggest day I ever
had at Driffield and it must, I think, be rare for the same trout

in the same stretch of water to make two large meals within a few hours.

Two-pounders were rare at Driffield but there were occasional stories of even larger fish, particularly at mills and in the lower stretches which were less fished than other parts of the river. The millman at Bell Mills close to the town once told me, for instance, of a fabulous monster that he had seen in the mill race, and I went to investigate. Standing in the tail of the race, I could see upstream of me a trout close under the wall below the building and shouted to the millman to look out of the window and tell me if that was the fish he meant. He said that it was, and the trout being in an easy place and lying in fast water, took my fly and was landed without difficulty. It proved to be an ugly brute with a big head and nothing much behind it. The big fish of the mill is often a fraud.

I did once find one of the mythical creatures which were supposed to haunt the lower water. There was a dam far away from any habitation in an open stretch of the river. Normally there never seemed to be any fish of much account in its neighbourhood, but one day as I passed I saw a long shape under the bubbles below the dam. The shape did not move and I was still uncertain whether it was in fact a fish, but at last it turned round and appeared to take something under water. It was surprisingly large, and I crouched under the bank, wondering what would be the best thing to try. The water coming over the dam would drown at once all floating fly, and as the fish had been seen to take or attempt to take food under water, it seemed best to try to present it with something sunk below the surface and large enough to attract its attention in the swirl under the bubbles. The fish lay with its head so close to the foot of the dam that it had no chance of seeing anything but objects that came down the fall. It was essential, therefore, to land the fly into the sheet of water that dropped from the dam. I tied on a wet fly with a silver body (Little's Fancy) and made shots with varying success at this falling sheet of water.

It was a long cast for I was well below the fish and it lay within an inch or two of the other bank, but my main difficulty

was to guess (for I could not see) whether or not it took my fly
under water. For some time nothing happened; and the fish
made no further movement so that I wondered if it had gone
to sleep. Then at last my fly landed about right and immediately
afterwards the fish turned, dropped downstream a foot or so
and appeared to take something. I struck and found it was my
fly that had been taken. It was the easiest place in which I have
ever hooked a big fish: there was one bush which might or
might not have dangerous roots on the far bank, but otherwise
there was no obstruction of any sort except the foot of the dam
itself. I was, however, squatting in a place where movement
was impossible either up or down, and handing my rod to a
companion, I jumped up the bank, retook the rod and ran to
the tail of the pool. The fish was soon pulled away from any
possible dangers under the dam or under the bush, and as the
current was fast he soon tired in trying to get back to his haunt.
The fight was disappointing, but the trout came up to expecta-
tions in point of size for he was over 4 lbs. He was not however
a good-looking fish and how he got there or what he lived on
remained a mystery. He was in any case the most spectacular
fish in point of size that I ever caught or indeed ever saw on the
Driffield Beck itself.

I remember specially one other: I had wandered far up the
Kingsmill Beck, a tributary joining the main river above
Driffield, and had come near its source to some bends where a
narrow stream ran between thick beds of watercress. A few fly
were hatching in bright sun, and after some sport with odd fish
who were taking nymph, I came round a corner to see half-way
up the stretch of stream above me a lovely fat yellow fish, poised
below the surface. He looked to me $2\frac{1}{2}$ lbs. and he was clearly
on the look-out for food. There was no covert whatever and I
had to crawl through watercress to get within shot. He never
rose but he sometimes swirled, presumably at a nymph, and I
put one on to the water just above him and let it float down.
He very slowly tipped up, examined it with the greatest care
and said, ' No, thank you.' When the same fly was tried again,
he thought about it for a moment, turned and swam slowly

downstream until he reached me. That was of course the end of the business for he saw me and bolted. He was a thoroughly sensible fish and I never could find him again.

A side stream, the Nafferton Beck, came into the main river at Wansford, some three miles below Driffield, and this rose suddenly in a clear pool in Nafferton village. At and near the mill just below the source the fish grew very big, but the most remarkable thing about the trout in the rest of this beck was their colour. There was nothing peculiar visible to the eye about this water: it was slow, looked almost like a canal and did not contain many fish, but these were of three quite distinct colours—white, red and black. They were nearly always in excellent condition whatever their colour, but there was nothing between those three distinct shades. On the very rare occasions when I caught one of the trout which looked quite white in the water, its true colour proved to be light grey, and the black fish were not quite so black out of the water as they looked in it. The fish of three colours did not each occupy particular stretches of water and indeed three might be found in line one behind the other, white, red and black.

I have no explanation at all for their coloration, which was not found either at the head of the Nafferton Beck or in the main Driffield Beck, or in the parallel side stream a few miles away—the Foston Beck, which was larger but otherwise closely resembled the Nafferton Beck. I only once fished the Foston Beck and that not on a very good day, but the trout seemed to me much more easy to catch than at Driffield, and other fishermen have told me that they found the same thing. Compared to Driffield it was easy but much less interesting fishing.

Sometimes I used to go with Capt. W. S. Medlicott at weekends from Driffield to stay with him on the edge of the moors by Goathland. It was an interesting drive for one crossed the open wolds, descended into the vale at Pickering and then climbed up again on to the moors, inland of Whitby, which were in those days full of grouse. A little moorland stream wandered down through a fir plantation near Capt. Medlicott's house, forming still pools in places and at others running between narrow banks clothed with bushes. There were not many trout, but those that existed were larger than one expects to find in such a small burn. Each trout presented a problem, for to begin with it was always hard to hit the river without hitting anything else: there was nearly always a tree in front and another behind, in addition to bushes and dead boughs brought down by floods and lying about in all directions. Generally there was very little fly and the fish probably depended mainly on large meals at long intervals when a spate occurred.

On most of my visits to this burn nothing at all was caught, but once on a Sunday afternoon there was enough fly to make all the trout sit up and the fishing was exciting. Each bend of the river had to be watched for some time, and even if a rise was seen, it was probably made by a cruising fish whose journeys might take him over a considerable stretch of water. The best plan was to take plenty of time over each fish, time enough to study its movements and habits, for casting was only possible in certain spots and it was important to learn whether a particular trout in the course of his wanderings went to places to which a fly could be got. If the trout had been visible all the time the business would have been easier, but they were not so visible, they appeared and disappeared in the varying light. Often when one had selected a spot from which casting seemed possible the fish would come cruising along to one's feet, spot the fisherman or his rod and bolt before anything could be done.

There was one fairly big pool shaded by fir trees on one side and with separate trees on the otherwise open bank opposite. Several fish were cruising up and down it, and one of them was larger than anything seen before. I crouched under the firs to watch and noted that occasionally this trout swam to the tail of the pool, inspected the surface and sometimes found a fly there: also that when he came to this end of the pool the other fish got out of his way. I could only see him occasionally from my hiding-place, when he crossed a patch of water with the sun on it, but his normal course was gradually determined, and when he passed me on his way towards the tail I flicked a fly on to the

[Photo : Giles Foster

7. The Upper Wharfe, Burdsall, Yorkshire.

Chapter Five

[*Photo : Oona Foster*

8. A butt and its architect, Ilkley Moor.

9. Jane and Ginger.

water and let it sit there, hoping for the best. After several vain attempts, the fly was sucked in and I wondered whether the right fish had sucked it. Luckily he had, but as there were roots and other obstructions in all directions he had to be held very hard and no law given in any direction. He was the best fish I ever caught in that burn and weighed 1 lb.

I once saw a fish there which was perhaps bigger still. A very quiet rise was seen once or twice under a root where the main current swept from a ripple at the top of the pool in a semi-circle along the far bank to the pool's tail. The place was over-hung with bushes, but the fish in rising made a pleasant deep plop and seemed to me much larger than most of the inhabitants of the stream. I crawled into position opposite to him against a tree and below a high bank, and waited to see whether he would rise again or whether he had spotted me and gone away. Presently there was another plop and my fly floated down past the root and was taken. The trout knew, however, exactly what to do, dived to the bottom, turned in under his root and at once smashed the cast against it—the usual end to a fish hooked on that little burn. The burn was very seldom fished by local people with a fly and no doubt in a spate a worm might be deadly, but that would not have given half the sport that I enjoyed in low water on a sunny afternoon.

My experience of the streams on the western side of Yorkshire has been practically confined to the Wharfe. Most of my fishing has been done just above Ilkley and that is not the best part of the river, which improves in its upper reaches. There must, I think, be some pollution in the water above Ilkley for the con-dition of the fish is very inferior compared to that of the fish nearer the source; moreover, the trout inhabiting the stiller reaches are covered with a most objectionable-looking louse. This creature, which I have never seen on fish elsewhere, is much larger and more unpleasant than the sea louse found on fresh-run salmon and sea trout. It is an inland variety, but from its appearance I should judge some relation of the sea louse. It gives the infected fish a grey appearance so that they look as if they were covered with a sort of fungus.

There is a still length of water opposite a hanging wood about one mile upstream of Ilkley, and after a dry period numbers of fish collect in this stretch and all of them seem to be more or less infected with the louse. Nevertheless it is an amusing place to fish and ordinary methods there are quite useless. Casting, owing to the trees, is almost everywhere out of the question, and ' dapping ' is the only means whereby these fish can be caught with a fly. For some reason, despite the background of trees and a steep bank behind, the fish are very difficult to stalk and every use must be made of tree trunks. The best method seems to be to watch for feeding fish from the top of the steep bank and then to slide down the bank slowly towards them and try to clamp yourself against a large trunk immediately opposite the fish. Some of these trees overhanging the water can be climbed, and many of the fish cruise about under their boughs, picking up small insects which fall from them. It is less difficult to approach the fish that are feeding actually under one of these trees, but even if the climb above them is made successfully the light is peculiar and they keep disappearing into deep shade.

The fisherman lies prone against the trunk or branch and generally has to use one arm to keep himself in position, and the water below him is very deep. He has to poke the rod slowly and carefully through the branches, trying not to get caught up as he does so, and then to let out just enough line to be able by lowering his hand to drop the fly on to the water. He clings there to his precarious post, watching for a fish to swim within reach immediately below him, and ready to lower his fly that dangles in the air, apt at any moment to be caught by a breath of wind and entangled in a twig or a leaf. He has another thing to remember: how and in which direction he can strike without hitting the rod against a branch; generally this means that the strike can only be made sideways and not up. All these things must be thought out before he actually tries to catch a fish. If he should hook one he must somehow scramble down from his perch to earth in order to play it, and there is hardly ever room for him to lift his rod clear of branches. There is one particular large tree on this stretch of water under which there always seems to be a good fish, but he is never alone, and even if he can be kept well screened by the branches there is always another trout in the offing, who may see too much and in bolting disturb all the fish under the tree.

The best plan, when this happens, is to have patience, get into position and sit tight ready for the fish to come back. I remember doing this once and the trout which I was after returned and began to feed again exactly underneath me as I lay prone along the trunk, one hand grasping it and the other holding the rod. I was all ready for him and dropped the fly right on to his nose. He took it with quiet confidence and all seemed well as I scrambled down to earth while the fish moved out into the river, away from the trees, which was just what I wanted him to do. He knew, however, where to go and the line soon caught on some deep hidden obstruction, probably a fallen branch. Anyhow that was the end of the business and the last I saw of that fly. I often tried subsequently for this fish for he still fed under the same tree, but he had learnt his lesson.

Off the opposite bank is a quiet deep backwater formed by a tangle of branches from a dead elm sprawling out into the river. In and around this spot a herd of chub was discovered. They were not always in the backwater and would cruise out from it and take a swim round in the main current and then return. I chose a moment, when they were absent, to crawl carefully out along the dead elm's boughs and balance myself precariously at their outer edge. Presently I saw the herd of chub returning, and somehow cast a large buzzy fly on to the surface of the backwater in front of one of them who looked as if he might weigh 3 lbs. He swam leisurely up and smelt the fly, then backed a foot or two, waving his fins and staring at it. While he hesitated another chub not half his size brushed rudely past him and seized the fly with a gulp. I caught him, but although I often tried for those chub again, he was my one and only capture. It was all very exciting, not least the tight-rope dancing on those rotten boughs.

Much the best fishing on the Wharfe is several miles higher up, and the river is particularly attractive at Bolton Abbey, where I have never fished, although I once tried unsuccessfully to show a Canadian officer, who was fishing off the bridge by the stepping-stones below the Abbey, how to catch a trout. My haunt on the upper reaches has been Burnsall, where from the hotel it is possible to get a daily ticket for, I think, ten shillings. Last September we went as a party by bus, which reached Burnsall about 11.30 a.m., and since there had been much rain and the river was only just beginning to clear, we thought that mid-morning would be early enough to arrive. We were wrong. I went round to the back of the hotel, where the water is fairly quiet, and over the whole of its surface were rises in all directions. We bustled for all we were worth to put up our rods and tie on our flies, and I slipped in long waders into the deep water above the bridge. The surface of the river, which was fairly clear, but still very high and dark in colour, was covered with a varied assortment of insects—several sorts of duns, spiders, and even wasps. Why they had all chosen that moment to appear and how long they had been there I do not know, but the fish were making a record meal and were, I could see, already getting particular or half indifferent—they had had about enough.

Close inshore by the back of the hotel, two fish, obviously trout, whereas many of those in midstream were grayling, were still taking a fair proportion of the flies that passed over them. It took a long time to make the lowest of these two trout notice my fly among all that company, and when he did so he made such a careless shot at it that he missed. The upper fish, who had perhaps come on the feed later, tipped his nose up with deliberation and confidence. He was properly hooked, and soon in the basket, and proved to be a beautiful bright fat trout. I hurriedly tried for another above him as well as several grayling, but all without effect, for they were already over-fed. Far out, what appeared to be a very good fish was still rising hard and I tried to wade within shot of him, but it was very deep and I could only just reach him. I failed to get any response out of him and gradually fish after fish stopped rising until there was nothing left but a few small grayling, who had probably been elbowed out of the way by their brethren during the height of the hatch. We ate a hurried lunch, cursing ourselves and the bus for not having arrived an hour sooner, when we should have come in for the earlier stages of the rise.

After lunch we went upstream to where the river runs through a sort of gorge. It began to rain, but at one or two spots some fish were feeding. The first batch of fish involved an awkward bit of wading out through strong current to a shingle beach in shallower water in midstream, and even from there the fish were a long way off. I lost one of them and could make nothing of the others. At the second place a steep grass bank behind me made it difficult to reach the fish, which were feeding on the edge of the main current running down the other bank. I did get one of them, another good trout, but the best of the company were, owing to the grass bank behind me, just out of shot and it was far too deep to wade. My terrier, Jane, who is the most important character referred to in this book, was sitting by my side watching every cast. During this performance a young retriever bitch, who takes no interest in fishing, started romping about on the steep grass bank and bundled into Jane: Jane charged, caught the retriever amidships, knocked her clean into the river and bit her as she crawled out. The photograph (Plate 7) was taken at the spot where the incident occurred. Jane and the retriever have been at daggers drawn ever since. It had been a tantalising day for us as well as Jane, but we had at least got something with a dry fly, although we had been told at the hotel that owing to the state of the water no one had caught anything on a fly for a week, and that the only catches had been made with minnow.

This particular bit of water is varied with quick runs and rocky pools alternating with long quiet stretches, and the country upstream is interesting and pretty. Moreover, the trout, and I have no doubt some of the grayling, are much larger than one expects in a rocky stream, and are, moreover, a beautiful shape and colour. I consider the upper Wharfe very attractive water and none too easy.

Some of my visits to Wharfedale have been connected more with grouse than with fish. Ilkley Moor is an example of ground frequented by large numbers of people, which yet holds a good head of grouse. Footpaths giving wonderful views of the West Riding traverse the moor from end to end, and particularly at week-ends the people of Yorkshire make as good use as any one in England of the right to enjoy their country. I have seen numbers of people using these paths, and the grouse seem to know perfectly well that walkers upon them are harmless and will often sit and in the spring fly cackling about quite near the paths. My host, who takes the shooting over a part of Ilkley Moor traversed by one of these paths, has himself built some very cunningly placed butts. He and his dog are shown in one of these butts in Plate 8. The ground falls from the upper part of the moor in a series of short steep slopes with wide flats between them, and grouse disturbed skim along these flats, and then generally swing back over one of the ridges to regain the main part of the moor above. There are slight necks at places in the ridges and the birds are apt to cross a ridge through one or more of these necks. A line of butts just below one of the ridges has been sited to meet this line of flight, and it faces at right angles to the line of beaters and to the direction of the drive.

I wrote beaters, but often there is only one beater—my host's wife—and four is the most that I have ever seen out on one day, always members of my family or other guests. Four guns is the limit and two the more usual number. I never remember to have seen a male beater, and seldom more than two grown-up beaters: there is no keeper. The really essential part of the whole business is the one invariable beater—she is worth an army of ordinary drivers, and if she has any assistants they are entirely subservient to her. I once witnessed a strike, when one of the under-beaters, a sister, was directed to cross a quaking bog. The head-beater makes good use of the public footpaths to get round the unsuspecting grouse, and knowing every inch of the moor, where the march is and where it is not (I am vague about the march myself and it seems to vary), when to show herself and where to use dead ground: she has a most uncanny knack of persuading (it is hardly driving) the grouse to fly over the butts.

The butts, which are sunk in the necks through a ridge, look

out over a flat that makes a difficult background against which
to see grouse skimming low over the ground. If the birds are
spotted in time, it is fascinating trying to guess which neck they
will select—if they mean to traverse the ridge. Sometimes they
swing from wide out on the flat towards the ridge and may lift
and come over high, but as often as not they fly low over the
flat or along the foot of the ridge and then suddenly turn and
come shooting up from below, to cut through one of the necks
only a few feet from the ground. Sometimes a covey or pack
will sweep along the slope just below the ridge and pass over
all three butts one after the other. All the butts are hidden from
each other by large rocks or by rolls in the ground descending
from the main ridge to the flat. A sharp look-out has to be kept
in all directions, particularly at the foot of the slope and out
over the flat beyond, and grouse may arrive from any direction
and at any angle. Perhaps the most difficult are those which
suddenly swing up from below your feet and curl over the ridge
to left and right.

The second line of butts is on a flat out in the main part of
the moor about forty yards short of a low ridge, which seems
to be a favourite collecting place for the grouse. The view in
front is limited to about forty yards, and the birds are over the
skyline and on you in a moment without warning. During the
drive one is kept in a constant state of excitement by hearing
invisible grouse alighting and cackling beyond the skyline, and
they are apt to collect in large numbers on this low ridge out of
sight and come over all together, when finally put up. For this
drive the beaters start to the left of and behind the butts, walk
in line along the march, often moving grouse as they go from
the centre of the moor, and then gradually work their way
round in a semi-circle towards the line of butts. My visits to
this moor have generally been in the late autumn, when grouse
are looking their very best and when they are apt to collect in
large packs. I remember an enormous pack of them coming
straight at my head in these butts. They looked packed so thick
that there seemed no space between them. There was, however
—not even a feather floated to earth.

My terrier Jane, who puts grouse top of all birds, has always been present as a matter of course. She is considered a trifle wild as a beater, moreover there is no difficulty in putting the grouse up, and she is therefore my companion in a butt, carefully and closely attached by collar and string, for she gets very excited. She sits bolt upright, watching and listening, her little tail wagging furiously. If she sees or hears a grouse, she makes a little murmur and if that is not enough rubs herself against my leg. She is very quick at finding a shot grouse, and I doubt if any bird leaves a better or to her nose a pleasanter scent.

The grouse at Ilkley have not yet become used to aeroplanes, although they have had no lack of experience of them. They behave to a low-flying aeroplane exactly as grouse do to an eagle, a bird which probably none of them has ever seen in Yorkshire, so that it would seem that the fear of an eagle and the knowledge of what to do if one appears is something which every grouse inherits. They all get up and fly generally down-wind, in fact a low-flying plane will completely clear a hillside of grouse. It may clear the ground about to be driven, but it may, on the other hand, put somebody else's grouse from across the march clean over the guns possibly from behind. I have had many shots at grouse coming from all directions on that moor, given me by an aeroplane.

There is no pony and no panniers, and in view of the distance the beaters have to cover, together with their sex and age, the guns are expected to carry home what they shoot. It is not a case of record bags, but there is sometimes a respectable weight to carry down the hill. The whole business has a character of its own, and scientific use of the footpaths is one of its most important items. On the fringes of the moor are thorn bushes, and both the grouse and the ring-ousels, of which there are numbers in autumn, get rich feeding from the berries in a good season. There is also, in addition to heather, bilberry and rush seed as feed for the grouse. Perhaps because of all this variety of food, the moor seems singularly free from disastrously bad seasons that have recently afflicted most of the Yorkshire moors. In the spring curlew and golden plover breed in considerable numbers on the same ground, and have given me some amusing days with a telescope, watching these birds run back on to their eggs.

I once went with some companions all the way to Yorkshire from the South for the express purpose of seeing Will Freeman hunt the Bedale. We got there too late: he had apparently caught the last fox and we had an absolutely blank day, but I remember his beautiful whistle. All his different whistles (he used nothing but his mouth) were pleasant to hear and they all meant something, which his hounds understood. It made me wonder whether huntsmen ought not to make greater use than they do of this method of communicating with their hounds, but whistling as good and as musical as Freeman's is not a common gift.

After our blank day with the Bedale we went to the Zetland country and found it covered with deep snow which made hunting out of the question. There were large numbers of wood pigeons and the only food that they could get were the tops of roots, in particular those where folded sheep had stamped down the snow. Our host, luckily for us, still wore the old-fashioned white nightgowns, and we raided his wardrobe and sallied forth looking like white ghosts, each to a separate root field. Thanks to the nightgowns, we were very invisible and the pigeons poured confidently in to feed. On one occasion, in a heavy snowstorm, I succeeded by crouching in walking through a flock of sheep right up to a flock of pigeons feeding on the roots. Presumably we saved at least part of the crop and we certainly shot a lot of pigeons. Shot pigeons are messy things to handle: moreover, it began to thaw and the root fields turned to brown slush, so that by the time we had finished with them the nightgowns had lost their purity.

I have never found a lack of something to do in Yorkshire, or for that matter in any other part of the country.

Six

THE CAUCASUS

"THE THIEN SHAN very beautiful, the Himalayas very beautiful, but the Kavkas is the most beautifullest of them all." So said Gabriel Eghieff, a diminutive Armenian, who had been with Mr. St. George Littledale to all of them. I have only seen the Kavkas, or Caucasus as we call it, but I accept the opinion of Gabriel, who is a lover of mountains. Incidentally he proved the most expert travelling cook and camp manager that I ever had the luck to meet. There will be more about him later.

I have been twice to the Caucasus in the autumns of 1910 and 1913, when the Tzar ruled as the Little Father of all the Russias, but judging by the trouble that we had in getting into his country at Volochisk, after travelling via Vienna, Cracow and Lemberg, I doubt if he had very different views about the desirability of admitting foreigners from those held by the Russians of to-day. My companion, Peter Haig Thomas afterwards referred to as P. H. T., and I were armed with every conceivable paper about ourselves and our belongings, including rifles, but I shall never forget the agony at that beastly little frontier station at Volochisk of waiting and waiting with our noses through a small aperture in a dirty ticket office for permission for ourselves and our luggage to enter the mysterious land of Russia. We got it only just before the train left for the East.

I have memories of an interminable plain just not flat enough to give a long view from the carriage window, absolutely featureless, so much so that after sleeping for an hour one woke up wondering if the train had moved at all. Every ten miles or so there would be a dirty village with dirty and sad-looking inhabitants, and a few trees dotted about, and a bit of shallow cultivation on rich black soil for a mile or so round the village, then just dull rolling steppe covered with short grass, and life-less for miles until the next village and its surroundings came into view. There were no hard roads, or practically none, merely cart-tracks, no inhabitants between villages—nothing. I kept looking out for great bustard and saw them once or twice from the train. Otherwise it was sheer monotony, broken at long intervals by meals, when the train stopped for a quarter of an hour at the most at such places as Ekaterinoslav (now Dniepro-petrovsk), Rostov, etc.

The meals at these stations were good and the service rapid and excellent. There were three bells: one five minutes before the train's departure, a second one minute before, and the third when it left. No one took any notice of the first bell except to eat faster: the bill came with the second bell and we all got into the train at the third. We learnt our first Russian word at those meals, the word ' sëychas,' which has exactly the same meaning as the French ' toute de suite ' or the ' touter the suiter,' as an Englishman emphasised it. As used by the Russian waiters it had more meaning than is usually implied by a French waiter: the Russians were commendably prompt, luckily for us, for there was very little time and stops for meals were few and far between.

I liked the country south of Rostov better than the Ukraine: it was flatter, you could see farther and there were a few rivers, ugly rivers but still any definite feature like a river was a blessing in that land. The main crop here, as a contrast to wheat in the Ukraine, was sunflower and it grew luxuriantly. The platforms at Rostov and at other stations, the floors of waiting-rooms, of railway carriages, and the streets were white with spat-out husks of sunflower seeds. Every Russian carried a little paper bag of them and munched and spat all day: the result was unpleasant. Hereabouts we saw a good many Cossacks and other horsemen: they rode well, and judging by the look of their rather small, rough mounts, they were good horse masters.

Then at long last, after that weary plain, we saw before us the great wall of the Caucasus and it was a refreshing sight. We left the train at Vladikavkaz (the gate of the Caucasus), and heaven knows why anybody should have been fool enough to change such a descriptive title into Ordjonokidze, after I under-stand some gentleman I never heard of. The endpaper map of the Eastern Caucasus shows the country we visited.

Vladikavkaz is the gate of the Caucasus for it lies at the spot where the Terek river leaves the mountains half-way along the chain at the northern end of the great military road which traverses the Dariel pass from Vladikavkaz to Tiflis—the only road in those days, and for all I know in these, that crosses the mountain chain, mounting to 11,000 feet to do so. We traversed it by motor car, and those hundred and thirty miles were interesting and in places alarming, for we were perpetually racing along ledges with a drop on one side that was best left to the imagination. My imagination was a bit overstrung by the time we reached Tiflis. I do not call the Dariel pass beautiful. It is too grim and stark, but the great peak of Kasbek on your right hand (west) is a fine sight.

On my second journey over this pass, three years later, when my father accompanied me, we stopped at Kasbek village and lunched with a dear old Georgian general who held the title of Count Kasbek. I suppose that his title and his property, including the mountain, were given him in reward for his services in the war against Shamyl, in which he fought on the Russian side. I had spent the journey reading up this campaign, and my mind was full of the story. It had taken the Russians a hundred years to conquer the Caucasus, and during the last thirty years their formidable opponent had been the Daghestan Moslem patriot, Shamyl. He had tried but never really succeeded in raising the Western Caucasus, as well as the Eastern, but his stronghold had been in that natural fortress of forbidding ridges and deep valleys that constitutes Daghestan, east of the Dariel pass and north of the watershed. Towards the end of the campaign he had crossed the main road in an unsuccessful attempt to rouse to revolt the Western Caucasus, and a general on the Russian side, named Freitag, had nearly but not quite cut him off after a forced march on the Terek plain. That was the beginning of the end, and after most of his followers had been bribed out of their allegiance, Shamyl gave himself up at Guneb in Daghestan.

There had been cruelties committed on both sides, but it is to the great credit of the Russians that they gave their captive a good home in the Crimea, to which he was allowed to take as many of his wives as he liked. He took, I understood, a number.

I discussed the campaign with General Kasbek at lunch and he was astonished that I knew the name of General Freitag. He said, "I always thought Freitag was the best general we had on our side, but we never mention him because of his name : he was really a German." Although he had fought on the Russian side as most of the Georgians did, Count Kasbek was a great admirer of Shamyl, and we were happy to find that although the Russians were quite obviously still none too easy in their minds about the Caucasus, they seemed to treat the inhabitants liberally and sensibly. The impression we got was that it was a happy country, much happier than Russia proper, and that the Russians were content to hold the approaches to the mountains and keep open the main road over the pass, but that otherwise they left the inhabitants to carry on, little interfered with in their mountain homes. Like most mountaineers, they looked down on the inhabitants of the plain, whatever their nationality, and nationalities are very mixed and their origins obscure in a mountain fortress which has from the beginning been a refuge from conquering hordes coming from all directions.

Count Kasbek told us that his possession of the mountain from which he took his title was of little or no value, in fact he offered it all to us. The peak was first climbed by Douglas Fresh-field as described in his book *The Exploration of the Caucasus*. He and his party had camped as high as they dared the night before on the northern slopes and had warned their native guides that they meant to start for the summit before dawn on the morrow. When the hour came the guides were not there, having possibly failed to hear the starting signal, and the Englishmen left alone to scale the slopes. It was late when they reached the top of Kasbek, and they feared to retrace their steps over some of the worst places they had passed, since the sun had by then melted the ice. Wherefore they descended by a different route on the opposite face of the mountain and came near nightfall upon two shepherds. They stayed the night with them and were conducted by them to the village of Kasbek next day.

At first nobody believed the story that they had actually reached the top, but the shepherds were insistent that they had seen the travellers come down one side of the mountain in the evening, and the guides admitted that they had seen them climbing up the other face in the morning. There were many false tales spread about, including one by the guides that they had climbed the peak themselves—an obvious impossibility for they were not shod for really steep ground. Finally, after much sifting of evidence, the Russians admitted that the feat had in fact been performed by the English mountaineers. It was the first of many great climbs on the virgin peaks of the Caucasus by Freshfield and other mountaineers.

I must pass on to Tiflis by the winding road through the interesting fortress village of Msket down to the rolling plain on which the Georgian capital is placed. I remember as we neared the city of Tiflis a great troop of Cossacks who were sitting stark naked on their horses' backs as they watered them in the river—a fine group of men and beasts. At Tiflis we were lucky in finding at the Hotel de Londres absolute comfort and delicious food. Herr Richter and his wife, both Germans, proved ideal host and hostess and had the pleasant habit of dining with their guests. We dined as men should dine after a five-day journey. I have not forgotten the meal or the red wine of Kahhetti, in middle Caucasus, that went with it, or the great white marble bath in which we washed off the dust of our travel.

Then on again by motor over the plain north-east, first by a comparatively good road past an interesting farming colony of light-haired Teutons, quite unlike the other inhabitants of the region. They were clearly first-class, prosperous farmers, and we asked how they had come to the country. The story goes that a sect in Germany had formed the belief that the end of the world was near, and that the right place to be for that event was the Holy Land. So they set off, but the journey was long, the end of the world did not come, and after crossing the Caucasus they felt tired of travel and petitioned the Tzar for land to colonise. At length it was granted and the ancestors of the people we saw had settled down at Marianpol, and the place still kept that German name. Near Tiflis the road was crowded with flock after flock of turkeys being driven in to market. Each flock containing, I suppose, one hundred to two hundred birds, was conducted by two little boys with sticks. The birds seemed very easy to drive.

As we progressed the country got wilder and the road less suitable for motor traffic. We were, in fact, perpetually bumping along the dry beds of streams and in other strange places, quite unfitted for motor travel, but the car was strongly built and we never really stuck. The attitude of the inhabitants showed that most of them had never seen a car before, nor had their animals. We passed endless bullock wagons and the result was always the same: the astonished beasts stared with wide eyes until the last moment and then bolted into the ditch, usually upsetting the cart and its contents. We expected violent reaction from their drivers, but not a bit of it. Most of them simply shook with laughter and not once was there any abuse. Some knelt down and prayed as we approached, but we never seemed to cause resentment or annoyance: the people were either amused or awed. Near the foot of the mountains the road ran beside a muddy river and collected on the bank was an excited crowd of people. They were gathered round an enormous black catfish which had just been caught and was said to be excellent to eat. It did not look it.

After winding up a steep hill we passed the picturesque little town of Signatch perched on the top, and thence arrived in due course at the village of Lagodecki at the foot of the mountains, about eighty miles north-east of Tiflis, and found it as delightful as its name. From that point the real meat of the trip began: we were at the gate or rather the foot of what was to be our home for a month, and it was delightful to receive such a welcome from Michael Ivkin, who was to be our head stalker, his family and others who will presently come into the story. To add to the excitement there were in the garden tame turr (the wild goat of that part of the range) and tame wild boar. In front of Ivkin's house was some fine sand spread about on the ground, and setting to with a pointed stick I proceeded to draw in the sand, one after the other, the animals we hoped to meet. The men crowded round and commented, and by the end of half an hour we had got fixed in our heads the Russian names of all the main animals. Finally I drew a ruffianly-looking man, and everybody laughed and said *razboinik* (brigand), an animal we heard more of than any other but never saw.

Above us as far as we could see stretched great steep slopes, all clothed in virgin forest, and after a night's rest we set off straight uphill by a mountain path, with a retinue of wiry ponies carrying our tents and kit. These paths, fit for ponies but certainly not for wheel traffic, traverse the range in many places between Daghestan and Georgia, and were much used, particularly by the Daghestanis, who came over with trains of light-boned but well-bred wiry ponies, bringing metalware from Daghestan to exchange for corn and other food with the inhabitants of the rich country along the southern foot of the mountains. We met many of these men and magnificent specimens they were.

The Caucasus is the home of the most becoming dress I know, including, I imagine, the origins of our frock-coat and possibly top hat as well. The men wore long coats cut like a square hunting coat, but bound in at the waist with a silver girdle, smartly-cut breeches and top boots. The coats and breeches were of different colours, one very effective combination being a light grey coat and rich red-brown breeches. They wore high conical hats made of kid skin with short woolly hair, some black, some brown, some grey. We found their manners charming, and when we pitched camp by one of the paths they would often call in passing and showed by clicking their tongues on their teeth great astonishment at everything they saw, in particular our weapons and glasses. They generally carried arms, but the Russians insisted on the rule that they should not take arms into a village: these had to be stacked on the outskirts—not a bad rule.

It was an exhilarating walk up through the timber. I had never been in virgin forest before and here were miles and miles

10. Bivouac in forest, Caucasus. Left to right: Rostom, Gadjeo, A.B., Michael Ivkin, Magomah.

11. Camp site on ridge in centre of Beliokhani.

Chapter Seven
[*Photos : the late Edward North Buxton*

Chapter Eight

12. Deer Ford on River Aline, Scotland.

of it untouched by the axe, set as a forest should be on steep slopes cut by steeper valleys, all facing to the south, and looking proudly out over the plain that stretches to Ararat. I was far too excited to ride, walking in such a place was delightful and the path was good: moreover, there was something of intense interest to look at all the time.

The lower forest was a jumble of every sort of tree as soon as we left the orchards, but as we wound upwards certain timber predominated. We came, for instance, at about 6,000 feet, to the home of beech. It was magnificent beech, but most interesting to me of all was the violent struggle for life in a place absolutely untouched by man. The corpses of fallen giants in every stage of decay littered the ground, and growing in the rich bed of the rotting trunks were lines of saplings feeding on the dead. The impression given was of tall hedges of young beech, all in line along the prone, straight trunk of their ancestor. There were huge patches of azalea growing tall and luxuriant, and masses of raspberry, blackberry and other fruiting plants. At the end of about four hours we were above the beech and into the country of oak, silver birch, and azalea, and finally we emerged into the open to reach a wooden hut just above the timber, with steep grass slopes up to the watershed, which is here at about 11,000 feet. It was a country to dream of, and I dream of it still, although the last time I saw it was forty-three years ago. We were too late for practically all the flowers, but in summer they must be absolutely superb.

We cannot have been very tired from our walk for my diary records that we were away from the hut by 5 a.m. the following morning. Michael Ivkin accompanied me and we worked round the edge of the Mosemchai valley above the timber. There was plenty to see apart from the view—first a chamois, then some female turr, and at about 9 a.m. we spied, lying in long grass just above the timber, a big herd of old billy turr. (There is a drawing facing page 57.) This sturdy goat (and he is a goat, although the shape of his horns suggests that he once thought of being a sheep) is a large animal weighing, I should think, nearly as much as a red deer hind, and the first impression I got

T.N.   H of him was that he was very bored having to carry about such a weight of horn on his head. The colour of old billy turr is that of a dark brown door mat, their wives being a lighter brown. Female turr carry small horns, and squeak rather like a doll when disturbed. Turr live on steep ground and, like all goats, are first-rate climbers, but the old males in particular look heavy and laboured in their movements. They struck us as distinctly stupid animals, which is rare for wild goats, and so far as we could see they had no system of sentries.

The individuals of the herd in sight of us were adopting every conceivable attitude that would allow them to rest their horns on the ground. They were lying (and they generally did lie) very close together, and the difficulty was to distinguish among such a venerable company which was the biggest. Moreover, the grass on this slope was very long and, although it made the stalk easy, it proved almost impossible to select a place at a respectable distance from which to determine the relative size of the herd's individuals. The result was that I got too close, had a hurried shot and killed a turr who, although old, carried horns far inferior to some of his neighbours.

I amended the mistake a few days later when we again found a large herd of real Methuselahs. Before we had completed our stalk they had moved, and we followed their tracks down into the timber. Then Ivkin made a brilliant spot of the horn of one of them lying down. They were in thick trees, and feeling that it would be impossible in such a place to pick out a real veteran, I stalked into a little open gully to one side of them, and asked Ivkin to move them quietly, after getting to the far side of the herd. It was a fluky business, but it came off, for about half the herd came clattering across my little open gully, and I got the two best right and left. Ivkin, when he came up, told me that there were bigger still in the rest of the herd which had gone off in the wrong direction, but I was content and turned my thoughts to the other wild inhabitants of the country.

Nothing has so far been said of birds, and the forest was full of birds. On the plain we had seen rollers, bee-eaters, crested larks, Egyptian vultures, and hen hen harriers. At the top of the Caucasus we had met only cock hen harriers, and in my experience hen harriers, except during the breeding season, maintain the rule that ladies and gentlemen are best apart. In the mountains were golden eagles, lammergeier (in great numbers), Egyptian vultures, lesser kestrels, hobbies, peregrines, both black and red kites and, I thought best of all, lanners, large pale falcons with the habits of a peregrine. The mention of a lanner brings me to his principal prey, *the* bird of the Caucasus, the great snow partridge of which there is a drawing facing page 116.

Of all the game birds that I have met I put this creature at the top: he lives in any case at the top and dislikes descending below 10,000 feet. He is a true partridge, in that he carries no feathers on the lower half of his legs, and he can run as fast as any French partridge, and that on the steepest ground. I watched an old cock one day through my telescope flirting his tail and performing all sorts of gymnastics on the rocks. In habits he is very like a ptarmigan, with the same tendency to swing off from the mountain side into space and then clinch in again to alight at about the same altitude as that from which he started. But the most striking thing about him is his size. He is not quite so big as a hen capercailzie but he looks it, and a covey of these great fat birds, grey and chestnut above and almost white beneath, flinging themselves into space and swirling round the crags is a glorious sight.

There is more in them than that. They have a ringing clarion call, a wild sound suited to the ground they live on and they make it to some purpose. It was perfectly obvious to me, as it had been to my father many years before, that they have an understanding with the game that inhabits their country. They fly over turr, chamois and other game yelling a warning, and the beasts act upon it. I never saw a lanner actually catch one, but they were after them. One day, while I was eating lunch near the watershed, a lammergeier became very interested in me or rather, I think, in my sandwiches. He kept circling round only about thirty yards off and I left some pickings for him behind.

I spent a day or two devoted to snow partridge and found

one of our retinue a keen and capable beater. He was a delightful
Georgian named Rostom, and was mad keen on all forms of
sport, but driving 'Indiushka goornaya' (mountain turkey), as
the Russians call them, was a new game to him. The ground
was very steep and it was extremely difficult to find any spot
from which one could shoot, firmly planted on two level feet.
That made it all the better fun. Rostom was the one and only
beater and I the one and only gun. Having surveyed the ground
and the wind, I selected a spot on a rocky ledge where I thought
that any partridges disturbed by Rostom from further along the
ridge would clinch in to the mountain and possibly come within
shot. Rostom went off over the top to make a circuit and came
back along the ridge towards me, while I made myself as
inconspicuous as I could among the rocks.

The view was glorious, the place intensely wild and most
abominably steep. I waited there alone, all agog, wondering
what was going to happen next, scanning the edge of the ridge
for anything that might come towards me. I forget and my
diary does not record all the details, but I remember seeing a
covey of these great birds come swinging along towards me. My
shooting, perhaps from the difficulty of placing and of moving
my feet on that steep ground, was a disgrace, but at the end of
the drive we picked up one grand old cock partridge, and to my
surprise and delight he carried spurs. He is the only partridge
I know that has won this distinction.

Then we descended to lower levels, the home of the dwarf
rhododendron, growing knee-high above the timber, and of the
Georgian black-game, birds extremely like our black-game, but
lacking the white behind and with tails slightly longer but less
curved. (Drawing facing page 116.) For these two reasons I prefer our own. We saw about fifty of these old gentlemen in a
corrie engaging in their autumn display, a habit common to our
black-game as well. My diary is truthful about the result of that
day's sport. With twenty-seven cartridges I killed one snow
partridge, five black-game (teteref) and three quail. It also
records that we saw a rock creeper and a dipper, both at about
10,000 feet, and that I and Rostom both thought it splendid sport.

Caucasian Snow Partridge

Georgian Blackcock. Chapter 6

Caucasian Red Deer.   Chapter 7.

I think so still, and wonder sometimes whether Rostom ever found any one else to whom he could drive snow partridges. Probably not, for 'shooting flying' is not much practised in those parts. When we cooked and ate the snow partridge we understood why the Russians call the birds mountain turkeys (Indiushka goornya). That was just what the flesh looked like, moreover it tasted like a fat turkey with a gamey flavour to it. It was perfectly delicious: so was everything else after it had passed through the hands of Gabriel Eghieff.

We were told that pheasants (we call them in England the old English pheasant) were plentiful in the lower forest on the edge of the plain, but as we never stayed down at these levels we did not see them. One day, while we were near the watershed, flock after flock of bee-eaters swept down from the north, crossed the ridge and screamed with excitement as they again saw trees, into which they dived. There was bracken in the upper forest and woodcock were very common, in fact it must be one of the main breeding grounds of these birds. There were plenty of jays, and great black, green and a spotted woodpecker: he was just not our greater spotted, but he was a very close relation. I do not think that he was the middle-spotted, a bird I met after-wards in Switzerland. There were hooded crows, ravens, and a white-necked jackdaw. The nuthatches, like the spotted wood-peckers, were not quite our nuthatches, but the great tits and the blue tits looked exactly the same. So did the cole tits, but the latter had one peculiarity. They seemed to have all the ordinary cole tit notes, but they had one extra note and it was apparently reserved entirely for us. Parties of them, on seeing such extra-ordinary-looking beings, came hopping one at a time down a branch to within a few inches of our heads. After an impertinent examination of us, each bird would utter a loud note of astonish-ment, meaning no doubt "Well, I'll be damned," and retire up the tree. I never heard an English cole tit do that, but of course human beings are not such a rarity in this country as they were in the Caucasian forest, and Caucasian cole tits may be more prone to bad language than ours.

There were accentors on the bare upper slopes, and their

cousins, hedge sparrows, in the forest, also song thrushes, missel thrushes, blackbirds, and wrens which made it feel homely, but we only saw one robin. Crested larks on the plain and a light-coloured lark on the tops, also wheatears galore and meadow pipits or a close relative of that stupid little bird. The warblers were not of course singing in October and most of them had probably left for the South. They were very difficult to identify, owing to their silence, but we saw willow wren and chiff-chaff, also a large brown warbler with white edges to his tail; he lived in long grass and giant hemlock, which grew to a prodigious height. The finches were maddening. There were chaffinches and bullfinches low down in the forest but not on the ground where we camped and stalked. Here there was a finch rather like, but not, a brambling, great flocks of lesser redpoll and a little finch rather like a siskin or a citril in long grass above the timber. I gave up the finches. My diary records that at the foot of the range I heard a cirl bunting.

One of my first puzzles in the forest was the appearance of some of the oaks. Their upper boughs were in many cases bent inwards towards the crown, as though a man had climbed the tree and pulled the boughs in towards him to get the acorns. Of course the explanation was bears (Russian Myedvyed: I have been told to spell it like this but it sounded like *medved*, which is easier), and in a thunderstorm I met one shinning down the tree under which I was sheltering. These bears are the ordinary brown bear of Europe; some of them had white patches on the sides of their necks, and most but not all showed some traces of these. We never bothered about bears, which were numerous; they just happened as a fluke. They fed largely on the great masses of wild raspberry, blackberry and other fruits, and varied that with a diet of venison. Naturally when fed on such rich food, they made delicious eating themselves. In fact, apart from snow partridges and quail, I thought bear was the best meat that I ate in the Caucasus.

We were soon instructed in the art of cooking ' shashliks,' and here is the recipe. Take a long straight stick and peel it, sharpening one end. Kick the fire into a low wide blaze (suitable for roasting chestnuts), skewer square pieces of meat and fat alternately on the stick. Then get a companion to hold the other end of the stick and twiddle it over the fire as you squat on opposite sides. It is a nice easy comfortable way to cook, makes a lovely smell and produces the best venison steak in the world. I am all for shashliks and we ate them by the dozen, just peeling them off the stick one by one. They cook meat in the same way in Turkey, where ' shasliks ' are called ' Kabobs.' In addition to bears there were plenty of wild pig (Diki Kiban), but when we were there most of them seemed to be concentrated on beech mast, below our hunting ground.

In order to reach more distant ground, we spent one night in a cave which provided perfect shelter and was very roomy, clean and comfortable. The cave was situated on ground much beloved of chamois (in Russian ' Serna ') and we enjoyed some excellent stalking. The chamois of the Caucasus is practically indistinguishable from his counterpart in the Alps and Pyrenees, but if I were shown three heads from these three areas I think I could pick out the Caucasian: his horns are straighter and narrower at the crooks, and in body weight I think he is the heaviest of the three.

I had crawled from below to within range of a buck lying alone on a steep slope. My first shot cut a groove through the long hair on his withers but did not touch him and he raced up the hill, and my last despairing cartridge was fired as he topped the skyline. To my undisguised amazement, for he was by then at least two hundred and fifty yards away, the buck collapsed and rolled down towards us. I turned to my companions and found them making low obeisance, as was their wont at a successful shot. My face was, however, too much for them and we all burst into laughter at that appalling fluke; the bullet had gone through his skull.

The next day we were watching through our glasses a herd of chamois does and kids romping and playing at ' King of the Castle ' on some rocks about two hundred yards above the timber. Suddenly play stopped and the herd bunched on the rocks, looking down intently below them. My men whispered "bars" (leopard) and we watched for any movement from the place to which the chamois' gaze was directed, but we saw nothing. The herd moved off uphill, whereas normally in that country chamois, on being disturbed from open ground, bolted straight downhill for the timber. I have little doubt that the men were right in their diagnosis of the cause of alarm, but although we found fresh tracks of leopard on several occasions we never saw one. One of our native hunters, a mountain Turk named Magomah, told me that he had killed five in his lifetime, all of them by following tracks in the snow, which generally led in the end to a cave. Since this leopard lives high up on the range and has to withstand a hard winter and deep snow, he is clothed in thick fur like his cousin, the ounce or mountain leopard of the Himalayas, but his colour is yellow, the same as an ordinary leopard's. Judging by his tracks, he is a big beast and we longed for a sight of him. A year or two previously a friend of mine on this same ground had seen one perched on a rock, and missed him clean.

On the train between Tiflis and Baku, at the end of our trip, I got into conversation with a Russian who spoke French fluently. To the south of us not far west of Baku we could see a range of hills jutting into the plain which appeared to be covered with long grass. The Russian said that in those hills were tigers. I asked him if he did not mean leopards (bars), but he was insistent that he knew all about leopards and that they existed in the Caucasus proper, but that the animals of which he was speaking were real tigers. I have no reason to doubt him, but wondered what tigers would find to hunt there—almost certainly pig and possibly gazelle. I have never cleared the matter up or indeed heard any confirmation of this report of tigers in that part of the world, but my Russian acquaintance was certain of it.[1] While on this train I saw a number of francolins for sale at some of the stations. On some shallow lakes visible from the railway, mysterious dark objects were seen swimming about: they turned out to be tortoises.

[1] I have just found confirmation of this in Douglas Freshfield's book *The Caucasus and Bashan*. He states that he saw in Tiflis tiger-skins from Lenkoran on the Caspian, which is at no great distance from the range of hills we saw.

The forest was full of foxes (lisitsa) which looked exactly the same as our foxes, and there were also wolves (Vork). We never saw the latter, but one night we heard them howling and the men were much annoyed, since they said that it would move the game. We saw tracks of lynx fairly often but never any of the animals, which are, I imagine, very nocturnal. I have forgotten the Russian for lynx.

After about a fortnight in the Lagodecki valleys we decided to mount to the watershed with all our baggage, follow the crest eastwards and descend again into the next group of valleys above the village of Beliokhani, situated like Lagodecki at the foot of the mountains. It was a good decision, for it gave us a wonderful view of the range. Gabriel Eghieff always celebrated the moving of camp by changing from his working clothes into a neat suit of dark-blue dittos. Anything less suited to the ground we had to traverse I never saw, but that did not detract from his sterling worth. We came in the course of our climb to the top and in our descent into the cirque of Beliokhani to some real ' mauvais pas,' at least for ponies. At such moments Gabriel was invaluable. He stood at the worst spot, a minute figure in dark blue, and as each pony came to the place he ran his hand firmly but gently along its crest and back without ever touching its head, and then with a firm grip steadied it by its tail—always the tail, never the head. Both the men and the ponies recognised Gabriel's as a master hand, and it was delightful to watch the confidence which his touch inspired. Gabriel was always having dreams which he related to us, and they often seemed to him to foretell what was going to happen to us on the morrow. I cannot, however, remember that any of them came true.

Prince Demidoff, by whose kind permission we were there, had reserved shooting rights in the Lagodecki valleys and did not allow grazing in them, but the watershed itself was grazed heavily with flocks in the summer, so that the grass was short and the impression it gave was of a great golf course with a few bunkers of broken rock. It was easy going on the top itself, and the view from the roof of the Caucasus was superb. To the north, the side ridges running out into Daghestan rose in jagged peaks to much greater heights than the true main watershed. Daghestan looked forbidding after the smiling forest on the southern slopes. Great black precipices dipped into cavernous valleys, and the timber line was thousands of feet lower than on the south side of the range. Moreover, the upper timber consisted of conifer, which were almost non-existent on the southern slopes. The steep valleys of Daghestan, in particular those covered with scrub, are the haunt of the true wild goat (*Capra aegagrus*), obviously the ancestor of tame goats, but we never had time to go after him.

Looking back in the opposite direction to the south, over the great forest through which we had climbed and which had been our home for a fortnight, was a great pink misty plain, bare except for some stretches of timber which sprawled out a short distance from the foot of the range on to the flat land beyond. But I was looking for something which my father had seen years before from the watershed some miles further west, when he had made an adventurous trip up through Daghestan and over the watershed coming out at Telav. Luckily it was a fine day, and jutting dimly out of the mist like a white ghost was a snow peak resting on a long snowy shoulder. It could only be one thing: it was Ararat, about one hundred and seventy-five miles away. This may sound incredible but it must be remembered that we were perched at 11,000 feet ourselves and Ararat tops, I believe, 16,000 feet. I do not think that I have ever looked on such a strangely mysterious and inspiring view. Lord Bryce once told me of his ascent of Ararat. He had an English companion and two Kurds: the English companion got a bad attack of mountain sickness, but Lord Bryce went on higher with the Kurds who finally refused to go further because they alleged that above the level reached the mountain was haunted. Undaunted Lord Bryce went on entirely alone, reached the top without any real difficulty and descended again, picking up first the Kurds and then his friend on the way down. The last long climb up the snow to the peak entirely alone must have needed some pluck.

The journey along the watershed was long and we were

forced to camp on the north slope for the night. The way down into the Beliokhani cirque on the morrow involved the passage of the worst place we had encountered, but there were no incidents and we descended to camp on a small piece of ground which made some pretence of being flat, just within the timber. Again Gabriel corrected the slope by cutting masses of heather and other plants, and with them levelling off the floor of the tents and providing a most springy and comfortable bed. It was a delightful camp and we woke up to the first powdering of snow (Plate 1—frontispiece). From it we heard what we had made that journey to hear, the roar of a stag, and a Caucasian stag is important enough to have a chapter practically to himself.

Naturalists may wonder why I have not referred to the largest European wild animal, the Europern bison, whose last natural stronghold was in the wooded slopes at the Western end of the Caucasus. I do not know if any still exist there, but in any case there were none in the country I visited and I imagine that it was too steep for such a heavy animal.

Seven

CAUCASIAN DEER

THE RED STAG of the Caucasus (drawing facing page 117) was the main draw for me to those mountains: everything else was incidental and had to take second place to him. Deer have always been a passion with me, and the red deer of Eastern Europe and Western Asia is to my mind the most beautiful deer and indeed one of the most beautiful animals in the world. For some mysterious reason, red deer get bigger eastwards at least as far as the Caucasus, Asia Minor and Persia. Our island red deer are small, as animals confined to an island generally are. Unlike the extinct Irish elk, whose remains are dug up in bogs and which was really a giant fallow, the red deer heads dug up from the same bogs show no exception to this rule; they are no bigger than the heads of Irish red deer of to-day. German and Austrian deer, again, are larger than ours, and those inhabiting the Eastern Carpathians are larger still, about equal in size to those of the Caucasus, Asia Minor and Persia. There is what we should call a red stag in the Himalayas, but strangely enough by the time that region is reached the increase in size has stopped. The Barasingh of India, marked like a true red deer, is not so big as his cousins in the Caucasus, nor do his horns carry so many points, seldom more than ten.

It is true, of course, that the wapiti of the Rocky Mountains and his cousin in Eastern Asia are bigger still, but they are not true red deer and to my eye they lack the quality of that animal. A bull wapiti (or bull elk, to adopt American nomenclature) is a coarser looking animal than a red stag, and a cow wapiti lacks the grace of a red hind. The deer of Eastern Europe, the Caucasus, Asia Minor and Persia differ slightly in other respects from their counterparts further west. The skull is straighter and comparatively longer and there is less dip between the eyes; moreover, in the autumn, there is no red in their coats, they are

Bear cub stung on the nose.

Caucasian Roe-buck.
Chapter 7.

Young Bull Elk.

Cow Elk.

Chapter. 9.

grey all over, like the colour of a Scottish deer's face, and their legs are very dark. The rump markings typical of red deer are very marked in the Eastern race, dark lines of hair bounding a very white stern. Moreover, there is a much greater relative difference between the size of stag and of hind in these Eastern deer, the stags looking quite double the size of the hinds. Weighing deer in the Caucasus was, of course, out of the question: we cut off what we could and it was hard enough work transporting that, the rest went to the bears and all the other creatures that liked venison, of which there were plenty. We could always feel that nothing was wasted and that everything was enjoyed by something; we wondered by what and by how many.

The difficulty of stalking deer on steep ground and in thick timber with hardly any openings in the trees, with the view generally restricted to fifty yards at most, is extreme and it is enhanced in dry weather, when sticks and leaves crackle under the foot. I have examined my diary to discover the number of days during two expeditions spent either entirely or partly in pursuit of stags. I have counted, in addition to the days entirely devoted to deer, the days on which mention is made of either seeing fresh tracks or of hearing a stag roar. In 1910 such days numbered thirteen and in 1913 they numbered fifteen: they were long days for we seldom left camp later than 5 a.m. and often considerably earlier, and although we generally rested in the afternoon, we stalked again in the evening until the light went. In the thirteen days of 1910 I had two chances, my companion, P. H. T., none. In 1913, when accompanied by my father for part of the time, he never saw or nearly saw, so far as we know, a stag, while I had four chances. I killed one stag in 1910 and missed another, and in 1913 I killed two stags and missed two other chances. That shows clearly enough the difference between stalking in Scotland and stalking in the Caucasus. It is the most difficult game I ever engaged in, and partly for that reason magnificent sport.

The deer are always in the forest and not on open ground, and therefore almost impossible to spy with a glass. Practically the only chance is during the rutting season, which is at its height in the first week of October, and we timed both visits on that. Then a stag's roar gives one at least the chance to locate his whereabouts in the forest. If roaring had continued all day there would of course have been good opportunities for a slow and careful approach by ear, but they did not roar all day. They sometimes roared all night, but on most days there was dead silence from soon after dawn until one hour before dark. That was the trouble and it was intensified by a factor connected with wind. All the country was steep, and although red deer and roe preferred the less steep parts, it was all steeper than any ground I have stalked on in Scotland. In such country the wind normally blows downhill at night everywhere, both along ridges and down valleys until about an hour after sunrise. Then comes a change: for the rest of the day in fine weather it blows *down* the *ridges* but *up* the *valleys*, until about an hour before sunset. Now those two moments of wind change were apt to be just the most critical moments of a morning or an evening stalk.

In 1910, before leaving the Lagodecki valleys and moving round to those of Beliokhani, further east via the watershed, I had had only one dealing with a stag. I heard a roar below our first camp in the Lagodecki country in thick timber, and then another roar closer to me. He was clearly a travelling stag and travelling fast, no doubt in search of hinds. I moved to intercept him, and in moving heard a third roar fairly close. I got into position to command an open space covered with thick, high bracken, sat down, watched and listened. I never heard him again and imagine that he passed to one side of me and very likely got my wind, but it may have been a near thing. We were to experience many near things.

The Beliokhani valleys were better stag ground than Lagodecki and we came to the conclusion that they contained quite a good head of deer; by that I do not mean anything like the quantity common in a Scottish forest, but quite enough for so large an animal, and enough to provide excitement galore. The amount of roaring, even in the height of the rut, varied enormously: mist seemed to silence them, but rain did not. They roared well on frosty nights with a clear sky, but they stopped much too soon in the morning and they started up again much too late in the evening. Far the best chance, and it occurred very seldom, was a day of pouring rain with heavy and loud drip off the trees, to drown the sound of movement. But why complain, the weather was generally glorious, the country a treat to see and be out in, and as I have said before, the excitement was intense.

Two of our men, Michael Ivkin originally from North Russia, and Magomah, a mountain Turk whose home was at Beliokhani, were first-class woodland stalkers. This woodland stalking is not understood in this country; they know little or nothing about it in Scotland and we have to go as far as Germany or Austria to learn the art. Michael Ivkin, mad keen as he was, never lost his head, and even at particularly thrilling moments remained absolutely calm. Magomah had a very quick temper, which subsided with equal speed. He had another peculiarity; one of his feet was a mere stump for he had lost the rest of it from frost-bite while hunting in the winter. He used to make up the rest of that foot with socks and any other material he could find, and stuff it all into his boot. It was amazing that he could walk that ground at all and walk it all day. He used to anoint his stump carefully every night with butter—our best butter. We got butter, honey and delicious brown bread from the village about every four days, by sending a pony down to fetch these luxuries. I never lived better on a trip in wild country.

I learnt much from those two men about the art of woodland stalking. It was Magomah who first taught me not to walk on my toes, which most people consider the right method of silent progress. He and Ivkin followed the opposite method: they put their heel down first in order to get the best grip on the ground and then lowered the front of the foot. They seemed to have eyes in their feet to tell them how to avoid twigs, but this is best done by feel for the eyes are needed all the time to look ahead. If I was in front and snapped a twig, Magomah used to kick me on the calf. I found that the best reply was to walk just behind him and wait for the rare moment when he, too, snapped a twig: I got a chance or two on most days and he took it very well.

Nearly everybody, in moving through a wood, goes much too fast: the pace should be painfully slow with constant pauses for listening.

The roar of a stag is a very hard thing to locate. To me, even when heard in a park, it is a thrilling sound. I have often tried to imitate the sound, but it is very difficult to make, simply with the mouth, anything like a loud enough noise. Giant hemlock grew in profusion in the stag country, and we used to cut lengths of the stem to produce magnifiers of our attempts at roaring, but I do not think that it was very successful. I remember Ivkin making an extremely accurate shot at the whereabouts of a stag who had been roaring all night above our camp. I suddenly realised that we had actually got there long before I expected to, and that a pair of horns was sticking up out of thick, tall bracken. As I unslung the rifle, that should have been unslung before, the stag jumped and I could seldom see more than his head as he bolted through the fern. I got off several shots but missed him. He did not look a very big stag, but I remember his great thick neck and heavy jowl, which gave rather the impression of a Jersey bull, and his beautiful grey colour. There were two hinds with him, and it is worth recording that the largest number of hinds I ever saw with a stag in the Caucasus was four—very different from the conditions in Scotland.

One of the pleasantest and most convenient camps we made was about in the middle of the Beliokhani cirque on a ridge that jutted far into the semi-circular valley or rather group of valleys (Plate 11). Either because of a storm or because herdsmen had purposely lit a forest fire in order to obtain grazing, there was a large open space nearly clear of trees on this ridge, and in it we camped by a spring. It commanded a glorious view of wooded ridges in all directions with a few, very few, open spaces in them.

I spent hours spying these open spaces, but with one exception it was a waste of time. One day suddenly in the field of my telescope was a stag feeding quietly with his back to me, head down, horns branching wide on either side of his body. I nearly jumped out of my skin. He was not more than about a mile away, and leaving P. H. T. and three men to watch, from camp, I went for him alone. It was a practically still day so that we could not judge by examining trees and grass with our telescopes how the wind would be blowing over the ground he was on, and I assumed that its direction there would be the same as at camp. When I arrived at the edge of the open space where the stag had been seen, what wind there was seemed to be in all directions: anyhow I never saw him, but those in camp whose glasses were on him all the time, had watched him suddenly throw up his head and bolt at full gallop. He had had a whiff and one whiff of man is enough for a red deer.

There was still plenty of light and I went on alone along a ridge thickly covered with trees in the hope of hearing a roar or in some way meeting another stag. At about 5 p.m. a stag roared below me and I went straight downhill pretty fast towards the sound, and in fairly thick timber on a steep bank suddenly saw a stag one hundred yards below looking at me. I sat down and shot him: he was an enormous stag but carried rather an ordinary head of twelve points. It was a wonderful moment, after all the near things and the misses and the disappointments—all the more wonderful because I was alone in that great forest. When I got home to camp in the dark, they could rag me about the first stag after which I had started, but I was square with them over the second. P. H. T. got no chance and I never got another during that trip, although we devoted all the rest of our time and energy to stags and were many times within an ace of getting a shot.

On the second expedition in 1913, with my father as companion but far too old a man for that stiff country, we spent the whole time in the Beliokhani valleys and did not visit Lagodecki. Gabriel Eghieff was, alas, engaged elsewhere and the cook interpreter, who accompanied us, was so inefficient that we got rid of him at once. Rostom took his place and as cook proved an excellent substitute, and necessity brightened up my Russian which was completely innocent of grammar and dependent entirely on ear for I had no dictionary or written aid of any sort.

Every night in camp as we sat round the fire, the whole company were kept in fits of laughter by my free use of that language and, having no qualms about making howlers, I was soon able to converse on any subject with the hunters, Ivkin and Magomah, and with the other people in camp. When I tried my Russian on strangers it was not nearly so successful. Most of our native companions are shown on Plate 10.

The other people in camp who stand out clearest in my memory were a good-natured giant whose name was Mourtouzali (Mourtou for short) and Nerula. Mourtou was head ponyman and very efficient at keeping them fit: he was careful in advising us just where to camp in order that he could find good grazing in plenty. He was always full of fun and seemed to think of the expedition as a perpetual joke. He was the camp butt, was ragged by everybody and enjoyed it: we all loved him. Nerula was a rather feeble-looking man but he belied his looks.

The military commander of the district insisted on sending a bevy of Cossacks to protect us from brigands. These Cossacks were noisy, lazy and useless; they were clearly there mainly in the hope of getting meat. I find my diary full of references to them. "The Cossack in camp was so over-eaten on shashliks, that he had a bad stomach ache and was useless." "Nerula sacked another Cossack." "Nerula sacked the last Cossack." The authority this old gentleman possessed with the military arm was mysterious and unlimited. We never got a new supply of Cossacks, because luckily nobody down at the village knew exactly where to find us, and the ponymen who went there for provisions took good care not to give our positions away.

After camping at various spots on the west side of the Beliokhani cirque and doing a little turr-stalking in thick wood and on steep slopes, we moved to the central ridge near which I had killed a stag on the previous trip. It was a delightful camp and there was good ground for stags all round it, for it was not quite as steep as most parts of the forest. On the way there we halted for the night by a minute clear stream, in which I caught seven trout on a dry fly; this so excited the men that everybody began to cut down saplings and try their hand. Ivkin caught two more trout on a worm, and another little fish, unknown to me, that looked like a cross between a roach and a grayling.

Some of the streams were clear and these seemed always to contain trout, but streams that came from sulphur springs were coloured yellow and had no fish in them. The sulphur springs, which tasted to me absolutely disgusting, were much appreciated by the wild animals and we always found tracks by them. One day while we were sitting eating our lunch a band of young ram turr came to lick the rocks round one of these springs. They were not more than forty yards off, and when they had finished taking their medicinal cure I picked up a stone and heaved it at them. It hit a rock just behind them and they came bounding across to within a few yards of us.

On the first evening that we camped on the central ridge real excitement began. My father and I went up in the evening to two different spots to listen, and after some time a roebuck appeared, which I shot, and we then moved further along the ridge carrying the roe. Presently blackbirds and jays began to swear, as if they had seen a fox or a cat, and soon we heard something barging about in the trees. After a pause there was a roar at about 6 p.m. There was little light left, so I answered to the best of my ability. For some moments there was dead silence and then we heard the stag coming uphill towards us, but the light failed before he appeared. Subsequently we found by his tracks next morning that he had passed just below us.

Next morning we both mounted to much the same places, I at 5 a.m., my father at 7 a.m. After waiting for some time without hearing anything, Ivkin and I moved quietly along the ridge to a high knob at the end of it, and again sat down to listen. All was mysteriously still and silent, and we again moved slowly on. Then suddenly Ivkin stopped and whispered "Olyeen," pronounced in the Caucasus ' ollen ' (red deer). "Samka" (hind), "Adin, dva, tree, tchiteri" (one, two, three, four). "Nye dalioka sametz" (the stag can't be far off). I moved forward and sat down. Then an excited whisper. "Tam pridyeot sametz" (here comes the stag). The deer were moving through the trees below us and across our front, and kept appearing and disappearing. Presently

I could see the stag's horns, but he got behind a tree: then he walked on clear of it and I could see his head, neck and the top of his withers. I got him in the neck and he hurtled stone dead down the hill, with the hinds skipping clear of his body. He was an eleven-pointer, not a very big stag, as they grow in those parts, and he had not yet begun to smell strong although his neck was swollen. Behind his withers was a patch of coarse hair growing forward like a wapiti's, and Ivkin agreed with me that this was very unusual with red deer. There was wild rejoicing in camp that night. The stag lay so near our tents that it was easy for my father to get to the spot to photograph him, and willing hands soon had all the meat home in camp.

The next morning I went off with Magomah in the opposite direction and had another eventful day. We began by seeing a couple of pig, and in following them jumped a really big roe-buck, which I missed excusably as he bounded off. We then mounted higher to the upper fringe of the timber, and found the track of a stag that had crossed the watershed to the south side, having come over from Daghestan. Magomah told me that there was a regular migration of stags from this direction at the beginning of the rutting season. We were crossing a steep slope bare of trees except for isolated clumps and covered with long grass, when I suddenly realised that a stag was staring down on us from above. He was off in a second at full gallop. It was not an impossible chance, but I missed him and probably failed to close the bolt properly, for I could not get off a second shot. Enough of him was seen to make us realise that he carried a beautiful head, wide and with grand long points on the top of each horn.

My father was finding the strain of the slopes too much for him, and a letter from my mother showing anxiety convinced him that he must start at once for home. Ivkin also was due to join another sportsman in Lagodecki, so that I was left alone in charge of Magomah. Stags were roaring at night all round us, but they refused to continue the chorus after dawn, and we wandered rather aimlessly about in the hope of hitting a track and being able to follow it.

While topping a rise very quietly, we came upon a bear within a few yards of us. He shuffled off behind an azalea bush and I put up the rifle and let it off into the azelea like a gun. I felt something hit my wrist after the shot, and discovered that it was the leather sight protector, which had blown off and, being attached by a leather thong to the barrel, had been flung back and struck my wrist. I cannot have even looked at the foresight, for I had never noticed that the sight protector was on the rifle when I fired. Stranger still, there was the bear at the bottom of the slope with a large hole in his side, made, I suppose, by a combination of bullet and leather: it was lucky that the rifle did not burst. The bear was in very beautiful coat with two large white patches on his neck; he was as fat as butter and quite delicious to eat. Then followed more days of listening and tracking in particular of a stag, who fairly made the forest wreak and bellowed all night: we followed him for miles but never saw him.

Then came October 2, a morning of pouring rain that followed a night in which we could hear at least four stags, and they were still roaring when we left camp in pitch dark at 4 a.m. and ran straight into a bear in the first half-hour. Bears were nothing to me that morning, and taking no notice of him, we stumbled straight on in the dark and the pouring rain towards a muffled roar that was clearly coming from round the corner at the far end of the ridge we were on. Just before we reached the corner we came upon the biggest chamois buck that I had seen. He stood in an opening, looking black as a top-hat, sturdy and hairy, and I took my hat off to him and went on.

Once at the corner the roaring sounded extremely loud and fairly close. The old gentleman was clearly in a grumpy mood. Sometimes he would give vent to a full-throated bellow, followed by a series of grunts, and then there would be a sort of grumble, as if he was continuing his music in his sleep. Thanks to his continuous roaring, we could locate his position with some accuracy; as it was still raining as hard as ever and the wind was still blowing straight downhill, we made for a position exactly below him. Here we jumped another chamois and then a red hind. I ran forward thinking that the hind belonged to the stag, but Magomah seized me by the seat of the breeches and cursed me for a fool, explaining that this hind was nothing to do with our stag. She was a huge hind and, I suppose, an old cast-off spinster. To our delight the stag roared again and, leaving Magomah behind so as to have only two feet with which to crack a stick, I moved forward alone across a gully uphill through long grass and open forest.

Suddenly I smelt the stag—a most exciting smell with something of a billy goat in it but much more inspiring—and felt my hackles go up. It is not often that the human nose can perform the function for which I suppose it was made, but on that occasion my nose did so and gave me the information I wanted, whenever, as I zigzagged up the hill, I crossed the wind of the stag. I experienced the sensations that a pointer must feel, and have envied them and other dogs ever since.

It was obvious that the stag was in a little hollow surrounded by a semi-circle of rocks, and full of the longest grass dotted with oak trees. I reached the entrance to this hollow just as the rain lessened and I wondered whether the sun would come out, and if so whether the wind would change and blow uphill instead of down, and do so suddenly. The fear of this made me decide, no doubt wrongly, to go straight on rather than mount the rocks on one side or the other of the hollow.

As I entered the hollow I almost stamped on a hind. As she bolted I ran forward, rifle at full cock, and there within forty yards was the biggest stag I ever saw, or hope to see, striding towards the edge of the hollow on my left. Three strides and he was out of sight over the edge before I could even let the rifle off. I raced up the rocks half left and found beyond them a precipice, impassable for stag or man. The stag and hinds had, unseen by me, turned short, baulked by the precipice, and if I had run half right instead of half left I should have cut them off in the open, as we found afterwards by their tracks, which showed that they had run round me in a right-handed circle. We never saw that stag again, but I often dream of him—a great grey beast, thick in the neck with a long and heavy head crowned by an absolute forest of points: the father of all the stags. Probably he was somewhere between a fifteen and a twenty-pointer, and it was worth the journey to the Caucasus just to see him, although the vision lasted for such a minute space of time. The sketch facing page 117 is supposed to be him.

It is no use following a stag that has been 'jumped,' and we went on over some poisonously steep ground towards where we had heard another stag roar, but the sun had now come out ; roaring had ceased: I had but little hope. We found ourselves approaching the spot where I had missed the galloping shot previously mentioned, and as we came into sight of the steep open space a small stag bolted from the edge of it below us, having no doubt got our wind. I looked across a little steep valley towards a clump of oaks on our level, and by them stood two hinds looking at the bolting stag. Then I made out under the shade of the oaks another form, dim but bigger than the hinds, and finally could just see that the beast carried horns. It was a long shot, but there seemed no time to wait, for the hinds might bolt at any moment. I did not even dare to try to get a rest or to sit down, but just took the shot as I stood.

At the shot the stag came out from under the trees and turned uphill after the hinds, mounting a bank so steep that the deer could not move really fast. I fired three more galloping shots, and in the middle of the business the stag lowered his head and drove with his horns at the hind in front of him, knocking her savagely out of his path. That struck me as unusual and made me think that he was hit and there was still one cartridge left in the magazine. He was leading now and just going to disappear, when I fired my last shot: that time there was an unmistakable thud and he ducked his head forward before getting out of sight. I ran on, reloading in hope of another view, when there was a crash above me and down came the stag apparently out of the sky above us, on to the rocks, and head over heels in an avalanche of stones without a check for three hundred yards below us.

With a 'whoop' from me and a 'gateau' (its Russian equivalent) from Magomah, we flew down that slope. How we kept our legs, heaven knows, but we got there so to speak in one, and I reached the stag only twenty yards ahead of old Magomah with his stump foot. Although there was not a whole bone left in the stag's head and hardly any in his body, only one top point of those beautiful horns was broken off and we found it nearby in the rocks. He was a lovely beast, and as we looked at the head Magomah became quite poetical. "Ochin, ochin kracewi," and I thought what a pleasant way the Russians have of saying "Very, very pretty."

Moreover, those long points on the tops were easy to recognise. I had seen them before; it was undoubtedly the same stag that I had missed a few days earlier in that same spot. The last shot and I think the first were both in about the right place. It took us five and a half hours' hard and steep going to get his head home to camp, and although I sacrificed a handkerchief and other things on his body to try to keep off marauders, Rostom, who went for the meat on the morrow, discovered that a bear had been there first and had made a hearty meal. Of course I ought to have been content, but the vision of that still larger old grey warrior remained and still remains with me.

I looked for him again next day, for he had roared in the same area at night, but all we saw was a little stag, who rose from fern in a hollow and stood staring in amazement at us from forty yards: he was the only stupid deer I met in the Caucasus and I let him go in peace. That night in camp during dinner, eaten while we listened to two stags roaring, we heard what we took to be a stampede of the ponies and ran out calling to them to stop; it was not the ponies at all, but a stag galloping past.

One more day is worth recording. I was awakened at 3 a.m. by a roar and we were off in the dark, led by the sound. We seemed to be getting near and crossed a small gulley with extreme caution, when we heard something moving on the leaves ahead. As we peered over the bank beyond the gulley a little bear came rollicking down the hill to within a few yards of us, and stopped himself with a jerk. He then performed a ridiculous circular dance in front of us, waving his arms and striking at his nose with his paws. There is a drawing of him facing page 124. I suppose that he had put his head into a bees' or a wasps' nest and been stung on the nose. Then he collected himself and shuffled off downhill, presumably after his mother, whom we never saw.

Soon after we hit the tracks of the stag and his hinds and could with some difficulty follow them. After a time Magomah saw the stag walking slowly away, and I sat down to try and get steady, but as only the top of his back was in view I did not fire and he passed out of sight. Then we lost time, since we got muddled by earlier tracks, so that the deer again drew ahead of us, but we righted ourselves at last and hit their fresh tracks. Soon we came right up to within fifty yards of two hinds, who stood still listening in a perfect light. Beyond them the stag's head was just visible with the rest of his body hidden behind a mound. I put up the rifle, but the sun was rising behind him and shining in my eyes so that I could see nothing of the foresight. Probably I was wrong to try the shot and if I had waited he might perhaps have moved out and shown his body, but the hinds were so close and seemed so likely to bolt at any moment, that to wait seemed too great a risk. I tried him as I stood and missed his head. He was a very big-bodied stag with a long and wide head, but so far as I could see his horns did not carry many points.

We never saw him again and that was the last actual chance I had, for a few days later old Magomah informed me that he must get home to his wife. Probably I had worn him (and especially his stump) clean out. It was hard to tear myself away, but he had served me so well and we had had such sport together that I felt I must comply with his wishes. It may be that his desire to go was partly caused by the thought of razboiniki (brigands), a subject never far from his mind, and one night we had seen a camp-fire on the opposite ridge which all the men imagined to be caused by some of these people.

I remember a particular conversation about brigands; Magomah was telling me of their exploits and I replied by stating that my father, who was then chairman of quarter sessions in Essex, dealt with more 'razboiniki' in England than

I had ever heard of in the Caucasus. This was received with shocked surprise. I was always being asked whether, if I saw a 'razboiniki,' I would shoot him. How any one was to tell whether he was a 'razboiniki' or not always puzzled me, and in any case my reply was that I certainly should not shoot him unless he had a particularly good head.

Something must be said of the roe (Russian Kazyol) shown facing page 124. There were quite a number of them and they were almost as difficult to deal with as the red deer. So far as I could judge they were exactly like our roe and seemed to me about the same size, but some of the bucks—not many of them—carried heads far bigger than anything seen in our islands. I saw two such bucks, missed one and got the other by an absolute fluke. We were descending the steep side of a gulley, Magomah just ahead of me, when I saw on the opposite bank a roebuck lying. I hissed at Magomah, who sat down and I fired over his head. He put his hands to his ears and looked round at me with a pained expression to ask what it was. I had nearly but not quite missed the buck and had only seen his two front points and not realised the fine length of horn behind them. He was a beauty, and Magomah forgave me for giving him an earache.

We went sadly down the mountain to Magomah's home at Beliokhani and he was, I think, sorry to say good-bye. Thence I drove to Lagodecki along the foot of the mountains, and wondered whether I would mount again and rejoin Michael Ivkin in the forest. Madame Ivkin, however, doubted whether I should ever find him, and so I gave it up and caught the public conveyance at Signatch. It was an eventful journey. We reached Signatch too late for supper, and the following morning the hind wheel of the public car came off and trundled down the hill ahead of us. We had to return to Signatch to get another wheel, and although we finally reached Tiflis safe and in respectable time, the journey was not comfortable for the point of a stag's horn was sticking into my back on one side, and that of a turr on the other.

My companion on the seat was a young Russian officer armed to the teeth and very nervous of anything to do with the

Caucasus. He carried two revolvers, one on each side of his belt, and was horrified that I had packed my rifles and had nothing in my hand but a walking-stick. From Tiflis I sent a telegram to my father, "Coming home content." It was not quite true: I had hated leaving and there was that old grey stag.

After enjoying the luxury of the Hotel de Londres I recrossed the Dariel pass, and arrived at Vladikavkaz station to catch the train an hour before it went. I asked for a ticket and the man in the office peered at my strange assortment of luggage. "Why go to-day?" he said. "There's another train to-morrow." Ideas of time are vague in the East, but I insisted and he let me go. Since those far-off days I have had but little news of the Caucasus, and I wonder sometimes what those independent peoples think of the new fashions. When I was there official Russia seemed to have penetrated but little into the mountains. Has the new Russia done so now, and what is the reaction? I wonder. Mountaineers are apt to think the people of the plain beneath them. They will remain in my memory as a picturesque and charming people, proud of the glorious country in which they live.

After experiences of stalking with a camera instead of with a rifle in Scotland, I have sometimes wondered what chances might have come my way of getting photographs of the game in the Caucasus. It would, I think, with a modern camera and a telescopic lens (not available in 1913) have been possible to photograph the turr and perhaps the chamois, but in all the encounters I had with red deer, either because of the lack of light or because of the shortness of time during which they were visible, there would only have been one chance of a picture of a stag and that a very young one. Moreover, I should have had to be very quick to get him. Nevertheless, the fact remains that a good photograph of a big Caucasian stag, taken in an opening in his virgin forest, would be a trophy far superior to a stuffed head hanging on a wall. The man who secures such a trophy can claim all the stalking skill and all the luck that any man ever possessed, and I shall want to see the result

Eight

SCOTLAND

WE WERE a party of eleven in August 1946, arriving at an empty house in Morven on the West Coast of Argyll with everything required for a month's stay—luggage, linen, stores, and all the rest of it. There was much to do to get things more or less ship-shape and mighty little time to do it, if the river were to be fished that night, and it was asking to be fished, as we had seen as we crossed the bridge at its mouth. Luggage was hauled up the stairs and heaved into different rooms; sheets and blankets were whipped on to beds, clothes were extracted and chucked into drawers. We worked with remarkable efficiency and still more remarkable speed, and we earned our tea. The first thing I unpacked was a cast, dropped at once into water so that by the time tea was over all should be ready except for putting up a rod and tying on a fly. In five minutes after tea I was off with the two terriers, Jane and Ginger, dancing along in front down the road to the river. Tea had been just tea and another needed meal was coming at 6.30, but there was an hour and much can happen in an hour.

Near the mouth of the river Aline in Morven is a pool called the Castle Pool that is a dream to fish, when it is in order. It was in order now—perfect order—and using a screen of trees to give me background, I slipped gently into its rippling throat. The place was alive with sea trout just in from the sea and they were in a merry mood—so were the terriers. The first trout that got a proper hold was brought after many rushes and leaps to fairly near the bank, and Ginger, with most improper haste, plunged in and somehow got it ashore. The same thing happened with a second, and Jane sat fuming and fussing on the bank, enraged at the manners of her son. She was not going to have any more of that nonsense and, when the third trout was being played, she shot off the bank clean over Ginger's head, landed in the river

140

just by the fish, snapped him up by the head, and with her little tail cocked and a grin on her face marched ashore. She gave one nasty look at Ginger, growled him off as he approached and played with her capture on the grass, pretending to prevent even me from getting a hold of it. We had time for two more trout, and Jane bagged both of them: then home for the real evening meal about 6.30.

The rest of the party then went to bed, but having whetted my appetite for sea trout, I was off again, this time without the terriers, which are in the dark more of a hindrance than a help. Things were as lively as ever, and during the last hour of light, when I took off Little's Fancy and put on a larger and black fly, the bigger fish had apparently told the smaller to go to bed, for the ones that came to me were all something of a handful. There is a long straight pool called George's, fast at the top but oily from half-way down to the tail, and although in full daylight it is difficult to get within shot of the quieter water without being spotted, it is as good a place as any on the river to fish when the light is grey. I timed my arrival just right that night, and crouching low on the grass bank I heaved my black fly well across and let it slide down near the far bank, and then across the stream to my side. When straight below me I pulled it back upstream with a series of short sharp jerks, giving it a lively motion both with rod and hand.

The first fish to come was a little slow on the uptake and got nothing but a toothache, but the second made a better shot and got a proper hold. I walked him up and kept him clear of the water below him and slew him out of the sight of the rest of the fish, and was soon into another who responded to one of the jerks near my own bank. He, too, was walked safely up the pool and his final splutterings were not noticed by the rest of the company. Then a lovely silvery creature flounced into the air right under the far bank. I had to put my muscles into it to reach him, but I got there at last and he took the fly savagely and screamed out line in every direction. He was not quite so big as the other two, but he was the best fun of all and had been nearly all over the pool before I got him. The light was nearly gone but there was enough for one more trout from the very tail to see the fly in shallower water. None of the four was over 2 lbs., but none of them was much short of it and my first evening's bag was eighteen—a hearty start for the season.

A few days later, on August 11th, I was fishing with a trout rod about midday from a bridge that spans the river near the top of the same pool, when I saw, near the fly which was travelling down close to the left bank, what I took to be the tail of a fair-sized sea trout. I waited and presently there was a thump. The thump struck me as rather big for the amount of tail I had seen, but the fish hung in the stream without much movement and I could not make out what it was. Anyhow it was no use standing still on the top of that high bridge with the fish downstream of me and, handing my rod to my companion, the head stalker and a keen fisherman, I raced down the road through a gate and over a wire fence to the river bank below the bridge, and told him to drop the rod, which I caught. Once level with the fish there was no need for further caution, and with a turn of the reel and a well-hooped rod things began to liven up, and it was soon obvious that the tail I had seen was not the whole tail or anything like it. Then we saw him and both yelled "Salmon" together. It was a very easy place for I could move in any direction and kept just below the fish all the time, but there was a bit of fun at the end for he chose to turn on his side and come in to the gaff exactly opposite a steep-sided, narrow ditch which here entered the river. The gaffer was at the mouth of the ditch, which was not a safe place in which to gaff a fish, but somehow he managed to heave it on to the flat grass above the lip of the ditch and in a second we both had a hand on it—a perfectly fresh fish of 11 lbs., and that is a rare thing as late as August 11th.

Higher up the river is a pool called for some unknown reason ' the pump,' deepened artificially by a wall made of rocks, held in their place by strong wire-netting. The upper part of it is very deep and complicated by an annoying back-water which lays hold of the line and prevents the fly working properly in the main stream outside the back-water. Under those conditions nothing ever seems to take my fly, and I suppose that it looks unnatural. I was fishing there one day alone in a spate; a quarter of a mile above me was a friend accompanied by the stalker, and at various distances downstream were different members of my family, most of them fishing and all hidden by a low ridge. As usual nothing came in the upper part of the pool, where the back-water was more annoying than ever and the fly would neither hang nor work, but there is a length of main stream just outside the back-water and slightly below it. When that is reached I expect something to happen, for the line can be held clear of the back-water, so that the fly slips down unchecked and eventually comes in to the near bank below. Nothing on that day happened at all and my hopes had been very high for the water looked exactly right. Lower down the pool there is a good chance of a sea trout, but not in my past experience of anything bigger. I fished on carefully, but with my hopes of salmon and grilse receding. Then as the fly swung into midstream there was a sudden yellow explosion and a hearty grab. That was no sea trout, and I screamed when the hook went home and continued to holloa my soul out in order to let all the world know what had happened and join in the fun, if they wished.

At the first holloa, my friend, who was lame, told me that the stalker, who had been sitting near him on a steep heather bank above a path, sprang up and turned a complete somersault on to the path, gaff and all, picked himself up and raced downstream towards me. The rest of the party out of sight below me had all heard too for the wind was right for them, and one by one figures began to appear, making best pace towards me. I worked my fish, which was a good honest, steady puller, away from the back-water to which he appeared to be wedded, and away from the stone wall with its dangerous wire that might catch the line. By the time I had got him almost to the tail of the pool the party was complete, terriers and all, so that about ten people were round me, every one in a mad state of excitement —Jane screaming, Ginger dancing about in all directions, and everybody jabbering and eyeing the water for a sight of the fish. We soon saw him, a good big grilse that we reckoned at 6 lbs. There is a quick rush of water, where it leaves the tail of the pool, that will knock the nonsense out of any fish, and on a short line I heaved the grilse into it so that he came walloping down on the surface of the waves at our feet.

All danger was over and it was merely a case of taking him down to a convenient spot in quieter water. I knew the spot and, seeing a nice shelving bank of shingle, I said to the stalker, "Don't gaff him, we will beach him." Jane and Ginger had been caught and were safely in somebody's arms, yelling and kicking, particularly when they saw the fish. I was moving down the bank's edge level with the grilse and guiding him exactly as I liked. It was almost too easy, but the crowd of all ages, the screaming terriers and the general hubbub and excitement made it capital fun. Then suddenly, one of my feet went straight into a deep round hole made by a winter flood and hidden in long grass. I crashed to the ground, but luckily my heel caught some projection or I think my leg would have been broken. I was unhurt and up again in a second, but the rod, as I fell, had given a terrible jerk to the fly in the mouth of the fish. However, all seemed well; he was still on and there were only a few yards to go to the shingle beach. Slowly the fish rolled over on the surface, and every one said "Ooh!" That roll did it: quite slowly I felt the hook tear out and it flew into the air, while the fish gently sank and disappeared from sight. It was a nasty blow to all the party, not least to the terriers, who rushed up and down the bank looking for the fish that they felt was theirs. A few days later I hooked another grilse in the same pool, and by then we had filled in that dangerous hole and no accident occurred. I gaffed him myself but there was only one spectator—the crowd was not there to see, and this success did not really make up for the previous disaster.

On the West Coast of Scotland the summer of 1946 did not show any shortage of salmon, grilse and sea trout, as did other parts of the country, in particular the East Coast. Indeed in Morven there was more than a normal run of fish, but, as is the case on the West Coast of Norway, there is no early run in these parts as there is on the East Coast and nothing happens in the west until late in June, when salmon begin to appear, followed by grilse and sea trout in July and August. Most of the large sea trout come first and smaller ones later, but I remember one occasion when during a spate in mid-August a number of large fresh-run fish were showing. I only hooked one of them and thought it was a grilse, but it proved to be a fresh-run six-pound sea trout. I could not tell whether the other fish I saw that day of about the same size were grilse or sea trout, but it may well be that a late run of big sea trout was occurring.

In 1946, salmon and grilse were constantly showing themselves in low water as well as in high, but August is a bad month to catch them. We were maddened by the sight of big fish leaping and even making head and tail rises, for they would not take. Constantly after fishing a likely stretch of water, one of these brutes would heave itself into the air just after the fly had passed, and presumably these exhibitions are from fish that have seen the fly, have never meant to take it, but yet feel some sort of reaction is required of them, with the result that they make these silly jumps. Eventually Jane, in her disgust, would turn her face away after seeing one of these maddening fish. She had given up any hope of them and so almost had I.

Loch Arienas, which helps to feed the river, was full of fish, but for some reason the fly which really excites them was conspicuous for its absence in August, 1946. Bibio pomone, a black fly with long sprawling legs which hatches on the moors and blows, I think, by a mere fluke on to the water, was almost entirely absent. There were a few duns most days but never a big hatch, and on those occasions when trout rose well for a short period the light was not good enough or the ripple too great to allow us to determine what caused the rise.

Rises in that loch never last long, and while they are on it is best to fish very hard, to be quick in playing anything hooked and to row upwind until the fish is netted in order not to disturb good water further on in the drift. On many days conditions seemed perfect and it was a delight to be in such surroundings with the constant expectation of the sudden start of a violent rise or the appearance of a gigantic fish, but such things never quite happened: we caught nothing like the bags we expected to catch. One thing was noticeable: if the smaller sea trout were taking the larger ones were not, and if a large fish was caught most of the others were of respectable size. For instance, the stalker went out alone one day before we arrived and in about two hours caught nine trout, none of them much over or much under 2 lbs. Sea trout resemble brown trout in that matter —if there is enough food available to tempt the big ones and they are in the mood, their inferiors are told to get out of the light and do so; they have to take their meals at times when for some reason their betters are asleep or at least not hungry, and those times are much too common.

Up in the hills of Morven is a pleasant loch inhabited by brown trout, that can be reached from home on foot in an hour. There is a boat on the loch, but from one side of it shelves and beaches run out to considerable distances from the shore: more-over most of the wading is sound and good. I prefer wading to fishing from a boat for it gives independence and a chance for initiative. The under-water geography is somewhat complicated and the water is not quite clear enough to allow a good view of the bottom, so that the way has to be felt rather than seen. That adds to the interest and it is surprising how far, when fish are rising, one can get from the shore without noticing the distance or even the direction. You see a rise ahead and move cautiously towards it casting hard, then another fish shows beyond and you go on and try for him and forget about the bank and every-thing else. The depth varies considerably, and there is no steady slope on the bed of the loch; the way back to shore may be barred by channels too deep even for long waders. The safest method is to find a ridge under water and follow it by feeling with the feet. My knowledge of the bottom of that loch is still incomplete but I have learnt some of it.

The worst trouble is caused by isolated outcrops of rock that may trip the feet and it is never safe to move at any pace. More-over, it is a mistake to do so, for anything but slow movement causes vibration and may put down the fish. Even if a rise is seen and covered with a cast, it often pays to be patient, if no response is made at once. These loch trout are all cruisers, and a fish that fails to see the fly at the first cast may have passed on out of sight, but he will probably return in the end to about the same spot. Wherefore patience and constant casting will often be rewarded.

I had a good day on that loch in 1946. There was a nice ripple but never at any time much fly or many rises. For a short while a small brown creature like a sedge spluttered about on the surface, and made things lively; moreover, his splutterings caused a splashy rise that could be heard. When I had spotted what was happening I put on a brown buzzy object and got several trout in quick succession. Then that performance ended and I walked ashore and ate my lunch, but in the afternoon a few dun hatched, not everywhere but in certain patches of water. I walked along the shore until I saw a rise and then waded in, and often found that where one fish had shown himself there were in fact several in a small area, all ready to take an intelligent interest. My bag was not large but it was larger than that from the boat, and although none of my fish weighed quite 1 lb., several of them nearly did and that is more than one expects from most lochs in Scotland. Another interesting thing was the colour variation of the trout. Those caught near rocks had very dark backs, while those from sandy bays were a rich reddish yellow.

One day I was fishing a narrow fast stream just below a ford much used by deer (Plate 12)[1] and above an old stone bridge, when something took the fly. There was a chance of other fish below and, believing it to be a small sea trout, I walked it fifty yards upstream without much trouble. When I thought the end of the business was coming, the creature differed from me, lost its temper and fled away down again and then leapt in the air. I estimated a grilse of 5 lbs. and changed my tactics, ran down to it reeling up and then, with a short line, crept along a platform placed for that purpose under the arch of the stone bridge. There was a nasty jagged rock projecting out of the water under the bridge, but I held the point of the rod out beyond it and passed

---

[1] This is not the same photograph as the one in *Fisherman Naturalist* but it comes from the same 40 ft. of film.

the fish safely through the bridge. A companion met me below
the bridge, and as the fish was now beat my only anxiety was the
terriers. I must somehow gaff the fish and hand it back high in
the air, so that when they sprang at it as they were sure to do
there would be no danger of their being pricked by the gaff. I
waded out into a small shallow and had a perfectly easy shot.
There was a good thump but the point of the gaff did not go in.
However, the fish was soon brought round again and I clipped
him into the air and on to the bank behind, but again the point
of the gaff had not penetrated. However, the terriers had him
by both ends in a second and all was well.

An examination of the fish showed at once why the gaff had
not gone in. He was a fresh-run grilse of $3\frac{1}{2}$ lbs., but so thin
that the point of the gaff had gone clean round him, and never
touched him. We ate him the next night and he was delicious,
and I sent his scales to Mr. Hutton, whose verdict was a typical
grilse but one which had apparently met with some mishap in
the summer in the sea, which had prevented him getting his
normal food. He was marked by a net and had lost a lot of tissue
in his tail, which looked like that of a wet cormorant. Con-
sidering his shape, which was worse than a kelt's, he had given
very good sport.

In *Fisherman Naturalist* I related the painful disasters, partly
due to my stupidity, which befell my daughter Jean in the matter
of big fish. Now at last the matter has been righted and she is
all square and set fair on her fishing career. In September 1947
after a drought lasting six or seven weeks the heavens opened
and discharged buckets of driving rain. On the first day of high
river I was fishing on the opposite bank to Jean, when she shouted
across "I think I'm into a big one." I raced upstream to the
nearest possible place to cross, while she took her fish down past
me and by the time I had reached her she was beginning to get
on terms. My advice to her was "Keep on hauling him down
and don't let him get below you. When you get to the tail of
the pool heave him out of it into the quick water and we will
gaff him in the next bit of quiet stuff below." It all went according to plan except that the fish moved out of the quiet water we

had selected as the spot for gaffing into the current again and was swept on down. I ran ahead and found another suitable spot and there he was coaxed in and safely gaffed, a grilse of 6 lbs. The turn of luck did not end there, for the very next morning she hooked a salmon in a big pool and after a hammer and tongs fight caught him too.

I had had to run round this pool to a bridge to reach Jean and some minutes after the salmon was on the bank, smoke and a nasty smell issued from my coat pocket. I delved into the pocket and fished out a burnt handkerchief and a burning pipe, threw the handkerchief under a rock, knocked out the pipe, cursed myself for a fool and started fishing again. Ten minutes later more smoke and smell was noticed coming from this same pocket, and this time my hand went straight through a large burnt and burning hole in my second best coat. The playing of a salmon always makes me see red and drives every particle of sense out of my head.

The long drought which preceded this spate made extremely difficult but interesting fishing. The river was reduced to a feeble trickle through rocks covered in green slime with occasional deeper holes in which all the fish were collected and were perfectly visible. In each pool the salmon and grilse seemed to occupy a different area to that inhabited by the sea trout. The best chance to catch a fish seemed to be, after a very careful approach with suitable background of bank or trees, to wait for the maximum breeze before casting at all. There was no stream whatever in the pools and the fly had to be given motion by the hand and rod. On some days it seemed best to let the fly sink, after it alighted, as deep as possible in the water even to the bottom of the pool, and then to pull it back and up with a series of sharp jerks. Sometimes a fish would take it as it alighted, sometimes as it was sinking and then the fish was difficult to feel, sometimes while it was being jerked back and then the fish was easy to feel but difficult to hook. Ninety-nine times out of a hundred of course nothing happened at all. My nephew, Arthur Dent, was much the most successful fisherman during the drought. He always was something of a wizard with a rod and long absence in Africa seems to have heightened rather than lessened his skill. He caught a salmon by these methods and lost another, and I do not think that he ever came home without a sea trout. I was extremely stupid at this form of fishing but I had one fine hour's sport in a minute pool reached by sea water at high tide.

I stalked the pool carefully from below using a tree as background and squatted on a little beach below its tail. A ' Little's Fancy ' was flicked into the pool, allowed to sink and then jerked back towards me. The fish could be seen when they turned on their sides to scratch off sea lice, and they could also be seen sometimes when they darted at the fly, but they were not easy to hook. If one was actually hooked the important thing to do was to pull him away at once downstream in order not to let the rest of the company see what was happening. I had no net and no dog and I beached each fish on my left between myself and a rock, pulled him over the sand to me by the gut, knocked him on the head and put him in the basket without ever moving my body at all. I got eight sea trout in this way one after the other and then foul-hooked one. I caught him but since he was impossible to control he flew through the crowd of other fish and frightened them which finished the business. Never before had I caught more than two sea trout at a sitting out of that pool. The largest fish weighed 1 lb. and when, after they had taken alarm and refused to play any more, I stood on the top of a rock above the pool, from which every fish in it was visible, I found that there was no other fish of that weight in the whole company of perhaps 150 little sea trout.

I also tried fishing with a fly in the sea, and caught one good sea trout wading out from the shore through the sea weed, about $\frac{1}{2}$ mile from the river mouth. During the last hour before low tide numbers of sea trout could often be seen jumping in the sea, but it proved very difficult to make them take. Once in a boat I drifted down to a spot where several fish had been seen jumping and saw a tight mass of little sea trout wriggling about near the surface. I put a fly into the middle of them but none of them took any notice of it. Perhaps we ought to have tried when the last hour of the ebb coincided with dusk or dawn.

On Sunday afternoon it has been our practice to take out as large and young a party as possible into the 'sanctuary' and try to get the whole lot of them really close up to deer. This affords good practice in stalking, and various members of the party, in particular the youngest, are deputed to take the lead and conduct different phases of the approach. With full responsibility on their shoulders they learn very quickly at that age, and it is obvious that far the commonest fault is quick movement. There is an instinct, that must be checked, to duck the head instead of keeping it perfectly still when a beast suddenly comes into view or shows suspicion. The most exciting phase is reached when one by one the whole party has to be manœuvred into position along a line of rocks or some other covert in order that they may all get a really good close view of deer.

I remember one afternoon when we spied about a dozen stags, and after a stalk in which various children took the full responsibility on their shoulders, we reached after a flat crawl a rocky ridge within about fifty yards of the deer. There was a convenient little hollow on one side of the ridge, but to reach it a hummock had to be passed just in view of the deer. I lay by this hummock and as each crawler reached it I kept his or her back flat with my hands. They were now all in line safely in the hollow, with two members of the party already in position watching the deer from the rocky ridge just in front and above. At a signal from these two that all the deer were quiet, the whole party then squirmed into position without being noticed. It was a hot day, flies annoyed the stags, and they suddenly rose from their beds and walked off round a knoll flicking their ears and shaking their tails. As the last stag passed out of sight our whole party ran in and went straight over the top of the knoll to within twenty yards of the deer. Red deer on an open moor do not expect a large crowd of humans to appear suddenly at twenty yards, and the stampede was spectacular. They have to get used to that sort of thing in the sanctuary on Sunday afternoons and it does not seem to do them any harm.

This chapter is supposed to deal with Scotland in general and not merely with sport in Morven, and I have been ransacking my memory for days at other forms of sport in different parts of the Highlands. There was a day, for instance, in early June when Capt. W. S. Medlicott and I, after looking at birds in the Forsinard country in Sutherland, got out of the train about dawn at Dalwhinnie. The engine-driver or the station-master, I forget which, produced some hot water and we gave ourselves a drink of hot chocolate and then set out on a perfect morning for the tops between Drumochter and Loch Ericht. We had one object in view and that was dotterel—the dainty little chestnut plover that nests on flat barren tops far from mankind and yet is the tamest bird in Britain. We were in dotterel country before most people have their breakfasts, and soon a dotterel came into sight whirling about in the air and calling. It kept appearing and disappearing, and we came to the conclusion that the centre of interest was a flat ridge about three hundred yards from us. Once we picked up with the glass a dotterel running about on this ridge, but it disappeared in the stones and we saw nothing more. After waiting some time we decided that I should walk to the place where the bird had disappeared, while W. S. M. sat still and watched with his glass.

When the spot was reached there was no sign of a bird and I began to walk about tapping the stones with my stick, when from almost between my feet the dotterel rose from its eggs, walked a yard or so, lay down, spread its wings and tail and kicked out its legs behind it. I held up my hat, and W. S. M. arrived to find me and the bird at my feet. We stood admiring its lovely shades of brown, large dark eye and pure white eye-streak, when it began to crawl away on its stomach, wings and tail extended and looking utterly helpless and ridiculous. We walked by its side for perhaps thirty yards, when it suddenly stood up in a normal position and stared at us. It had done its trick, decoyed us away from its nest according to the rules, but the rules apparently stopped short at this point. It had not the faintest idea what to do next and just stood there thinking, if a dotterel can think. We stood by or rather over it, and after a long pause it walked quite slowly, bolt upright, back to the nest, and we walked by its side. When it reached its destination it sat quietly down on the eggs again, taking no more notice of us, and we sat down by it. We should have liked to stroke it, and I dare say it would have allowed us to do so, but we were not going to take any risks, so moved discreetly away and left it sitting happily on its eggs. It was a strange sensation up there at 3,000 feet to be alone with a wild bird that had probably hardly ever seen a human being before and yet remained, after obeying its instinct its rules or whatever it may be, seated on its most precious belongings, with two enormous strange creatures staring at it and talking to it. There is no use in trying to fathom a dotterel's brain; it must be a very different organ to that of most birds.

Those particular tops and the stony slopes below them are capital ptarmigan ground, and many years ago four of us with six beaters went after them during three days of brilliant sunshine at the end of September. My host, Mr. George Albright, and the keeper knew the art of ptarmigan driving from A to Z, and of all forms of shooting in Scotland I should put it at the top. Most of the ptarmigan ground in Scotland is within the sacred precincts of deer forests, and stalkers, if not their masters, are generally afraid of disturbing the deer. In my experience, if deer can see what is going on, they do not take much alarm and are apt to watch the proceedings, apparently with interest, from a distance. It has always seemed to me waste of a good thing not to drive ptarmigan on the high tops on deer ground in fine weather. We at any rate had no such qualms and let what deer there were be disturbed or not as they chose.

Ptarmigan have the habit of swinging off wide into space from a hill and then clinching in again to it where they meet a contrary wind, and the main art in ptarmigan driving consists therefore in spotting where this clinching in will take place. In this particular year there was an exceptional stock of ptarmigan, and on the last of these three days a golden eagle was conveniently hunting the far side of the hill, which was off our march. This eagle produced two excellent results; he kept putting somebody else's ptarmigan on to our ground and he was constantly giving us driven shots both at grouse and ptarmigan.

I remember two drives in particular. In the first we lined the upper lip of a steep, semi-circular corrie that is visible to the north-west from the Highland railway between Dalnaspidel and Dalwhinnie. The beaters scrambled across the rocky face below us and the ptarmigan suddenly appeared from out of the corrie under one's feet. The second drive was a long one with the top beater on the crest and the bottom beater on the upper line of heather, all parallel with the line of the ridge. A low subsidiary ridge that ran down the slope at the right angle was selected as the spot the guns should line, and we were given twenty minutes to make our own butts out of stones, of which there was no lack.

From these butts we had a perfect view of the more distant ground to be driven, but there was dead ground in front of us where a slight hollow ran down the face of the hill from the crest of the main ridge to the heather. This made it all very exciting, for the grey and white birds could be seen flying towards us in the distance, were then lost to view, and reappeared within shot in front. Where we were the light wind was from behind our backs, so that the birds were flying into it, and they swept along only just above the ground. My butt was built in a shallow dip which crossed the little ridge we were on and led to the dead ground in front, and a large proportion of the birds followed the line of this dip. Covey after covey flew towards us and each covey seemed to pick up others from the ground as they flew, so that by the time they reached us, the birds were in packs, some of them perhaps of fifty birds or even more. I have never seen such a sight of ptarmigan and, except for a few birds that swirled down the hill from the beaters or guns above, those that came to me came straight at my nose along the little hollow and, if the birds were spotted the moment they appeared out of the dead ground, it was possible to get a right and left in front of the butt. We shot the same ground or practically the same ground on the three consecutive days. I have no record of the actual bags, but I can remember it within a bird or two. It was about this : first day, 33 brace of ptarmigan; second day, 39 brace; third, 43 brace, and there were a sprinkling of cock grouse with them, for I can remember a right and left of a grouse and a ptarmigan. This may sound rather murderous, but on the last drive of the last day we seemed to see more ptarmigan than ever. That may have been partly due to our very efficient eagle. I hope that he had as good a day as he helped to give us. That kind of sport might be had on large areas of Scotland, where it is never practised, and, if a fine day can be picked, it is the most sporting form of driving conducted on the highest ground in Scotland, worth the climb whatever the bag.

I have never liked shooting over dogs and think that August 12th is too early to shoot grouse in Scotland. Grouse sit to pointers and setters for a very good reason. The parent grouse, who give the signal to get up and go, delay that signal because of the youth of their brood, and while they have those feelings it seems to me too early to go after them. I like watching a good pointer or setter at work, and good ones are pretty rare, but I have a qualm of conscience about the whole business which disappears later in the season. My conscience is an odd thing, for it seems to remain quiescent, when as sometimes happens I go after grouse with a terrier. The principles of the business are the same but it is a much more lively form of sport, for a terrier that winds grouse does not stop to point; it gallops as hard as it can straight for the birds it winds. There is no quiet walk up to a point, but a race to get to the grouse as quick as the terrier.

There is good sport to be had below high-water mark on the shore, where nothing is needed but a shooting licence. I must confess, however, that it is very hard to keep below high-water mark, for so often the only cover or the only way of approach to fowl lies just above it. A friend and I were once offending by a few yards, since we were sitting in gorse bushes which are not apt to grow below spring-tide mark, waiting for pigeons that we had seen drinking at a burn. While we squatted in the bushes two ladies came down the burn fishing, and the one on the far bank hooked a trout, but her companion on our side of the burn held the only landing net. The situation was serious and our gallantry got the better of our caution. We rushed for it, seized the net, waded the burn and landed the trout. The ladies were very grateful but rather worried. "We are not quite sure whether we ought to be fishing here at all." We assured them that they were perfectly all right and could fish where they pleased, and they no doubt took us for thoroughly well-mannered landlords.

There are in certain places on the coast in the last half of September and in October numbers of teal collected on the estuaries—presumably birds that have bred in Scotland—and sometimes a good sprinkling of wigeon with them. It is very hard to get near them and my best chances have generally occurred at spring tide when sea-water covers fresh ground and, what is more important, ground within shot of a sea bank or some other cover. On one such occasion a companion shot a wigeon that fell in the sea and he took off his clothes, swam in and retrieved it. He emerged on to the top of the sea wall with his prize and nothing else but himself face to face with an old lady who was making hay. She looked up and said without surprise, "It's a gran' day for bathin'". On other parts of the coast, in particular on the Solway, enormous numbers of golden plover congregate in September, no doubt birds that have nested on the moors and are about to start on their autumn migration. I have never been able to be at the right place and free to spend a day after them, but wonderful sport is there if covert can be found on the line they are taking. Golden plover are easy to call, and the other day while motoring along a road near the Norfolk coast a little flock of them swished over the car, and away towards the sea. I hung my head out and whistled at them, and they came whirling back to within a few yards of the car.

In two places in Scotland, one on the East and the other on the West Coast, I have had sport with geese. On the East Coast firth in mid-winter these birds seldom feed above high-water mark except during frost, when they come down on to clover stubbles, but on the West Coast, where there is apparently no good feed on the estuary, they come inland every day at morning flight from their roosting grounds on sandbanks out at sea. The best plan of campaign seems to be to spy the fields for feeding

geese from high ground, and when a flock is found to stalk to a
position as near them as possible and dead upwind of them, for
geese cannot apparently get the wind of a human being. My
companion, the keeper, is an expert at moving geese for he never
frightens them. He used to walk about casually with his dog at
heel, looking like a shepherd to whom the geese are accustomed,
and if, as sometimes happened, the birds flew a short way and
alighted again, he gave me plenty of time to crawl into a new
position, if I wished to do so, before again moving them. Like
any other bird, geese must rise upwind and they cannot turn for
at least thirty yards. Therefore if an approach can be made safely
to within fifty yards of a flock, a shot is certain when they are
put up. At one hundred yards there is an even chance, but if no
approach is possible to within that distance, it is mainly a matter
of luck. This quiet method of moving geese disturbs them very
little and they will probably return to the same feeding ground
the next day. I like to use an ordinary twelve-bore and No. 2
shot, and think it better sport to try to get really close and
never take a long shot.

I remember once getting within about thirty yards of the
nearest birds of a flock of over a hundred greylag. They had no
suspicions and I could hear them talking quietly as they fed,
while I crouched behind a low rock. I was dead upwind of them
and knew that when they were moved they must come straight
over my head. A right and left seemed certain. There was a roar
of wings as they rose, and the whole flock came straight over me
at about the height of a French partridge. I shot at the leader,
an enormous bird, at a range of twenty yards, and missed him
clean. I did get him with the second barrel but it was ridiculous
not to have got two. Geese are quite easy to miss, sometimes
they are going very fast and sometimes they are almost standing
still, but the real trouble is that they are geese and that is enough
to upset most people's nerves. Such a combination of stalking
and moving is a fine form of sport, and far too difficult for there
to be the smallest danger of any one shooting too many. In the
early mornings on the Solway these grey geese go flighting about
over the ' merse,' as saltings are called in that country, and one

morning I tried to intercept them. There was only one bit of cover and, though flock after flock passed me, hardly any came within shot and I only got one of them, but for half an hour the excitement was intense and one never knew which way to look.

This chapter began with legitimate fishing: it shall end with a more doubtful form of that sport. Our excuse was a lady who had never caught a salmon and our chance was a spell of dry weather and a low, clear river. The lady held the rod and I held the fly, which was very large. We walked up the bank until we saw a salmon, which was not in the least difficult to see. Then I slipped in downstream of the fish, stalked him slowly, dropped the gut over his back and gave a jerk. It was great fun the first time but it palled, for it was much too easy. We caught five salmon in the afternoon, one of them twice, and the only thing to be said in our favour is that we put them all back with nothing but a slight prick generally near their tails.

Nine

SCANDINAVIA

THE MAIN PURPOSE of nearly all my visits to Scandinavia has been fishing, and most of this chapter therefore relates to that form of sport. Plate 13 shows a typical Norwegian Fjord and Plate 14 gives an indication of the impatience of my daughter Elizabeth to get to her fishing.

The first foreign visitor to the river in which I have fished year after year in Norway was, so the inhabitants say, an Englishman and the oldest of them remember his arrival. He came in a yacht and lived on it, but he fished the river, whether with leave or not I do not know. He did one thing to which the inhabitants objected and for which he is chiefly remembered. He shot at cats outside the houses from the deck of his yacht and has been known as ' the mad lord ' ever since. After him, Lord Methuen and a friend came there and had capital sport. They did not shoot at village cats, and were better liked than the ' mad lord.'

Ever since these days English fishermen have been given the title of ' The Lords Fishers,' and at the annual Sports Day, when all the children turn up and we arrange races, etc., give prizes and make speeches, one of the events is a tug-of-war between 'The Lords Fishers' and their 'Kleppers' (gaffers). The kleppers always win, but on the last occasion when I took part the village broke in to give us a hand, and everybody that could get there got a hold of the rope on one side or the other. The result was inevitable; the rope broke and everybody on it rolled over on their backs.

There has been a revolution in Norwegian fishing, and I happen to have been for many years to the river where the revolution started. I am in no way responsible for it, but have benefited from it and began to do so in its early stages. Major Archie Morrison started the revolution one hot August, when the river was low but full of sea trout. The fishing there used to be done almost entirely at night and with a big rod: he intro-duced day fishing with a dry fly and a small rod. The revolution has not travelled very fast or very far for fishermen are extra-ordinarily conservative creatures, but it will spread, and my object is to show what a frantically exciting thing dry-fly fishing for sea trout is, without in the least detracting from the sport of catching the same fish with a wet fly either by day or by night.

To do that I am going to rely mainly on my diaries, which have been written up every day and therefore give the impressions of the moment, but in order to paint first a general picture it seems best to begin with the summaries written at the end of each fishing visit. The figures relate only to fish of 3 lb. or over.

The first fact that emerges is that dry-fly fishing for sea trout in a rapid river is a game for the young, in particular if the water contains big fish. In 1912, when I was only just over 30, had very good eyes and was quick on my feet, I caught in a month's fishing in Norway seventy-eight sea trout, of which sixty-nine were caught on dry fly and only nine on wet. In 1923, a remarkably good season, in thirteen and a half days, my bag was fifty-two sea trout averaging 5½ lbs., the proportion of fish caught on dry fly being still very high. In 1925 there was a large run of big fish early, but very few small fish and a great shortage of fly, with the result that more fish were caught at night on a wet fly, the proportion being thirty-nine on dry and thirty on wet in fifteen days' fishing. In the next season the river was very low, and again there was a large early run of big fish and remarkably few small ones. Out of fifty-two large sea trout all but ten were caught on dry fly.

In 1927 and subsequent years we went through a bad spell, as was to be expected from the lack of young fish in preceding years, but conditions began to improve again slightly in 1930 and 1931. From 1931 onwards my length of stay on the river each year was about three weeks. 1933 was a fairly good year, and my diary records that I did not miss quite so many chances as usual; my bag was sixty-eight big sea trout, forty-six on dry fly and twenty-two on wet. In 1934 fish ran very early and we only saw latecomers, my bag being forty-three sea trout, of which twenty-three were on dry fly and nineteen on wet. In 1935, for the first time, I caught more fish on wet fly than dry —seventeen on dry and twenty-nine on wet fly, and that sort of proportion has continued since. The reason is obvious: my eyes were beginning to fail and my legs could no longer go the pace required to keep ahead of a fish racing down the river, and these fish run further and faster by day than by night.

When I first visited this river we were all still experimenting with flies and took with us innumerable different patterns. Slowly and painfully, as my diaries show, we have discovered what we want and reduced our needs to the minimum in different sorts of flies. I took home some of the natural flies in a bottle, and expert fly-tiers in England produced an imitation good enough, and what is equally important, something that could be seen in rough water and in most lights. Under any ordinary conditions we have come to the conclusion that a 'tup' made with very stiff hackle is good enough to represent the pale dun about the size of a yellow Sally that hatches on Norwegian rivers, and although there is also a small iron blue and a kind of miniature alder, we do not bother about them, because their imitations are not sufficiently visible. The other fly of real importance is the large brown sedge that hatches at water-line on rocks about sunset, and to imitate that a good big dark fly, that can be made out of a crow's wing and no doubt many other feathers, is good enough with which to fish wet at sunset and after dark. In very high water it seems worth while to have a few larger dry flies, and those tied with deer's hair have been found effective. For the rest, if I want to fish wet by daylight, as I often do, I use mainly a Little's Fancy with a hook about as long as my second finger-nail. In certain conditions in Scotland, where the light and the colour of the water is quite different, a black buzzy dry fly has been found effective, but I have never tried it in Norway and doubt if it would be sufficiently visible in that rough water.

One of the main things brought out by my diaries, which are, I think, quite truthful, is the enormous proportion of fish missed or lost compared to the number caught. That is due first, of course, to stupidity, secondly to the amazing eyesight

and activity of a sea trout, and thirdly to the violence and pace
of the river. Here is an instance of what happens, taken from
the account of a wonderful day, when I was probably in good
form. It tells what occurred in one pool only at the peak of the
rise of a great hatch of dun about midday, when high clouds
sometimes intervened and covered a bright sun.

"Then to G.[1] (G. is a pool by the side of an island covered
with trees) which was a sight to see: fish great and small rolling
up at duns in all directions. I began by losing two beauties in
the tail of the pool, one strong fish racing all round the pool,
down to the tail and up again round a rock, where he broke me.
The other who was probably equally big (5 or 6 lbs. anyhow)
played upstream like a gentleman and heaven knows why he got
off. I think it was an ineffective barb. A little higher up a great
yellow fish missed it twice from sheer abandon but I got one of
$4\frac{1}{2}$ lbs. above him." One caught out of four rises under the most
perfect conditions.

Here is another day which speaks for itself. "A nice day of
sun and cloud, light upstream wind. Every bit of bad luck was
crowded into the morning. I raised two big fish in Oinahol
(Island pool) and left a tup in one. The other, who was seen
scratching lice off his stomach, had two shots at it and missed
each time. At L.K. the light was bad and little fish kept missing
it. Then what I thought was another small fish by the tiny rise
did not miss it and proceeded to march solemnly up the pool.
He turned at the top, heaved slowly and irresistibly out and then
down the pool totally uncontrollable and terrifyingly heavy. I
screamed for Hyelmar (the gaffer), who was away down coffee
housing with M. (my wife) and down we went over the bridge,
the fish anywhere and racing on for the rock at L. where I felt
a jar. But the line came free, and on reeling up I found him in
L. Then more heaves and jerks and at last out came the fly.
Neither of us ever saw him, but he must have been very big.

"I then hooked one of 4 or 5 lbs. and lost him fairly soon. At
the very top of the pool a grand yellow fish made a perfect rise

[1] In these extracts I have generally only given the first letter of the name of the
pool, since it will mean nothing to most people.

and I seemed to get him just right. We went downstream side
by side, when I gave it him hot and he came in half-way over
the bridge across the side stream and I hauled him into slack
water. Just as Hyelmar was getting out the gaff, out came the
fly. We put him at 9 lbs., but he felt light after No. 1.

"A very big fish missed it at the tail of J. and two decent ones
higher up. Above the rock I hooked one of 4 or 5 lbs. who flew
downstream. I passed the rod to Hyelmar at the rock and we
ran down to above B. where the fish smashed the cast. Another
fish had a look higher up the pool and yet a third missed it. In
the tail of K. I got apparently well into a fish of 4 or 5 lbs. and
he got off unaccountably. So homewards looking for a fish to
change my luck."

A morning of disaster relieved by a brace in the evening.

That is not an isolated instance of the heavy odds on the side
of a big sea trout hooked on a small rod and IX. gut in a river
full of hazards. The following is an account of a battle on what
is perhaps the most difficult and sporting water in the river. It
is all quick rippling stuff running past three long narrow islands,
all covered with trees, and the reader must picture himself
standing at the top of the lowest of these islands. As he stands
there with the trees of the lowest island shading him from the
sun to the south and the east, he sees, as he looks upstream, a
long straight stretch of fast water racing towards him between
the next narrow wooded island and the true left bank on which
he stands, both sides covered with trees to the water's edge. To
his left upstream of him is the main river, faster still with big
waves in the centre, with most of the water from the side stream
joining the water from the main stream on his left, after cas-
cading in a series of miniature rushes and falls over a long submerged bank formed of rock and shingle. There is a continuation
of this bank of similar formation curving across the top of the
side stream on his right to join the mainland on the true left
bank. The shingle bank steadies the rush and just above it there
are both to left and right of him narrow bands of quieter water.

It is a spot which will tingle the senses of a fisherman with an
eye to water, particularly if he has learnt the look of those places

in which sea trout delight to be and in which they may be induced to pay attention to a fly. He will see more than that: he will realise that a big fish hooked in such a spot is going to be fun. Unless the river is very low, the weight of water is too great to allow wading across the bank of rock and shingle to the island above him. His operations are therefore confined to the water on his right front for he can reach that side of the tail by wading across the top of the side stream on his right, but there lies a danger.

With no immediate background of trees as he wades he will probably be spotted by the fish, for in order to let his fly float on the water of the tail of the pool above him he must fish from the rock and shingle bank itself, in order to avoid getting his line caught in the rush of water over the bank; if it is so caught the result will be immediate and fatal drag. To fish from the shingle bank involves getting too close to the trout. What is he to do? The best plan, in my experience, is to wade across this side stream well below the submerged bank and out of sight of the fish, and tuck himself under the trees that line the far bank: there he will be invisible with the trees behind him and may be able to spot a big fish lying level with or just below him. That is what I did on the day recorded in the following account. Plate 15 shows me playing another sea trout in the water above described. The particular trout referred to in my diary was lying a little up-stream of the place where I was standing when photographed.

"We went up to the pool made by the beginning of the lowest side stream, where lay all alone a great dark-brown fish near the tail of the pool. I got out of sight under the trees and put a tup over him, without result; then a Little's Fancy, to which he paid no attention, then a sort of 'blue pill,' and after several casts he wobbled slowly round after it, but did no more. Then an alder and then a young salmon fly, and he departed hurriedly down-stream and out. While wondering what we should do, he came paddling up again to a higher position. Again I tried a tup right over his head down a line of ripples. No notice. Then I put it down a line of glassy water two feet inside him, and he wobbled over and looked at it. Again the same thing happened, and the third time, about two feet inside and six feet downstream of his lie, he made a tiny, lazy rise and missed it. He went back apparently quite happy and at the next shot a small fish seized the fly. I pulled him quietly away and slew him in secret out of sight, but the big fish would not subsequently pay any attention and we left him.

"Near the tail of the top island were three big fish but they would not take, and H. (another pool) gave its usual dull response, so I returned to my friend. He was in exactly the same position, and at about the fourth cast he repeated his wobble sideways and downstream, and very softly—so softly that I hardly realised that it had happened—he sucked in the tup. We both (Hyelmar and I) yelled with excitement. The fish heaved his way slowly up and out, and an awful strain was on the line. I walked back and drew him down and inshore, but he bored slowly up to the trees, and then began to tire and drop back downstream kicking. I yelled to Hyelmar to cross the side stream to the young waterfall into the main stream, and the inevitable head-over-heels business down the waterfall began. A great head came up and dropped into the foam, a tail waved in the air and down he went crunch-bump, and with a final splosh landed safely into the pool below. One gasp and a kick and he was near in, trying to get his wind, and before he got it he was on the bank—a great long hen fish with brown spots and a dark back. Thirteen pounds and a bit and looked long enough for 20. A great bit of sport, and the point about the glassy water is important."

That was twenty years ago, but I agree, and if more attention had been paid to the remark about glassy water in subsequent years, more fish might have been induced to see and take the fly. It is a tip worth remembering for a sea trout will move quite a distance sideways to take a floating fly, and, if he is lying under waves with smoother water to the side of them, it is worth letting the fly float down the smooth surface, instead of letting it dance over the waves. Sometimes, however, a sea trout, if he likes, can make amazing shots at flies in waves.

There are in most Norwegian rivers (and the one where I have chiefly fished is no exception) salmon traps belonging to landowners. These traps, which consist of wooden boxes with stout fences directing the current towards them, are set out from the bank, where a stream runs inshore of a shelf of rock and shingle and a plank bridge gives access to the trap from the shore. (A salmon trap is shown in Plate 16.) One day when I was accompanied by two ladies, but for some forgotten reason by no gaffer, a good sea trout was hooked on a dry fly in a pool upstream of one of these traps, and in the course of the ensuing battle the fish was bowled over a kyer (low pier of stone and wood), and came racing down the channel inshore of the trap and was swept through under the plank bridge which formed a sort of open door over the water. There was not a second to waste in hesitation and I sprang into the river in my waders, sat on the waves and was wafted through the bridge, to be caught up like Absalom in the branches of a birch tree which overhung the river.

My two companions were running down the bank parallel with me, both of them completely overcome by laughter at the sight of me sitting on the crest of the waves being danced down the river and caught up in the birch tree. I screamed for assistance and one of them raced back and gallantly helped me in passing the rod from hand to hand through the branches of the tree. What was the sea trout doing? Luckily for us, nothing at all, and for all I know he was laughing too as he sat tucked up round a rock downstream of us, with slack line washing about anywhere in the river.

Once clear of the tree, I ran on winding up the line, re-established touch with the fish, galloped him on with much holloaing and excitement downstream to where we reached a road, and there my lady helper, spurred on by me, gaffed with a brilliant shot the first fish she had ever slashed at. That was a proper hunt, and we got two more big fish that morning, besides losing others.

So much for dry fly and something must now be extracted from the diary to illustrate evening fishing with a wet fly, when darkness intervenes.

"After looking in vain for a decent fish and catching two or three small ones just out of the sea, I went back to Oinahol in the dark and fished it abolutely blank, went down to S. also blank, and thought of going home but just didn't, and returned

to O. High up in O. there was a quiet pull and, when asked by
Hyelmar whether I thought it was a big one, I replied that it
might be. When I reached the shore, to my disgust the line went
slack, so I reeled up and found that the fish had merely come in
towards me and was still there. When I reeled there was a hearty
heave and off he went with a rush out and then up as if his point
was the next pool upstream. With all the weight of Oinahol
stream on my side, I fairly let him have it, but he took a terrible
lot of stopping and we knew then that he was really big. He
finally sailed downstream and we left the pool majestically side
by side, I along the bridge, the fish in midstream, and walked
rather than ran down the rapids to above S. Here he pulled up,
but a good heave sent him off again into the stream and he
swung at a rare pace into S. I lay back and he came round all
right, to be gaffed in the tail of S. Fourteen and a quarter pounds
and a real beauty absolutely fresh-run and very fat."

Here is another account of an evening:

"The rest of the evening was deadly dull until M. arrived,
for the fish in S., of which we saw four big ones, were all asleep
and at N.T. a fish I moved in the tail of the pool went clean up
it, frightening everything. (That is a point to remember, it
often happens.) After fishing with a salmon rod with no result,
I reached S. at 9.30 p.m. and fished it down with the little rod
and a black doctor. One of the big chaps took it with an angry
thump and was off like a streak for the main stream. I fled down
and the line screamed out, but I got on terms just above the
Black pool (about three hundred yards below N.T.) and he came
into the water just outside the kyer and so to the tail of the pool,
where we saw him—a big fish. I walked him up ten yards, but he
was a nasty-tempered brute and bored out again to the current.
I hauled at him and worked him in again at the tail of the pool,
and it looked as if all would be well. He gave a sideways lunge,
however, and reached the current and was swept down again.
Again I hauled and he came into a bit of stillish water lower
down, but I failed to stop his next lunge and off he went into the
waves, and I knew we were for it.

"The reel shrieked as the river took him in its arms and we

tore along, the fish far below and the reel screaming all the time. I had to take to the water owing to bushes on the bank, and spluttered and stumbled along in the dark. I dropped my cap in the river and retrieved it brilliantly, and emerged above the bank pool, with the fish somewhere below it. Sweating and puffing, I crawled up the steep bank, and finally came to a stop with the line fast in a rock opposite a wire fence. After ten minutes' pulling from all directions and floating a branch down the line, we got the backing in and the line tight. I hand-lined from deep in the river, and finally the fly came clear with a bit of moss on it. A wonderful hunt, not less than six hundred yards and perhaps eight hundred. Ye gods, what a fish!" The only thing I could remember about it until I looked up the diary, was dropping my cap in the river and retrieving it again. That was pretty clever in the dark, but I doubt if the cap was worth it.

One more of these extracts, and it is included because I think it shows the sensations that are given to a fisherman when a big fish runs right up a strong current above him and it feels as if nothing would ever stop him.

"As I returned to Oinahol about 1 p.m. I saw what looked like a big fish rise in the quick black water above the run into the pool. I waded up and at once caught a small one. Then came a great clumsy walloping rise. I restrained myself and timed him just right, and with a scream he tore out line straight upstream without a check against a great rush of water. I stood fast and wondered as half the backing left the reel, and still he went on. Then came the usual kicking and angry wobbling and he began to come back. I tried to hold him in the pool and away from the rocks that lie in the fall to Oinahol. He turned again and once more went upstream but slower, and then to my horror something on the backing made it catch in the point of the rod. I took the rod by the centre, reached up and just eased it. When all was clear once more, half the backing lay in Oinahol and the rest, including the fish, heaven knew where. I reeled it all up and to my delight found him still there, about in the place where I had hooked him, and off he went again. Gradually he dropped back downstream and we, the fish and I, began tumbling and

rolling together over the rocks down the fall into Oinahol.
There he lolled about gasping and we got him—9 lbs. A great
fight, and I sent for lunch, fishing a pool lazily with a Little's
Fancy until it came."

The diary records on this particular day that about two hours
earlier I had "sent for beer and jolly good it was." As a matter
of fact this fishing is such terribly hard work that on most days
I am in my shirt sleeves, and always have a glass of beer and a
bit of cake about 12 noon, followed by an enormous lunch, when I
get home at about 2.30 p.m.

The extracts show that quite a number of the fish are seen
before a fly is put over them, but it took me a season or two to
learn the art of spotting them, and some people never acquire it.
There are exceptions. One young lady, Miss Nancy Hugh Smith,
saw them at once the first time she came to the river, but that is
very rare. They look like grey ghosts in most lights and appear
to be transparent, but sometimes in bright sun there seems to be
a tinge of pink on them. The first Norwegian who pointed them
out to me, always did so (and still does) with the remark, "Here
stand a fiske," but it is no use looking for an upright figure
standing on its tail: they would be much easier to see if they did.
In fact they lie glued to the bottom of the river, and if they rise
to a fly they do so like a grayling from the bed of the river and
do not lie cocked up near the surface like a brown trout feeding
on flies. The sort of place to look is just upstream (not downstream) of a rock, which breaks the current and so creates a quiet
cushion of water just above it. Sea trout love such places, and
unlike salmon and brown trout, they dislike back-waters, and
always seem to want to face the way they mean to go.

I have often seen fish travelling up the river. They move,
contrary to most people's ideas, quite slowly—so slowly that it
is difficult to walk slow enough to keep alongside of them, and
they constantly stop apparently for breath and then move on
again a few yards. It does not seem the faintest use fishing for
these travellers; they take neither fright nor notice, they are
concentrating on getting up the river to the lake, and flies and
other objects mean nothing to them. It is the lake that makes

this river so absolutely gin-clear for it filters the snow water that comes down from the roof of Norway. The water is so cold that if you fall in, as you sometimes do over the top of your long waders, there is only one thing to do and that is to run home. Nobody but the very young can walk about in that water without waders, but it is lovely stuff to dip your face into on a boiling hot day. My wife and sister, on one such day, found a clear pool in a wood by the river, slipped off their clothes and jumped straight in. It was so cold that they could hardly get out: they never tried that again.

Perhaps, with many years of experience, I may be permitted to give a little advice to those who wish to fish for sea trout in Norway. Go when you are young, when your eyes are good and your legs are strong, and get straight out of your head that this is coarse or easy fishing. The pace of Norwegian rivers is apt to make people think that they can catch fish anyhow, that any old fly lying any old how is good enough. A sea trout, whose eyes are better than theirs, will put them right on that matter. To do any good they have got to be fishing at their very best; the fly has got to land just right, it has got to cock quite true and to float down without the smallest semblance of a drag, there must be no gut loops lying in the air and, more important still, the fisherman has got to get within shot of his fish without being seen, and that is no easy matter. It is no more easy to keep out of sight, at least in daylight, with a wet fly.

The moment when I always get a rise to a wet fly is when I wade forward a step and forget to pull in the slack. They always take it then and of course are not hooked, but it shows how effectual wet-fly fishing without drag would be. Now and then I have tried to effect this by fishing wet upstream and have had a little success, but it is the greatest art of all forms of fishing, and my eyes are no longer good enough for it. An expert at it (I only know one—a Frenchman) would, I believe, be deadly with sea trout in Norway. It will be interesting to see whether in the future keen young people will develop this form of fishing and become sufficiently expert to reap their reward. Those who do will, I think, always be very few, but it is worth a try. I last met the Frenchman mentioned above in the summer of 1947 at his home on the Ain in the French Jura. Maurice Simonet, in addition to being a maker of sabots, is garde-forestier, garde-chasse, and above all garde-pêche at Ney near Champagnole.

One day as we reached the Ain another fisherman was seen wading below us and Simonet being suspicious warned us to keep out of sight and only to start fishing when we had got out of sight round a bend of the river, while he stalked the fisherman. He rejoined us an hour later and to my question, "Eh bien, c'a marchait?" he replied, "Mais *oui*, c'a marchait bien. C'etait le *Président* de la Société de Pêche a Champagnole, et il n'avait pas le droit de pêcher la bas. C'est loué. On peut pardonner le simple soldat, mais *pas* le *Général*. Je vai certainement faire un procés." We had left Champagnole before the case came on and I have not heard the result. When I told him that our local chauffeur claimed to be a fisherman his comment was, "Lui, pêcheur! Il pêche dans l'assiette."

Most fishermen associate Norway with salmon rather than with sea trout, and in looking through my diaries I have come across the account of the best day's salmon fishing I ever had or expect to have. Here it is (the river was the Sundal):

"July 22, 1935. Mist on the hills at first (that's enough to make any Scotsman squirm) with sun at intervals after 11.30 a.m., and a stiffish upstream breeze. River down a bit. A fish just touched it in the tail of F. He did the same thing again, just scraping the fly apparently along his side. We changed the fly, but he would not come, so I tried the first one again—a sort of blue doctor—and he took it wide as soon as it touched the water. We landed out of the boat and I took him down and out of the tail into the pool below where we got him—12 lbs. It seemed a pity not to fish this lower pool while there, and we did so. Peter (the gaffer) saw a fish swim twice after the fly. The third cast he took it wide, like the first fish; he weighed 9 lbs.

"Went up again to F., and in a jolly merry stream near the top of the pool I got one of 16 lbs., and twenty yards lower another of 22 lbs. who was a very merry fish. The 16-lb. fish had sea lice on him. Then in the tail on the right bank I got another of 13 lbs. who was rather a fool. He took the fly at the end of the cast when lifted several times through the water before picking it up. They seemed to shut up after that and it had become very sunny and hot. Peter was a splendid companion, and the incident which we both enjoyed most was when, just after he had got the net under a fish, the fly flew out as I raised the salmon's head out of the water. The fly flew into the air and stuck in the top of the tallest tree, whence Peter, after a long climb, retrieved it by cutting off the bough in which the fly was stuck. A great morning!" 'The fly flew out' illustrates the state of my mind. I must have been pulling that salmon's head pretty hard to hitch the fly straight into the top of a fir tree. I must have been thinking, let's catch this chap quick and get into another.

"Went out again at 7.30 p.m. and fished upper G. with rather a weak evening sun on it. Got one of 22 lbs. near the tail who went down and was walked up again. In lower G. had a fine boiling rise in quick water and fortunately did not move the line, for five yards further down in the same cast there was a thump and there he was. He pulled well but he walked better, and we killed him where we wanted to—17 lbs. Nothing more till the last cast of the evening, when, as I was lifting the fly and letting it down again in stillish water, a fish seized it and made a very fine run downstream. He then turned up and got round a snag and, although we tried everything, we could not get it free and eventually broke the cast. He felt heavy. That made seven fish in the day."

A cryptic account, probably because I was too excited to spend much time in writing up my diary. We found out what the 'snag' was the next day. It was a complete large birch tree that had fallen off a cliff into the river—a mouthful of a snag. The extraordinary thing about that day was that, except for the fish who got round 'the snag' and broke the cast, I not merely hooked but caught every fish that I was conscious of moving. That is luckily very rare in any form of fishing, and those salmon must have been in a proper state of mind.

The above account of a successful day's salmon fishing may

give the impression that I am extraordinarily skilled at it, always have been and know exactly where my fly is and what it is doing. That is not true. I started salmon fishing late in life, and one day in Norway, when I was still in the early stages of using a big rod, a friend lent me a beautiful spliced greenheart about 18 feet long. It was rather dark; I was standing on the steep, rocky bank above a pool and trying to throw a long line to reach well out into the stream. I could not for the life of me see where the fly was going, there was a nasty wind the wrong way, and, to make things worse, some wretched bug would keep giving a savage bite at my left ankle. I went on fishing but kept making grabs with one hand at the bug. Every time I cast it seemed to bite, and the harder I cast the worse it bit. At last I made a successful grab and got it fair and square in the finger— my own large salmon fly, which had been sitting all the time on my ankle waiting for me.

So much for fishing in Scandinavia—too much perhaps, and fishing is not the only form of sport in that delightful part of the world. I once went up after ryper to the Hardanger Vidde, a high rolling plateau in the nose of Norway. Most people imagine that we alone of all countries can boast of grouse, but a dal (valley) ryper of Scandinavia is a grouse, even though he goes in for the fashion of weaving white feathers on his wings and breast. If you turn him out in Scotland, he drops this fashion and turns into an ordinary Scottish grouse. In fact he is a grouse.

Most unluckily, the British Minister in Norway, who was going to take me and my sister up to the moors, was at the last moment prevented from doing so by a royal visit, so that to our great disappointment we travelled alone. It was a varied journey, partly by train, partly by boat up two long lakes, and partly by motor car. The incident I remember best on the journey was the landing of some bulls off the boat on to a pier. They were beautiful little beasts, but as the pier was far above the deck of the boat, we could not imagine how any one was going to get a bull ashore. There was a steep series of steps from the water to the level of the pier, and each bull, led by a man, walked across the gangway from the deck to these steps and marched confidently up them, as though they had done it every morning of their lives. It was really rather disappointing, we expected a lot of fun.

We eventually arrived at a 'saeter' (summer farm) on the Mysvand, a lake the shape of a narrow Y, and found there the British Consul, who the next day introduced us to ryper, but then had to return to Oslo, leaving behind two men, a gardener and a policeman, whose normal police duty was outside the Storting, the Norwegian House of Commons. Neither of them pretended to any knowledge of ryper, but they looked on the whole business as a holiday and I never met a keener pair of beaters.

It was already September and the birds were as wild as hawks, but there were swarms of them for it was a very good season. We were not alone in our quest of them: golden eagles had also discovered that this particular bit of country was full of ryper. The ground looked very like a Scottish moor, but it was covered by other plants besides heather; bilberry, blaeberry, cranberry and other berry-bearing plants were growing in profusion, so that there was any amount of feed for the birds. The trouble was to get near them, but we soon discovered that the best plan, in which the eagles often assisted us, was to move the birds into some long narrow birch woods, which lined low ridges. When we had succeeded in doing this, I used to go on to the end of a birch wood, place my sister as a stop on one side and then let the two men walk through the trees towards me. It was surprising how large a proportion of the birds took the line of trees as their flight and came over me at the end of the wood. There were a few woodcock and in the open an occasional snipe, including a few double or great snipe, a bird I had never seen before.

One of the troubles was carrying enough cartridges, and another was getting the ryper home, but our two beaters' main ambition in life was to carry more ryper than any one had ever carried before. We gave them every opportunity and they lived up to it. We found elk tracks on several occasions, but never saw any of the animals; nor did we see any reindeer. There were a few teal and I tried flighting without much success. One sentence in my diary is perhaps worth recording. "Bag 7 ryper, 5 teal, 1 hare, 2 snipe. Spied the snipe with my telescope, stalked and shot them both sitting with one shot." I never did that before or since.

In another part of Norway said to be frequented by reindeer, my wife and I stopped the car in which we were travelling and sat down to spy. Presently my glass found a herd of the animals and in the herd were some very fine bucks. We were running our glasses, in great excitement, up and down the herd discussing which was the biggest buck, when we came to the tail of the herd, and there in the field of the glass was a man and a dog walking quietly along behind them. That was a nasty shock: we thought we had found the real wild animal.

In all my visits to Norway I have only once coincided with a lemming year. Everything was after these defenceless little animals which look like miniature guinea-pigs, at any rate in colour. Birds of prey, foxes, village dogs and cats, all spend their time catching them, and have no difficulty whatever in doing so. Normally lemmings live high up on the barren tops, and just once in a while, at intervals of fifteen or twenty years, they have an abnormal breeding season, when the surplus population moves by regular routes from the tops to the low ground and even into the sea. The oddest thing about their attempt to find a new home is that it invariably ends in complete failure. Despite the toll taken during the journey by predatory animals, by drowning and by every sort of disaster, individual lemmings do settle down in the low country, and find or make a hole under a rock or somewhere. We used to see them in August in such places apparently contented at last and in good health. I was assured, however, that by next spring not a single one of these animals would be alive.

I asked Dr. Nansen, who was among many other things an expert zoologist, about the whole strange phenomenon, and he assured me that none of these lemmings that had found a home and settled in the low ground ever survived the following spring.

They all die of some mysterious disease, to which they appear to be immune on the high tops, but which is invariably fatal to them when they reach low altitudes.

A lemming that had settled in a particular place would be seen frequently outside his hole and would take precautions not to get caught, and go down his hole if he saw a human being, a dog or a hawk too near him. Not so the lemmings which were still on the move: they took no precautions whatever. If one of these travellers were met on a path or on the bank of the river, the ridiculous little animal would sit up and squeak just like a lead pencil on a slate and order the human being, the dog or anything else to get out of its light. Naturally a dog ate it at once: one evening, when I was fishing a turbulent stretch of the river with a very fast current, a lemming came down to the river's edge just by me and squeaked at me. I paid no attention and it carelessly plunged into the river by my feet at the very worst place. It was carried down a long way by the current but it floated like a cork, swam strongly and got safely across, for I saw it land.

One of our party motoring along a mountain road saw a lemming crossing just in front of the car and pulled up to let it pass. The lemming stopped in the middle of the road, sat up, looked at the enormous car and gave vent to a series of furious squeaks. My informant swears that it literally burst with rage on the road in front of them.

My sister-in-law, who had been fishing, returned late one night in a carriage, and we heard laughter and excited noises outside the door and went out to see what was happening. She had caught two lemmings and brought them home in the box seat of the carriage, and she and the driver were trying to extract them. The lemmings were squeaking defiance and biting their hands.

There is another parallel case of periodical migration and attempt at colonisation in a different country, which also always fails. It is the case of Pallas' Sandgrouse. More rarely than lemmings these birds, which live in the Middle East and are not normally migratory at all, make a great journey to the West,

13. A Norwegian Fjord.

14. Elizabeth hurrying to the next pool, Norway.

Chapter Nine

15 (top). A. B. playing fish between lower and middle island, Norway
16. Salmon trap, Norway.   *Chapter Nine.* [*Photos : Peter Clarke*

and some of them even reach these islands apparently in good health. But nothing ever comes of it, they never establish new colonies, they all die: it is as big a failure as the migration of the lemmings.

I have never hunted elk in Norway, but I once went on a visit to a friend in Sweden, who is now one of the leading lights in the Swedish Diplomatic Service. To go to a foreign country, to be shown round its capital (and Stockholm is a wonderful capital) by someone who knows all about it and is proud of it, and then to be a guest in different country houses, is a wonderful way to see a country. Sweden is a comfortable country and its people look happy. Well they may; the houses are not only good but beautiful and enjoying the benefits of modern inventions without, so far as I could see, any diminution of beauty in the buildings. The farms struck me most: I never saw such farm buildings, furnished with all the latest devices. Having never been to Canada, I am not in a position to give a comparison, but others who know both Canada and Sweden say that the two countries are much alike. I can well believe it. The impression I got was of farms running out into openings in the woods, and of woods running out into the farms. It was half-timber, half-cultivated land and there seemed to be a sort of friendly rivalry between them, and both farms and woods were equally well kept.

It was extraordinarily interesting to enter, as I did, into the life of a country home in Sweden. It struck me as very unforeign. The butler wore white gloves, but he looked and behaved exactly like an English butler. The keeper lived in a house in a clearing in a wood, just like an English keeper and he looked the same. We had lunch in his house, and the interior was just like the interior of an English keeper's house. There was one difference at lunch, or rather at the end of it. Everybody stood up, bowed to the host and said, "Thank you for my good lunch." I thought that a pleasant touch and typical of the manners of Sweden, where everybody takes off their hat and says good morning to everybody else.

Dinner was a wonderful meal. We sat first at a small table near the fire, and on it were little glasses and little plates. I have

T.N.   M never seen or tasted such a delicious collection of hors d'œuvres and of little drinks to go with them. Some of the hors d'œuvres were hot and some cold, and they varied every night. By the time I had finished with them there was not much room for anything else, and the dinner proper, for which one moved to the large table, was fortunately short. I thought it hardly necessary. The Swedes are not foolish enough to pretend that they do not like their food. The main thing that struck me about Sweden was the looks of the people. Scandinavians generally are a fine-looking lot, but the Swedes are at the top of the tree in appearances. As you land in England or in Germany, after a trip to Scandinavia, there is an absolute crash in looks, and that crash is most violent if you come from Sweden. They are outstanding in appearance among all the people of Europe.

I had been invited to Sweden partly for elk-shooting, and therefore arrived in the short open season. This open season is fixed in each county each year according to the estimated stock of the animals. If the authorities of a county think that their stock of elk is too low, they do not have any open season at all, and none is allowed to be killed. If, on the other hand, it is considered that the stock of elk warrants it, the open season may last a week or even a fortnight. During it every one is after elk. I was told that there are more of these animals in the more thickly-populated country in Southern Sweden than in the North, where supervision is more difficult and poaching almost impossible to eliminate. This system seems to work well, for I was told that the stock was on the increase rather than the decrease.

I had two very interesting days, during which we followed a party of a bull, cow and calf elk. The best of the sport fell to me for I did most of the tracking. We found this party of elk in a wood not far from a farm, and indeed there were people at work on timber and on the agricultural land wherever we went. At one moment we tracked the elk over the open fields in front of a farm, but no one had seen them. Late in the afternoon of the first day the keeper had a shot at the bull, and after the shot someone of our party saw the bull and the calf, and did not see the cow. This made us fear that the keeper had hit the cow by mistake.

Next morning we took up the tracks again, and shortly afterwards were fortunate enough to cross perfectly fresh tracks of the same party, after they had made a circuit during the night. The tracks of all three animals were there, so that we knew that the cow was all right. Some of the tracking was perfectly easy for on wet ground the elk sank in deep, but on dry pine needles it was a different matter, and the only thing to look for was a different shade of pine needle, where it had been turned over by the toe of an elk. That part of the tracking was intricate and interesting. It was noticeable that the animals travelled freely through bogs in the woods, but took great pains to avoid ever going down a steep slope: they always took the easiest gradient. No doubt this was because of their long legs and heavy bodies. They also trotted over and did not jump obstacles such as fences and palings, which they can do owing to the length of their legs. I saw the bull once, but then only for a second and did not shoot, but in the afternoon of the second day we marked them into a certain bit of covert, took up positions and the keeper went in to move them. My Swedish companion had an easy chance and killed the bull, which was a large one. I had enjoyed the tracking but was rather glad not to have to take a shot, indeed I should have been happier if we had not killed the bull at all. Not many wild animals would, I think, have stuck to such a comparatively small area when they knew, as they must have done, that they were being followed. Probably the explanation is that in that country they are always meeting people, and become more or less accustomed to being disturbed by human beings.

We heard tales of a savage cow elk which was said to have attacked several people in the summer, including a keeper, who had fired his rifle in the air and only avoided the charge of the cow by jumping on to a high rock. I was a little sceptical about these stories, but one day we saw a solitary cow elk in a clearing in a wood about two hundred yards away: she had obviously seen us but did not move although one of my companions

was whistling softly from quite close to her to attract our
attention to the animal. The cow looked at all of us in turn,
curled her lip and raised her head. My two companions, brother
and sister, suggested that this might be the savage cow and that
I should shoot her from where I was. I thought that there might
be a bull with her which we had not seen, and so waited where
I was, watching the cow through my telescope while they went
round to stalk her, and trying to draw her. (Sketch facing
page 125.)

They got within very short range before she spotted them,
when, instead of bolting, she threw up her head proudly and
took a step forward towards them, and then walked slowly and
sulkily away. She looked, I thought, nasty. They thought so
too and shot her, when she proved to be a very old barren cow.
After that we all believed the stories. I was told that in particular
near thickly-inhabited places a bull elk sometimes becomes
dangerous, but that a savage cow was very rare. The great sharp
hoof of an elk could deal a nasty blow, and the attack is made,
I understand, with the forefeet.

The most interesting thing in elk behaviour that I saw was
the way in which a cow elk directed her calf. We were having a
sort of drive and I was posted to command a little valley in a
wood. A greyhen flew out of a tree and a blackcock rose from
the ground when a cow and calf elk came trotting over the
skyline into this valley, followed by a young bull who was
calling softly. The calf wanted to come straight on over the
valley, but for some reason the cow held a different opinion.
She curled her great roman nose round the neck of the calf and
piloted it back, making it face in the opposite direction. The
head of an elk is a queer shape but it is well suited to the execution
of such a turning movement. Elk, wild boar and bison are some
of the most antediluvian looking of all the animals of to-day:
they seem to belong to a world long past.

There is an idea at any rate in Norfolk that enormous numbers
of wood-pigeons come over every winter to our islands from
Scandinavia. I do not deny that large flocks of these birds reach
us from overseas, and have indeed on several occasions seen them

arrive, but in Norway I have never seen a single wood-pigeon
and cannot remember seeing any in Sweden, although it does
look a possible pigeon country. I have no idea where the pigeons
which reach us from overseas come from, but suspect that it is
further south than Scandinavia.

In the part of Sweden that I visited there were a number of
lakes with reedy shores suitable for mallard and I saw a good
many, but do not remember any other duck. The fir forests were
full of crested and cole tits, and there were great black wood-
peckers and nutcrackers, which are a sort of sooty-coloured jay.
We saw a certain number of capercailzie and blackgame.

In the part of Norway where I have fished, the two birds always
in evidence are fieldfares (not redwings, which live further north)
and white wagtails. To the fisherman the white wagtails are
very important birds, for on fast water, where fly is difficult to
spot, these wagtails give away a hatch at once. If a hatch is
going on they are certain to spot it and will all be by the water
hawking about and catching the fly as it leaves the river. If there
is no hatch, they are away in the fields. My first tip to a dry-fly
fisherman in Norway is, watch the white wagtails.

My last tip in this chapter is to writers of books. I put the
manuscript of this and other chapters into an old bag with a
hole in it, and a mouse proceeded to gnaw the paper and make
a nest of it. It may be a suitable accident to occur to me, but it
caused me much annoyance for I dislike having to write something twice. That mouse and one of its children have been
caught, but it has taught me a lesson about receptacles that are
not mouse-proof.

Ten

NORFOLK

THE PEOPLE of Norfolk are prone to think of those who live elsewhere as foreigners and they even have that feeling about their nearest neighbours in Suffolk. This, coupled with a certain reserve, which some might call lack of enthusiasm, makes them a difficult people to know, much more difficult than say the inhabitants of Yorkshire. One of the most interesting things to me in Norfolk is the language, which I have always considered the pleasantest in England. Having visited Norfolk frequently since my earliest days (and those are the days when sounds and intonations and figures of speech are easiest to acquire), the language has never presented any difficulty to me, but newcomers to the county find it an impossible dialect to get their tongues round. It presents insuperable difficulties when an attempt is made to turn it into writing.

There are sounds in it which are absolutely un-English but which seem to me remotely connected with French. For instance, the long Norfolk U, if that is the way to write the sound, is like a Frenchman saying ' du ' with a slurred drawl. The word ' do ' or ' du ' means ' otherwise ' and a good many other things as well. "Goo yew along, du yew'll be late." Another Norfolk sound rather like the last and almost impossible, so far as I can see, to put into writing is contained in the first syllable of the word *beau*tiful.

Having told stories about other parts of England, it is difficult not to give a few from Norfolk. Norfolk people will hear the sounds they involve, but others, I fear, will not. The first I heard myself a week or two ago sitting on the Bench, and as soon as the lady, who was complaining about her husband twice as old as herself, began to talk I seized a bit of paper from under the chairman's hand and wrote her remarks down word for word.

"He aggrawate the loife out o' me. Him and me, man and woife and he hent (hasn't) spuk to me for tew yare. T'other mornen' at 6 o'clock he come douwn like a roarin' lion. He used hoigh weerds, your Weerships, an' a werra low language." She gave no illustrations of her last sentence, which went up at 'hoigh weerds' into a typical Norfolk squeak and then dropped sympathetically at the 'werra low language.' A man up before an uncle of mine for being drunk and disorderly, when asked if he had anything to say, replied, "Oi oont say as Oi warn't full of bare, but Oi hedn't *noo* disorder." Another uncle of mine, the Rev. Charlie Digby, rector of Warham near Wells, was visiting a widow, who described to him what had happened the night before. "Ooh, Mr. Digby, Oi had sech a wonderful dream last noight. Moi oold man, he com and set by moi bedsoide and he looked so lovely: he weere such bewtiful clothes and he say such bewtiful weerds. Now, Mr. Digby, what d'yew think, they tell me that's a soign o' rain." That is typical Norfolk: they gulp down enthusiasm as it rises.

Norfolk people believe in understatement. A gun at a shoot in coverts always heavily stocked with game said to the keeper early in the day, "I suppose you have got masses of pheasants as usual." "Well, Oi doon't know, sir. Yew might see tew or three hare an there." Another keeper, exasperated by a spaniel, which was running in in all directions, expressed himself, "Oo daire, Oo daire whewever dew belong to that haire mucky little dawg." They can be very expressive. When I was trying to learn the art of using a quant (the Norfolk form of a punt pole with a crutch at the end of it), the old boatman explained the theory of the business by the sentence, "Yew koind o hould the water, wi' your feet." Those who know how to quant will appreciate how well that description hits the mark. The last story shall be short: it is of a boy throwing stones at a toad and saying, "Oi'll larn yew to be a dutty tood."

Having described in *Fisherman Naturalist* the wild inhabitants that live about my home at Horsey, I propose to deal in this chapter simply with recent news of them and of other happenings in my neighbourhood. The summer of 1946, the first one of so-called peace, showed, as I thought it would, the intense popularity of the Broads as a holiday area. Naturally the firms which let out boats were short of labour and short of craft, and there were difficulties inherent in rationing, yet I do not recall any boating season in which people seemed to derive more pleasure from their holidays. I remember a particular Sunday afternoon when the sun shone from a cloudless sky and there was a strong breeze. About twenty sailing boats were racing about all over Horsey Mere. For some reason they all seemed to be in skilled hands, possibly because the wind was too high for beginners. For whatever reason, it was all skilled sailing with a polish to it, and I never saw a happier crowd. In many cases bathers lying on logs were towed behind, which must, owing to the pace the boats were travelling, have involved a breathless passage and none of them could stick it for long. Tucked away in a corner in his boat on the edge of reeds was the millman, one of whose duties it is to look after the boating fraternity. He was sitting there enjoying the fun as much as I was and as all the rest of the party were.

Some people seem to object to these holiday crowds on the water, but Horsey Mere looks to me at its best with boats racing across it and people laughing as they sail. There is more in it than mere sailing. A clerk from the Midlands, basking on the deck of a motor cruiser moored in a remote corner with a background of reed and sedge and not a house in sight, said to me, "What I like about this place is that I never look at a watch. I haven't looked at mine for a week."

During the war there were, of course, no boats or practically none, and the authorities who are supposed to keep the channels open were short of labour. The result of these two things and especially, I think, the absence of boats, has resulted in great outgrowth of vegetation restricting the open water. In 1945, in expectation of a large crowd of holidaymakers in 1946, I put on two expert reed-cutters to cut back the outgrowth in Horsey Mere to at least its position before the war. It took them about ten weeks to do the job, but they did it well. In my opinion the war has proved that the boats themselves, and in particular the motor boats, cut through outgrowth of vegetation, hold it back and keep the channels open. More power to their keels for they do a lot of good.

I am not strictly one of the boating fraternity, but my children are and they and many others have first learnt to sail on the Broads: there is no better or safer place to learn. There is nothing hard to bump against except another boat, and anyone can run ashore anywhere with impunity, even though it may involve asking for assistance to get free of the hover (floating table of vegetation) which lines the shore in most places.

A Broads Conference has been in session, and so far as I can judge the essentials for a happy future for the Broads as a holiday resort are these: A single authority whose duty it will be to preserve the Broads, and if possible improve them for the visitors, most of whom want to enjoy themselves from a boat. It should be the job of such an authority to keep Broads and the channels connecting them open, to maintain the present character of the district, its vegetation, its wild animals, and its general appearance, to prevent the hideous and insanitary growth of bungalows sprawling along the banks, to deal with sewerage, policing, regulation of size and pace of boats, and to do so without ostentation or anything that detracts from a holiday spirit.

So far the Broads holiday traffic has developed on its own, without planning and almost without regulations. It has outgrown that stage, the business wants tackling in a businesslike way, but in a way that will not detract from the fun and freedom of a holiday. It seems to me that the number of visitors to the Broads is going to increase and that more water is needed to avoid overcrowding. There is more water there but much is not available, for some Broads, including ones that would be suitable for sailing, have become choked with reed and some are kept closed by the owners. It is perfectly natural that the owner of a Broad should like to keep it for himself and his friends: I have those feelings myself sometimes. For instance, I resent it when a boat come stealing on to Horsey Mere in the winter and upsets the duck. In the summer I have got used to seeing sails and hearing human voices. I should miss them if they were not there, and the nature of the Broads, the ' ronds ' of tall reed and bulrush with their edge of ' hover ' act as a deterrent to wandering, and keep visitors more or less to firm ground and open water. Of course if they wandered all over the place, the wilder creatures would dislike it, but so far holidaymakers have not prevented the shyest birds and beasts from living and breeding in the Broads.

I wonder if some compromise is not possible that would give the visitors more room and more water and yet would preserve the Broads as a stronghold for all those animals, birds and plants that need that type of country. I would suggest that owners who have closed Broads suitable for sailing might well be asked to open them from, say, Easter or Whitsuntide until the end of September for the benefit of the visitors, but that for the rest of the year they might be closed. It may be argued that duck and other water birds need some quiet spots in the summer and this is true, but in my opinion there would remain enough undisturbed water unsuitable for sailing but good enough for duck, and that on the whole no harm would be done to the natural history and sporting facilities of the Broads. I am a naturalist and a naturalist keen on sport, and if I thought the above suggestion would do serious harm to either aspect I should probably not have the pluck to make it. At the same time, the holidaymakers seem to me to come first and private owners second.

However that may be, 1946 from the naturalist's point of view was a good season, and I find it difficult to decide what to put in and what to leave out. We had one nasty disaster which gave me and my men concerned in preserving wild creatures a bad headache. A certain old hen marsh harrier with a red tail and a lot of white about her, who had reared two families of six chicks on my land in previous years, turned up with a particularly good-looking husband and settled down early in April just where I wanted and expected her. She laid her six eggs as usual, and six is a big clutch for her kind, and one fine day a couple of naturalists were taken by my keeper to have a look at her nest. That night or the next day those eggs were stolen by a man in gumboots, as we found by the tracks. It was the first time I ever lost a harrier's nest on my land, and my men and I saw red. No doubt the little party of three had been seen going across the marsh to the nest, and seen by somebody out for a set of rare eggs, either for himself or to sell to an egg-clutcher.

There is no wilder bird than a marsh harrier, and I expected that the unfortunate pair would at once leave the neighbourhood. This did not occur and, I suppose, the old hen has become wedded to the place: at any rate within fifteen or sixteen days from the taking of the eggs she had nested again and began to lay afresh at no great distance from her first site. This time she laid five eggs and, as is her excellent custom, she hatched every one of them. Unfortunately when the oldest chick was about three weeks old and the youngest about a fortnight, two men not employed by me were cutting weed in a dyke three hundred yards from the nest. I suppose that the parents were shy of being seen taking food into the nest to feed the chicks. Anyhow lunch was late, the nursery party became impatient, the big three killed and ate the small two. That, I regret to say, is not an uncommon practice with young marsh harriers—they are apt to be a little abrupt and let their feelings get the better of them. It was the last disaster—the big three eventually flew in grand feather.

They were not the only ones. In another area a mile away were two hens and one cock. One of the hens was a dirty blonde and the other a dingy black. The cock preferred the blonde (so on the whole did I), and although the black sat in ridiculous attitudes on dead boughs with her wings and tail spread in dejection and supplication, and advanced to meet the cock in the air with her feet out ready to take his gift of prey, he took not the faintest notice of her and always passed the food to the blonde. The black bird had to fend for herself and we thought that she would never acquire a mate but we were wrong, utterly wrong. Very late in the season a magnificent cock, the best-looking bird of the lot, arrived and took pity on her, probably because there was nothing better to be had. Both these pairs nested successfully and reared, the blonde four and the black two chicks. The black and her handsome mate preferred, I discovered, old partridges. I visited their chicks on two occasions within a week, the first time only just after prey had been deposited at the nest: it was an old English partridge, intact except for its head, which had been removed. At the second visit the nest contained the remains of another old partridge and a redshank. Most of us prefer *young* partridges, but not that pair of harriers.

I was disappointed by a pair of Montagus; they had settled to nest on one of my marshes in an admirable position, which I could survey with comfort from a hide built up in a birch tree. Then the water rose, they changed their minds at the last minute and went across the boundary to Hickling. I found their nest with my telescope from the look-out, but I lost the fun of having them under constant supervision. A composite photograph showing a hen Montagu alighting on a dead tree we had rammed down into a marsh for her benefit, together with a film extract of another hen flying home with her kill is shown in Plates 19, 20.

We had a good store of bitterns but they were unevenly distributed. For instance, near my southern boundary I counted six boomers at no great distance from each other, whereas there were only two on the rest of the ground. We found the nests of these two and of two more out of the six, but even my poaching instincts were not quite strong enough to allow me to search for the other four. All those that we found reared respectable families, and judging by what I heard of other localities in Norfolk and Suffolk bitterns had a satisfactory season. I was told that a keeper in another area of the Broads saw during morning flight in October five bitterns one after the other fly over his head.

This uneven distribution of bitterns was copied by the water-rails, which were thick on the ground occupied by the six booming bitterns but rather thin elsewhere. I suppose all this was due to food supplies. The water-rails seemed in good breeding form, for five second nests built in June contained 10, 10, 9, 9, 9 eggs or 47 in all. From what I know of these birds, it is doubtful if all those eggs were allowed to hatch, for a brood of young water-rails is more than a handful from birth and nobody has reason to know that better than their parents. I know of a case in which a water-rail, possessing a nestful of nine eggs, hatched seven and decided that that was enough. The bird made quite certain that there were not going to be any more by poking the two remaining eggs into the water and ramming her bill through them. Both these eggs contained perfectly good chicks. Having witnessed the devilment contained in these little balls of black velvet, I do not blame the parent. In the autumn of 1946 we had water-rails all over the place, and with them spotted crakes.

Spotted crakes are, I think, the biggest mystery in the bird line at Horsey. We see or rather hear a few of them each spring going through, but heaven knows where they go to, where they come from, and where they breed. In the autumn, in October and November, we are spluttered with them, and again are ignorant where they come from. I do not know but imagine that there are just as many in other parts of the Broads, but they are impossible little brutes to see, and unless the notes are recognised nobody would guess that they were there. At Horsey they skulk about along the edge of the Mere and in other places where there is thick marsh vegetation, and catch, I believe, mainly shrimps. Sometimes they are very silent, but if one of them says anything, they all start talking at once. They make a number of different noises but the commonest sound is a sort of 'click' or 'clock' not unlike the call note of a greater spotted woodpecker. Almost the only way to see them is to get a dog to hunt them up and make them fly, which they will do rather faster and more readily than a water-rail, but you want a dog that has no objection to water or the thickest of covert. When I can get square with a pair of these mysterious little creatures I shall feel better about them than I do at present. It is quite untrue to say that a spotted crake is a rare bird in this part of the world. There are dozens of him but I have yet to meet anyone who can tell me anything about him.

Something happened to shoot up the mouse population. I know that among other reasons from the jump in kestrels, not only at Horsey but all over Norfolk. It is a sudden rise in the kestrel population, which has been low for years.

In the winter of 1946-47 there were the largest number of short-eared owls on the Horsey marshes that I ever saw at that time of year. This incursion of owls was no doubt due to an increase of short-tailed field-mice, which had for a long time been scarce, and we had had none of these owls breeding at Horsey in the summer of 1946. It was difficult to estimate the numbers but I saw five on the wing at once, and whenever I went out on the off-chance of duck at evening flight I was invariably taken for a post by one or more of these owls, as I sat motionless by the side of a dyke. In fact, I had to make a movement of a hand to prevent them sitting on my head, which might well have produced a nasty scratch from a claw. On one occasion a bittern flew past within five yards of me, so that even in the dusk I could see its eye, and it was closely followed by two of these owls which, on noticing me, stopped chasing the bittern (who seemed to be taking no notice of them) and turned in the air to examine me and then to bark at me and at my terrier, Jane, who was sitting by my side.

A strange incident occurred on this evening with the duck. I shot four mallard coming to a shallow splash, and Jane, who had marked them with great accuracy, found three of them in no time when released from her string. The fourth was a runner, and she and her son, Ginger, took up the line some ten minutes after the bird had been shot. After following the line, not as usual down a dyke but *across* two dykes and out on to a large open marsh, the terriers disappeared in the dark, and my son, John, and I waited for their return. Ginger came back first, followed some minutes later by Jane, who looked as if she had something to tell. We told her to carry on and kept the light of a torch on her. She led us straight across the middle of the large marsh, keeping a straight course: then she stopped and bit Ginger, a sign that we were getting hot. She then continued her march, walking faster and faster, and finally ran in. There was the mallard dead in a cloud of feathers, four hundred yards from where it had been shot. It had gone straight across country all the way, ignoring the dykes. The incident of Jane biting Ginger is common. Nothing is allowed to touch what

Jane finds, it is hers and she will only allow me or John or some other special person to take it from her.

The summer of 1946 was remarkable for the number of golden orioles seen in Norfolk. In the last week of May four separate orioles, one pair and two single cocks, were certainly seen and reports of others were received, which may or may not have been correct. One of these four birds was heard by me while I was shaving in a bathroom with the window shut and facing north. The note, coming from the other side of the house, just caught my ear and when I reached an open window facing south he let out a single magnificent whistle from the bottom of the garden. That was the last of him, so far as I was concerned, for a gardener was at work in full view and close to him, and he passed straight through and away to the north.

He was not the last of these birds. In the third week of June, which is very late for travelling orioles in Norfolk, my son, who had never heard an oriole, was on the lawn and I was writing in the house. He shouted at me, "Is that an oriole?" and hearing that the sound had come from the other side of the house, I went out of the back door. From the trees not twenty yards away came the soft whistle of a cock and the cat-calls of a hen oriole. For the next hour my family and I watched below the trees they were in, listening to their conversation : that of a happily wedded pair. If proof were needed that an oriole is a difficult bird to see, we proved it. They were never silent, so that we always knew exactly where they were, and we were never fifty yards from them, generally much less. We all got glimpses but never once did we get a proper clear view of either of the birds. The lateness of the date and the behaviour of the birds convinced me that this pair had settled and were not mere travellers; moreover, a week later the whistle of a cock oriole awoke my son at 5 a.m., but on that occasion he did not hear the hen. My reading of the incident is that this pair nested or attempted to nest somewhere in Norfolk and that Horsey was just within the extreme limit of their journeys from their home. Perhaps on the occasion when they first visited my garden the hen was laying, which gave the pair a chance for a long day off duty, and on the second, when the cock came alone, she was sitting and he found time to do a little travelling. I poached in all directions at unearthly hours and never got caught, but failed to solve the mystery. Some of the birds seen were as far inland as Norwich, which proves that they do not merely hug the coast. Not many people in Norfolk know the note of an oriole, and I suspect that the vast majority pass through unnoticed.

The determined expression on the face of the cock (photographed at Geneva, Plate 17) is true to life. He is a bird that will not stand any rot, least of all from creatures larger than himself. This particular pair used to get annoyed by a family party of carrion crows that would trespass on their preserves. I saw the cock oriole charge them as they flew past, catch a crow fair and square in the ribs and turn him clean over in the air—a fine feat for a bird no heavier than a missel-thrush.

In the winter of 1945-46 great numbers of pochard spent the day on Horsey Mere and there was also a large flock of coots, but very few tufted duck and not many golden-eye. At Hickling, on the other hand, there were plenty of tufted duck. This leads me to think that the food of pochard and tufted is not the same. By luck one pochard coming off the Mere was shot at evening flight, and this gave a chance to discover what he had been eating during the day on the Mere. His crop was absolutely full of the seeds of a weed called *chara hispida*—not the weed itself but the seeds: he had also eaten quantities of small snails. In the autumn of 1946 flocks of pochard up to the first week of November looked at the Mere but without alighting. They dipped over the water to examine it, but apparently considered that it did not yet contain what they needed. I imagine that the chara seed was not yet ripe, and in fact they did not populate the Broad until the end of November. In some years large quantities of wigeon alight on the Mere in the daytime, but they did not come in the winter of 1946-47 although there were a number in Norfolk.

My keeper, Mr. G. Crees, saw a green plover pick up one of its chicks between its legs and carry it back about one hundred yards into a marsh from the position to which it had strayed

17 (top). Cock Oriole.
18. Hen Oriole. *Chapter Ten*

19. Hen Montagu's Harrier alighting, Norfolk.

20. Hen Montagu returning to nest with prey, Norfolk.
Chapter Ten

close to the main road. Presumably it considered the chick to
be in danger from the traffic on the road. This is the first time
that I have heard of a green plover carrying its young. One day
in my motor car I had to pull up to allow passage to a family
party of partridges with the chicks only just out of the nest.
The little balls of fluff all squatted on the edge of the road in
line by the side of the car, and the cock mounted to the top of
a lump on the verge of the road and called to them. Cheered
on by the hen, they jumped off the road on to the verge and
proceeded on their way—a thoroughly well-drilled party.

While staying a night at Holkham, Lord Leicester introduced
me to two tame partridges on the lawn by the house. He had
taken the eggs from a deserted nest and hatched them under a
bantam. The rest of the covey had, much to his annoyance,
been decoyed away by a pair of partridges which had presumably
lost their own family, but these two young birds had stuck to
him. They were absolutely tame so far as we were concerned,
but they kept a watchful eye on the sky and bolted under a fir
bough when a jackdaw flew over. While we were at breakfast
they walked into the dining-room, and after going behind a
screen, started to play. The screen did not hide them from me
and I sat fascinated by their games. One of them would suddenly
hitch its shoulders, which made the feathers ruffle and produce
a little sound like a minute umbrella opening: it also executed
a little jump. The other bird responded with similar movements
and made a little jump to one side. The game, which always
went on during breakfast and always behind the screen, seemed
to consist in making your neighbour jump, but the play was
rather dignified and restrained: they never went to excess or
made any attempt to fight. No food or other inducement to
enter the dining-room was provided: the partridges came there
only at breakfast time entirely of their own accord, apparently
for the purpose of playing behind the screen. Lord Leicester tells
me that after I saw his partridges his motor mower back-fired
and this was too much for them! They left and were absent for
ten days, but then returned looking rather crestfallen and
hungry.

T.N.   N

During the summer otters deserted Horsey, possibly because the traffic of boats upset their nerves, but I am always afraid that somebody may be trapping them for their pelts. In any case, the otter paths, which are extraordinarily regular being in exactly the same position every year, lost their well-worn appearance since the traffic along them had diminished. When quiet was restored to this bit of country the otters began to return, and at morning flight on the Mere I saw the wash of an otter and heard him in the reeds, but did not see him.

Many naturalists visited Horsey in the summer, and it was interesting to see the different ways in which they employed their time. A large number seemed simply bent on seeing and recording the largest possible number of different sorts of birds in the day and did not appear interested in what particular birds did. They just wanted to count. Examination of publications by naturalist societies throughout the country leads me to think that this practice is very common to-day, and it strikes me as a dull form of natural history. It does no harm and I am not quarrelling with it, but the people who engage in it seem to me to treat natural history as a business and to lose the fun, which they might get out of it, if they took the trouble to become more intimate with the creatures they saw and realised that birds and indeed all animals are individuals with individual tastes and characters.

Other visitors, with whom I found myself much more in sympathy, liked spending most of the day getting a really good view of a particular pair of birds and learning how they spent their time, and how they went about their business of rearing a family. Very few people seem to have acquired the art of using a glass or of accurate marking, and it is clear that good nest-finders are rare among naturalists. They seldom understand the importance of sitting still and of selecting the right place in which to sit—most of them will go wandering vaguely about, making a noise and preventing the birds from carrying on in their natural way. These criticisms will not, I hope, deter visitors from coming to Horsey, for as long as they enjoy themselves in their own way and do no harm the more that come the better.

Naturally photographers are frequent visitors. I like to encourage photography of wild birds and beasts, for it has done perhaps more than anything else to spread an interest in natural history among a wider public; but there are dangers inherent in it and some photographers that I have met have shown themselves either ignorant of, or indifferent to, these dangers. Coming generally on a short visit, they are apt to be in far too much of a hurry in moving hides up to the nests of shy birds, instead of getting the birds completely used to the hide before they start work with their cameras. Some of them, moreover, are not strict enough about the rule not to enter or to leave a hide without taking a companion to put them in and to take them out, when they leave. They are also apt to watch developments from far too close to the hide. The interests of the birds should come first, photographs second, and those who reverse that order give a bad name to an honourable profession.

I am shocked that so many modern scientific publications are unreadable, at any rate to most people. Authors who are or who are supposed to be scientific use a jargon which is extremely undigestible and, I think, quite unnecessary in particular in the matter of ologys. Ecology and other weird 'ologys may mean something to somebody but on the rare occasions when I take the trouble to look one of them up in a dictionary the word is generally not there at all, which makes me suspect that it has been invented in the idea that its use implies knowledge. It implies to me that the author is unable to write English which anybody can understand. This scientific jargon is on a par with Government slang: ' In this connection it is interesting to note,' ' discussions at the highest level,' ' fruitful collaboration,' ' contacting ' and all the other expressions which give me a stomach ache.

Any account of what happens at Horsey would be incomplete without some mention of the creatures which dominate so much of our lives—the two terriers, Jane and her son, Ginger (Plate 9). Due perhaps to an increase in voles, we were fortunate, at least in my view, in having a minor invasion of stoats in the spring and we made the most of them. One hunt stands out from the others, and my son, a boy friend and I were all there to enjoy it. So far as I can remember, we were supposed to be looking at birds, but we also carried a spade and the terriers hit off a stale line, which was obviously that of a stoat, for the dogs kept taking it over dead logs and through other places that are attractive to stoats. They kept hunting along the margin of dykes, which their quarry had hunted before them, and then turned into an extremely wet bit of country covered with tall reeds. When they reached a dead bush with trailing horizontal branches the pace suddenly increased, and no doubt the stoat had been drying himself on one of these branches. From now on they raced through the covert generally invisible, but we could occasionally hear the reeds rustling as they passed, and Ginger's exhilarating squeak kept us right when they reached a thick patch of sedge. Jane, who is normally mute, screamed as though in fury at not being able to force her way more quickly through the tangle.

They pushed the stoat out of the sedge, and after another turn all round the marsh, shot down the only more or less dry track through it and marked to ground on the track. The spade now came in useful, and since the ground was absolutely sodden it was clear that we should not have a deep dig. No other hole was visible, and once the stoat almost bolted out of the hole at which we were digging, but doubled back before Jane could grab him.

On such occasions Jane always seizes the best hole and Ginger is shouldered out to find the second best place. In this case there did not appear to be one and it looked as if one more spadeful would end the business. The stoat knew better, the hole ran in a circle and he bolted at the spot where we had started to dig. Ginger just got a view and plunged, but thick covert grew close all round and the stoat reached it safely, and off we went again, sometimes on land, sometimes in deep water; in fact, the stoat must have been swimming much of the time. There were many dykes of an unknown depth intersecting the marsh and we all fell at different times into them before the dogs hunted into a narrow promontory of sedge with short grass all round it.

They were obviously very close to him and we hoped that

he might be induced to go away over the open. He did, in fact, look out, but he funked it wisely and turned back along an overgrown bank. Here for a moment the terriers divided, and I fancy that we were wrong in going to Ginger, who had, I believe, changed on to a fresh stoat. Dark was coming on and the line lay into country more impenetrable and boggy than any we had encountered. We had been running for two hours. I was about beat and quite incapable of negotiating this new bit of country, and therefore gave the order to stop them. Somehow or other the two boys waded in and from the midst of impenetrable sedge caught the two terriers and carried them out in their arms. That hunt gave a good illustration of the staying powers of a stoat and of the difficulty of catching him in covert so thick that it was almost impossible for the terriers to get a view, but the moral of it is look out for holes that run in a circle. If we had remembered that we must have caught him.

In the hard weather of January-February, 1947, when the state of the roads kept me at home, I devoted some of my time to stoats. After hunting a stale line up to a hole in a bank, Jane marked and I began to dig, when I saw the orange foot of a mallard sticking up out of some dead reed, cut from the dyke and laid on the bank. Lightly buried in this litter was a freshly killed, fat and healthy mallard. There was no shot mark on it, but the bird had been seized at the back of the head and bitten all down the front of the neck to the breast, a small part of which had been eaten. I continued to dig according to Jane's instructions, and ten feet along the hole came upon a live but hibernating toad and another pair of wings, which I am practically sure were also mallard's. I was, however, in a hurry and so was Jane, and without further examination I covered them over with earth. Eventually the stoat bolted into the terriers' mouths and was chopped, which was very unfortunate, for he was a beautiful buck and would no doubt have given a great hunt, especially as his hole was in the middle of the cream of my country.

I took home the mallard, which we ate with relish, but how did the stoat catch it and still more how could he hold a strong healthy bird far larger and heavier than himself? I can understand a stoat making either a successful stalk or a successful series of clown's antics to within springing distance of a mallard, but even when his little teeth went home it is an extraordinary feat for such a small animal to hang on to a heavy bird that had, at least for the moment, the use of its wings. Perhaps it did fly and he hung on and flew with it until it fell.

Some years ago I found a freshly killed teal, also uninjured, dragged right down in a stoat's hole. Once in the snow near Norwich, a mysterious smooth track which I investigated was noticed in a garden. It led to a little hole in the snow under a bank, and in this hole was a freshly killed full-grown rabbit. I then followed the track backwards and found where the stoat had caught the rabbit, after a short chase. A careful examination of the mysterious tracks made by the stoat dragging the rabbit showed a series of semi-circular smooth depressions in the snow, some curved to the right, some to the left, with a few tracks of the stoat's feet showing clear of these depressions, but most of the feet tracks had been obliterated by the smooth track of the dead rabbit's body, pulled over the snow by the stoat. The semicircular depressions seemed to show that the stoat pulled its heavy burden in a series of jerks, sometimes directed by a righthand pull and sometimes by a left-hand pull. The snow was fairly deep and soft and it must have been a laborious business hauling the rabbit over a distance of about one hundred and fifty yards. I felt a little ashamed of removing the rabbit and taking it in to my hostess. I had no dog and could do nothing about the stoat that I had robbed of his lawful rations.

I have managed to teach Jane that in the spring when she winds a hen pheasant sitting on its nest it is bad form to catch it. She must just indicate its position and stand still. This is still too much for Ginger, and no doubt it is difficult to understand that you may pounce on any squatting bird in the winter, but that in the summer it must be left strictly alone. In most cases but not in all I was able to avert disaster.

Hares come and go in an astonishing manner in this marsh country. One week the marshes are full of them and the next there are practically none. In October I took the two terriers out alone without a gun and they found three hares during the afternoon. There happened to be a screaming scent and they ran into the first hare after half an hour—a nearly full-grown leveret. The second of the same size was killed in about the same length of time. The third was smaller and they caught it more quickly. I thought that was enough for one afternoon and we went home with our tails up.

Many people imagine that there are no trout in Norfolk but in fact several of its streams hold trout. There is a short length of the Bure at Blickling, near Aylsham, which runs from south-west to north-east under an abrupt bank. When the wind is north-west, fly floating down the stream from above is drifted by the wind along the surface close under this abrupt bank, and in such a wind but not at other times this stretch of water is worth watching. Some years ago I was there one morning when the wind was right and mayfly were hatching and drifting down, not in large quantities but just enough to excite my attention. After watching for some time it became evident that three fish were taking the fly very quietly as it trickled down within an inch or two of the bank. I slipped round to below the lowest fish and got into position, squatting against the bank, with Jane sitting by me quivering with excitement for she too had noted the rises. The first fish, who was not very big, did all that he ought and was caught, and that without disturbing the other two above him.

I then noticed that the upper of these two was something out of the ordinary: he was in the corner at the point where the current came round in a curl before flowing straight down by the steep bank, and now and again he made a deep sort of ' glok ' with his mouth when he closed it on a mayfly. Big fish are not very common on the Bure, and missing out No. 2, I crawled to within shot below the top fish, and waited again to mark his exact position by the next rise. He took a fly in a little bay within an inch or two of the bank and I managed to make mine hit a bit of overhanging grass just above him, and then with a little flick got it to fall off the grass and alight softly on the water. He took it perfectly and tore off upstream. Jane, who

knows all about the importance of big fish, and what they do
with a reel and line, flew along the bank, leapt into the water
and swam at a furious space after the trout.

Perhaps the fish took Jane for an albino otter, at any rate it
raced upstream and across and, flinging itself in a mad leap into
the air to get out of Jane's way, landed fair and square on a bit
of black sticky mud on the further shore, showing itself to be
a great fat yellow fish, if not 2 lbs., wonderfully close to it.
Jane, breasting the stream, was swimming for all she was worth
to get to the fish, and I had to make up my mind in a moment
what to do. She would, of course, grab and kill the trout that
lay gasping on the sticky mud, but what would she do after
that? Stop there and chew it to bits or try to retrieve it to me
and in the attempt drop it, particularly when she reached my
steep bank, which would be very hard to negotiate with an out-
size trout in her mouth? I forgot that, although at this place
the river was very deep and the bottom muddy, there was a ford
only about three hundred yards away that I could have waded
and reached her and the fish by running in about five minutes.
I did the wrong thing: I pulled that trout very gently back off
his bit of mud, from which he could never have got off by himself, and into the water, and worked him away downstream,
Jane swimming like a fury behind him.

As I walked away downstream, hauling the now beaten fish
after me, I came to the end of the steep bank and to a gently
shelving bit of mud—a suitable place for Jane to land the fish.
I held him there for Jane, but just as she was going to grab him
and end the business, the fish dived and got the gut hitched in
a great mass of grass that some fool of a bullock had half-
detached in slipping clumsily into the river, so that the grass
lay in a thick mat trailing under the water. Jane knew exactly
where the trout was, although she could not see him because of
the grass, and she trod water and dived repeatedly under the
surface to try and grab him. The gut was fixed in the grass so
that I could not pull it free and get the trout into open water
where Jane could see it. She continued to tread water and to
dive, and at last in her efforts struck the gut, probably with her

foot, and broke it. She was as mad with rage as I was but it was my fault, not hers, for pulling the fish off the mud where his terrified leap had taken him. Anyhow, but for that clumsy bullock kicking lumps of grass and bank into the water, the trout would have been ours, and he was about the biggest fish I ever hooked at Blickling. I never saw him again and he may well have died of shock at the sight of what he believed to be a furious white otter.

It is difficult to write with restraint about Jane, now nine years old, for life here would not be the same for any of us without her. She obviously feels for each one of us the same devotion (coupled with amusement at our several peculiarities) that we feel for her. Each one of the family is certain of the same welcome every time they return after a period of absence, and Jane has one or two other special friends whom she treats in almost the same way. One of them she connects partly, I think, with a long dog which he sometimes brings and provides combined sport for the two. Another has his home in Yorkshire where there are grouse and a large retriever, who is a friend of Jane's. A third is a lady, not connected with any form of sport but equally popular: they are very special people to her, and when she meets them she becomes definitely flirtatious. Like all animals, her memory is vivid: she never forgets either a friend or a place.

She once offended me deeply: it was at the birth of her first litter. At that moment she became for two or three days a wild animal: she disappeared from the house and was discovered secretly and furiously digging out a hole under a garden shed just like a vixen. Nothing would persuade her to return to the house, but at the last moment she was with great difficulty induced to have her puppies on straw on the floor of the shed instead of under it. She decided that only two people knew anything about puppies : the keeper, Mr. Crees, and our family nanny—a very good choice: none of the rest of us, including myself, was trusted at all. She even growled at me when I approached her hiding-place. I was very nervous, but everything went as it should and she was a perfect mother to her four puppies. Two days after their birth she became normal again and, rather shyly at first, began to take a pride in showing us her treasures. She was splendid at bringing them up and playing with them, and she and her son, Ginger, who is still with us, have never ceased to romp together. Her fitness is partly due to him for he is a dog that revels in a game, and he can still make his mother join him in the sport of coursing and rolling each other over on the lawn. Ginger goes in circles all round her, but Jane bides her time and when she does charge she seldom fails to catch him amidships and bowl him over. When in particularly high spirits, caused by my putting on old clothes, and in particular the right sort of boots, both of them roll about purring and gurgling at my feet, and Ginger gives vent to his feelings by rushing for one of his toys, old bones, my shoes and other objects, and throwing them over his head and down the stairs, pretending that they are alive.

In her later years Jane has become much more talkative. She practically never barks but has a pleasant little murmuring conversation which is perfectly easy to understand, and also other means of conveying her wishes, such as little taps on your elbow and wriggles round your legs: moreover, she can say almost anything with her eyes. Ginger's method of conversation is quite different—much gruffer and more abrupt. Whereas Jane asks, "May I come in, please?" he says, "Open the door," but Ginger has a first-class fund of humour and nobody takes his apparent grumpiness seriously. He is always on for a rag, either with Jane or with us or with one of his toys, and it is some comfort to feel that when the dreaded day comes for Jane to go, we shall with luck have something left of her in her son. We hope, too, that one day Ginger may have a daughter, but the difficulties of finding what I call a good terrier are enormous, and the creatures which are called fox-terriers in these days bear no resemblance to the real thing. Apart from their revolting appearance and their size, which makes it quite impossible for them to go to ground, they have no brains and no nose. I apologise for this violent diatribe, but it is about time that somebody pulled the leg of the modern terrier and the people who have produced it.

I had meant to end this chapter here, but the behaviour of a certain harrier, who dominated the parish of Horsey in the summer of 1947 needs recording. Obviously the same hen marsh harrier referred to earlier in this chapter, which had her eggs taken in 1946 and laid again, returned to the same marsh in 1947, accompanied by the best-looking cock I ever saw. His colour scheme of black, blue-grey and red-brown was so perfectly arranged on such a clear-cut pattern, that a neighbouring keeper wondered whether he really was a marsh harrier at all. Owing presumably to his dashing appearance, he acquired, shortly after his first hen had begun to lay, a second wife and settled her in about five hundred yards to the south of the first. I proved this to the hilt, for after passing prey just in front of me to hen No. 2, he picked up a reed and placed it in her nest, while she was eating her meal; then went off to another marsh, picked up a second reed and placed it in the nest of hen No. 1. A most unbecoming young cock then floated into view and tried to flirt with hen No. 2, but was, I am glad to relate, sent straight off about his business.

Another pair of marsh harriers settled on a different part of the property and all went well until the moment when the third chick had just hatched. Then the cock disappeared, and the hen had to start hunting for prey for her three chicks, and therefore failed to hatch the last two eggs. She seemed to be managing to find food for the three, but gradually they lost condition and it was some time before we discovered the cause. The cock marsh harrier owner of two wives was at that time feeling the full weight of his responsibilities for he was having to cater for two hens and seven chicks (three in one nest and four in the other). This was too much for his morals: in addition to legitimate hunting he took to scrounging or, to put it bluntly, he stole the kills of others. He was actually seen on several occasions to steal the kill of the marsh widow (I wonder if he had murdered her husband), and not content with that, he stole the kills of a pair of Montagus harriers who lived a little further to the south.

My main concern, apart from trying to ensure that no undesirable character should find their nests, was to induce the best-looking members of the party to sit for their portraits on convenient posts within camera shot of a hide. The result has been *nil*, as it generally is, but once if any one had been in occupation of one of these post hides, he would have had the chance of a life-time. An osprey which had caught a perch on the Mere, after first wedging the fish into the fork of a dead tree while he dried the feathers wetted by his plunge, finally decided that the most comfortable seat for his meal was that provided by me within 15 feet of a hide. There in front of the empty hide he slowly demolished all the fish except its tail, and then still more deliberately preened himself.

Eleven

SNOW

THE HARD WEATHER of February-March, 1947, and the long period of snow has induced me to end this book with a chapter on the effect of such conditions on wild creatures, and the chance they give to a naturalist to see things that are in other weathers hidden from him.

I should have thoroughly enjoyed this hard spell which, thanks to cancelled engagements, left me freer than I have been for months, but for the constant feeling of the straits to which animals and birds have been reduced by these exceptional conditions. The corpses of the victims were a constant reminder of the toll that was taken, and the corpses that one saw were a minute proportion of those that lay frozen on the ground. I kept wondering what had happened to the duck frozen out of our waters, to the bitterns, the herons, the water-rails, the woodcock, the thrushes, the fieldfares, the redwings, and all the hosts of birds that must find some soft place if they are to get a living. All this made me uncomfortable, and the small attempts to provide food for a lessening population in a minute area seemed, as they were, hopelessly inadequate.

Nevertheless there were compensations. Nothing shows up the life-history of animals like snow. On it they write their lives, and since my earliest days I have studied tracks, in particular tracks written in the snow. It may perhaps help other naturalists, particularly young ones, if I say something about the tracks of animals and birds and the way in which they show not only the structure of the creatures which make them, and their different paces, but their habits and the manner in which they get their living. I must, however, in all honesty warn readers that the next ten or twelve paragraphs take a bit of digesting. They need a background of snow with the tracks of different creatures imprinted on it.

As an instance, look at the difference between the track of a fox and that of a hare. The track of a fox, travelling at its normal pace—a walk—consists of a series of double impressions caused by the fact that each hind-foot at each pace comes down on the top of the impression made by the fore-foot, but not exactly; the hind foot comes down to the ground so as to cover about two-thirds of the track of the fore-foot that has left it; the impression of the hind-foot nearly but not quite overlaps that of the fore-foot, hence in every case a double impression—not as appears at first sight a single one. The impressions of the left and the right feet are almost in line because a fox, like a cat, is extremely narrow both fore and aft—through the chest and through the hind-quarters. A fox's track is ridiculously like a cat's, much more like a cat's than a dog's (a dog is much wider in the chest), but there is an obvious difference—a fox's toe-nails show plainly in front of the imprint of the feet, while no toe-nails show on a cat's track, because its claws are retracted when walking. I love the track of a fox; it has a purposeful look as though it were going on and on for ever.

The track of a hare (or of a rabbit or other rodent) is very different and conforms in all these animals to a certain type. This is due to the fact that their hind-legs are far longer than their fore, so that at each pace the hind-feet come to the ground beyond and outside the places where the fore-feet have been planted. They move, in fact, in a series of hops and not in a series of steps. The track of a hare, therefore, when moving at its normal slow rate, shows at each pace two larger impressions level with each other and fairly wide apart (the hind-feet) and *behind* and inside them, one a little in front of the other two smaller impressions (the fore-feet).

So much for the tracks of fox and hare moving at their slow and normal pace. When galloping, the tracks of both look very different. As pace increases, stride lengthens and the hind-feet of both fox and hare come much further forward, far in front of the fore-feet; the form of the two tracks is then more alike than at the slow pace, and indeed the gallop of the two animals is not very different, whereas the slow hop of a hare bears no resemblance to the walk of a fox. All that is shown in the tracks. With each animal the hind-feet at the gallop do not come down level with each other, nor do the fore-feet (as they used to be drawn by artists before the days of photography), and the distance between each set of four footmarks is much further apart owing to the lengthened stride. Although the form of track made by a galloping hare and fox are rather alike, there is, of course, no difficulty in distinguishing them by the shape of the actual footmarks; the rounder foot of a fox shows an imprint very different from the pointed foot of a hare.

The tracks of other rodents, rabbits, rats, mice, squirrels, etc., all show the same typical form of track caused by the structure of their limbs—longer hind-legs than fore, with the resulting movement by a series of hops. Rats and mice show the impress of the tail as a straight line behind each set of four impressions of the feet. A squirrel makes a pleasant track which is easy to distinguish. It moves in a series of bounds, long bounds if it is moving fast, and the hind-feet are very wide apart and reach the ground only just in front of and outside the place where the fore-feet have landed: its tail does not generally mark the snow, being held above it. In fact, a squirrel's track looks like a wide foreshortened rabbit's track. There cannot be any doubt about it, for if followed the track is certain soon to end temporarily at least at the trunk of a tree.

The stoat family, which includes otters, stoats, weasels, pine-martens and polecats, all make similar types of tracks, which show the structure of the animals and their method of travelling. They all have long bodies and four short legs, and their normal pace is a canter, and though they all can walk they seldom do. When cantering or galloping their feet all come to the ground near the same spot, so that at first sight each set of impressions looks as if it had been made by only two feet, whereas in fact it has been made by all four feet, the hind practically overlapping the fore-feet. The distance, particularly with stoats and weasels and their nearest relations, between each set of impressions is remarkably long, and when they are going at full gallop almost incredibly long for such small animals. That merely bears out the fact that, despite the shortness of their legs, there are no more beautiful movers or indefatigable travellers than the stoat tribe. Apart from other differences such as webbed feet, an otter has five toes whose marks can be seen on the ground, whereas a fox or dog has only four, the fifth being up the leg as a dew-claw.

Since deer, sheep and goats have been mentioned in this book, something shall be said of their tracks. The prettiest track, to my mind, made by any of these animals is that of a roe, which is very neat, narrow and pointed. In red deer the track of a stag, in particular a big stag, is much blunter and more rounded at the toes than that of a hind, whose hooves are narrower and more pointed. The footmarks of sheep, wild or tame, are relatively shorter than those of deer. To me they are rather dull-looking tracks, and so are those of goats, which have, however, feet of a more purposeful appearance. This is natural, for goats, wild or tame, are great climbers and know where to place and what to do with a foot. I have spent perhaps more time in tracking wild pig than any other animal. In a pig's track the two heels, if this is the right word, make clear marks in snow behind the foot, and all doubts will soon be dispelled by the constant marks of routling and also of wallowing and scratching against a tree.

In reading tracks, the first thing to remember is that the faster the pace at which the animal is moving, the longer is the stride and the deeper the impression. If the tracker will take first a few steps at a walk, then break into a run and look back at his own tracks, the difference in the two sets of footmarks will be at once apparent. The deepest impression of all is naturally made on landing after a jump.

The next thing of importance to learn is the difference between fresh tracks and old, and that is far more difficult to describe. Moreover, the appearance of tracks is enormously affected by the weather of the moment and the weather at the time when the tracks were actually made, and subsequently. Fresh tracks made

21. A convenient perch in the marsh, Norfolk.

22. Squirrels just before my visit and—

23. —about two months later.

Chapter Eleven
[*Photos : Joan Bridgman*

in powdery snow can be distinguished mainly by the colour of the snow displaced by the feet and scattered round the tracks. It looks much whiter than all the rest of the snow and, generally speaking, freshness of a track is partly denoted by colour or at least by shade. If there is bright sun shining on the snow or if it is thawing hard, a track will not look fresh for long. Even on dry pine needles the toe of a deer will turn over a needle and its under-surface will look a different shade from that of other needles which have not been displaced. Perhaps the best thing to say about the matter is, "Fresh tracks look fresh" and to leave it at that. They somehow look fresh on soil as well as on snow, and old tracks look tired and weather-worn. It is a thing that must be learnt by eye. I give up trying to write it. If there is any real doubt about the matter, droppings will probably be found, and their appearance will give a clue as to how long a time has elapsed since the animal passed that way.

I specially enjoy following the track of an animal that gets its living by the chase, such as a stoat, an otter, or a fox, for with time and patience it is almost certain that the tracker will come to a place where the story of a stalk or a hunt, and possibly of a kill, will be found written on the snow. While writing this chapter I went out in the snow for a short spell and happened to retrace my steps for two or three hundred yards under some scattered oaks. In walking back I heard some large bird get out of a tree, but the trunk prevented me from seeing it. Under the tree from which it had flown were twenty or thirty woodcock's feathers, but no track of a bird on the snow—nothing but the the scattered feathers. Of course, what had happened was that after I had passed the place some bird of prey, which had caught a woodcock, had carried it to the tree and was plucking it when I returned below the tree and disturbed it. It did not drop the body of the woodcock, and must have carried it away.

For the tracker, particularly if he is following in the wake of a hunting animal, there is always the chance of unravelling some riddle or of reading a detective story in the snow. He may come to a place where the fox he is following, as it quarters the ground in quest of prey, has stopped, then moved in a straight line and at a cautious pace towards some definite point. Then a sudden spring, and possibly at the end of it a little blood and a few feathers or a bit of fur.

Once while following the tracks of an otter for quite a short distance over ice and snow, I discovered that he had in that short space of time killed and eaten two hen pheasants and a mallard and then gone rollicking home down a dyke in a series of gallops and slides, for all the world like a schoolboy revelling in the sport of running through snow and sliding over ice.

The tracks of birds, which are almost impossible to see under normal conditions, are fascinating in the snow—in particular the beautiful fingering of their wings, where they get up and alight on snow. Birds' tracks are divided at least in my mind into two main divisions, the walkers and the hoppers. I like the appearance of the walker's tracks the best, and of these there is nothing better than a pheasant's steady, determined march. Each foot planted firmly down almost exactly in front of the last and at absolutely regular intervals, with neat impressions of the well-spread toes.

A woodcock's track is very pretty: a long toe straight to the front and a short one behind, with the two side toes pointing out at a wide angle, much the same as that of the side toes of a pheasant. There is never doubt for long about a woodcock's track, for in hard weather, even in the daytime, he progs for food with his bill as he walks and all along his track are holes in the snow. When he gets a bite he routles about with his bill and this makes a larger opening in the snow. The impression left, therefore, is a series of small holes in the snow all round his neat little footmarks with occasional larger holes. Some drawings made during the snow are given of the tracks of fox, hare, stoat, squirrel, otter, pheasant, woodcock and blackbird. I should have shown photographs rather than drawings but the latter may perhaps help to explain the text.

During the frost which has induced me to write this chapter I have had the luck to enjoy the sight of a woodcock day after day and almost all day on the lawn in front of my window, at varying distances between fifty and one hundred yards against

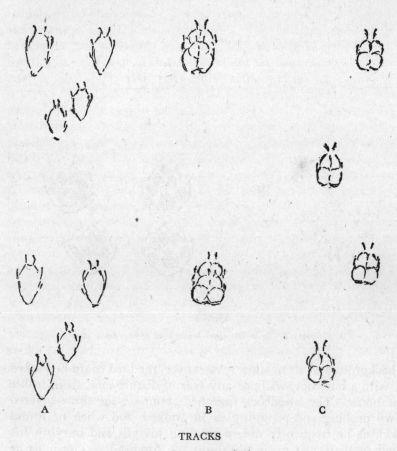

TRACKS

A.   *Hare moving slowly*
B.   *Fox walking*
C.   *Fox galloping*

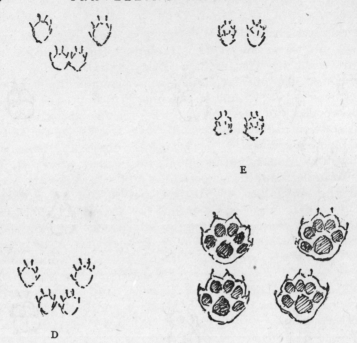

TRACKS

D. *Squirrel;* E. *Stoat;* F. *Otter landing out of river on to snow*

a background of clean snow. Moreover, the bird could be looked at with a telescope, without any fear of disturbance, from inside the house. The woodcock marched about on the snow-covered lawn probing and progging as he walked, and when he found food, as he frequently did, wriggling his bill and burying his head so that as it came up again the forehead was seen to be powdered with snow. He reminded me of an old man bent double picking up paper and orange peel with a spiked stick off a ' beauty spot.'

One morning while I was watching the woodcock, a blue tit, who was perhaps as much interested in him as I was, alighted by the woodcock on the snow. The woodcock obviously thought that this was cheek, for it raised both wings aloft and then jumped into the air and relit on the snow. The blue tit fled and that no doubt was what the woodcock intended it to do. In the afternoon of the same day I was again looking at the woodcock out of the window, when a kestrel stooped at him. The reaction of the woodcock to the stoop of the kestrel was exactly the same as his reaction to the blue tit, and so was the result—the kestrel lifted and flew away. The woodcock stood quite still and cogitated for some moments about this incident (so did I), but then it calmly resumed its operations: I did the same and went on writing. If another woodcock had arrived, it would, I believe, have done exactly the same thing, for these birds, like grey shrikes, robins and certain other birds, seem to have individual territories in the winter and object to the company of their own kind. One day the woodcock, noticing perhaps the collection of birds at the bird table, rose from the lawn and flew straight at the window out of which I was looking. Just as I was fearful of his crashing into the glass he swerved and lit apparently at the kitchen door.

Most small birds are hoppers, and make tracks with the two footmarks side by side, but there are exceptions. For instance, a wagtail walks and does not hop, while a starling generally walks but can hop. Pigeons walk on their short legs with a rather ridiculous waddle and make stupid-looking tracks with side toes planted at a narrow angle. Water-rails and water-hens make pleasant tracks, but those of a coot are ludicrous—almost more ludicrous than its actual feet, which are nevertheless useful paddles. A bittern makes an enormous track with long sprawly feet with the three tree toes displayed on a narrow front: even in its tracks a bittern cannot help looking like nothing on earth. A heron's track is similar, but the side toes are wider spread and the track does not look so ridiculous as a bittern's. The web feet of ducks make, of course, a tell-tale impression; there never can be any doubt what made their tracks. One could go on for ever about the various bird tracks, but this at least may be said for them—they are easy to learn. In hard weather a little food will attract a large company; individual birds can be seen to alight on or get up from a particular bit of snow and the tracks can be subsequently examined. There are of course far more bird tracks than animal tracks to be identified, and to attribute them all correctly takes time, but it can be done, for they can be seen, so to speak, in the making.

The best and longest day's tracking I ever had was in the Jura, just on the French side of the Franco-Swiss frontier. It was mid-winter, my friend Captain W. S. Medlicott was staying with me at Geneva and we decided to spend the week-end after pig. Accompanied by my terrier, Tinkle, we motored across the plain in the early morning in thick mist and left the car at the foot of the range. Snow lay right down to the edge of the plain, and as we climbed slowly up the steep slope covered with pine the snow got deeper and deeper. Having reached a considerable altitude, we turned along a narrow path which traversed the slope at the same level. Our object in doing this was to cross the tracks of pig which had fed during the night on sweet chestnut growing at the foot of the Jura and had mounted to spend the day in the fastness of the mountain forest.

Before very long we hit the track of a large herd of pig which had crossed the path in their climb up the slopes. Tinkle, who was held on a cord like a miniature Norwegian elk-hound, proclaimed that the tracks were fresh enough to follow, and in fact this was obvious to us as well, for snow displaced by the feet of the animals was brilliant white. One set of tracks was larger, wider and blunter than any of the others and sank deeper into the snow: it was clearly the track of a big old boar (un vrai solitaire). The pig had climbed straight uphill, and as we followed in the mist through the pines the snow got deeper and deeper.

Quite suddenly we emerged at about 3,000 feet from the mist and looked out to the east over the plain to the lake of Geneva and to the Alps. Below us was a great flat white sea of mist and above it glistening in the sun the mass of Mont Blanc, the castle of the Pic du Midi, the curved needle of the Aiguille Verte, and the whole battlement of the Alps. The mountains looked as if they were floating on the sea and every line of that majestic

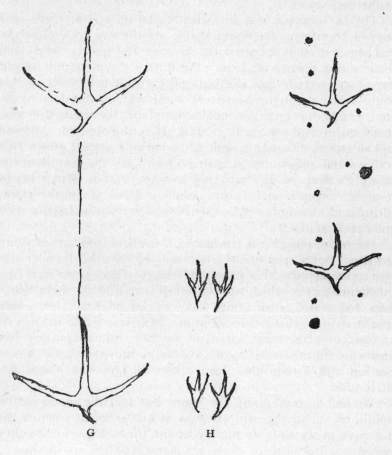

TRACKS

G.   *Pheasant*
H.   *Blackbird*
I.   *Woodcock*

company was brilliantly clear. We sat on the snow and gasped at the majesty of it.

Tinkle, however, was impatient to be up and at them, and we rose to take up the tracks again. As the day grew older the sun began to melt the snow on the trees and undergrowth, and there was a shower of drips. Pig dislike those conditions and our particular pig had climbed and climbed to get above this drip. When about three-quarters of the way up the slope to the crest and about 3,000 feet above the plain, the tracks led to a small spring and some soft ground. Here the pig had wallowed and scratched themselves against the bark of a great pine. This wallow and subsequent scratch is, I believe, the best moment of a pig's day. At any rate they had tarried, and Tinkle began to strain eagerly on her cord as she stepped along the track, tilting and waving her nose, ears cocked, every muscle taut, nose and nerves aquiver.

Presently some of the tracks ceased to climb and turned along the slope, but a brief examination showed that the old boar was not accompanying this party: his large tracks were with the other smaller lot, which had continued to climb. At this altitude drip had ceased, everything was gripped by frost, but every frozen twig in that dead-still atmosphere was liable to snap or at least to make some sound if touched; moreover, our feet scrunched on the frozen snow. We had to move with the utmost caution and Tinkle also seemed careful how she placed her little pads.

We had been climbing for hours, but still the tracks led on uphill, so that we began to wonder at one moment whether the pig were going to cross the top of the Jura. Then at last they ceased to climb, turned along the slope, and the tracks showed where they had begun to spread about instead of following on each other's heels. There was every sign that they were thinking of settling for the day or of pottering about to feed. We were getting close; the supreme moment might come at any time.

After crossing a steep, rocky ridge we came out on to a little bit of flat ground deep in snow and with some open spaces clear of trees. We were close to the top of the timber. The tracks led across the flat and Tinkle lifted her nose and sniffed, then pulled on her cord, pressing eagerly forward. She had got the wind of the pig direct and not merely of their tracks.

Moving dead slow, we began to cross the open flat towards some thick bushes beyond it and below some steep rocks, praying for some sort of breeze to ruffle the trees and make a sound to deaden our steps. There was not a breath, the silence could be felt. Then suddenly it happened. Twigs snapped, there was the sound of scrunching snow in the thicket ahead, a few galloping steps and then again dead silence. Tinkle bounded on her cord and whined, but we saw nothing—it was all over: they had got us and gone. A near thing, but we needed a puff of wind or some other spice of luck to get within sight of pig on a day when the smallest sound of trodden snow or scratched twig carried a certain warning, and pigs' ears are first class.

It is no use following jumped pig and the tracks showed that they had fairly galloped, so we began the long descent. In walking down a steep slope some frozen twigs flew back in my face and one of them caught my eyeball. It did not hurt much at the time, but in fact I had to spend a week in a dark room as the result and my eye was always liable to cause trouble at any time for several years. Anyhow that day was worth while, despite the bad luck with the pig and the damaged eye. The climb out of the mist into the brilliant sun, the panorama of the Alps, the long long track, the dead silence of the forest, and at last the scrunch of snow as the invisible pig jumped for safety.

Experience taught me that if I got one pig a year by fair stalking with a rifle in the Jura, I must consider myself lucky, but it was grand sport in glorious surroundings and muscles had to be strong to stand it. Moreover, the life-history of the pig, and there is none more interesting, was written on the snow.

The hard weather in England in 1940 and 1947 has taught me something about the effect of frost and snow on different creatures. I used to think that birds and beasts of prey were little affected by such conditions and it is true that they feel hard weather much less than most of the creatures on which they prey, but some even of these hunters have had to change their habits. In the frost of 1947, for instance, the owls and the kestrels at Horsey have found mice difficult to catch, and have certainly paid more attention to birds than they normally do; a little owl was seen to catch a small bird in full flight. The owls have hunted all day instead of at dusk and in the dark, and I have discovered at least one reason for this change of habit. One day the road through the village was so dangerous that we ourselves opened up some of the heaps of gravel to spread it on the icy surface, when the overworked roadman was unable to reach us. These heaps of gravel were full of voles, either hibernating or at any rate in a very sleepy state. Moreover, I noticed that, despite the large population of voles and mice, very few of their tracks showed on the snow. The owls and the kestrels did not get many chances to pounce on mice and had to look for other food, such as birds.

In 1940 the otters at Horsey remained but they turned from fish to fowl, and in 1947 conditions were so hard that they left us altogether and probably journeyed either to the coast for sea fishing or to the lower stretches of rivers kept open by the tide. A mysterious animal was reported in the middle of Yarmouth which I have no doubt was an otter. Just before the frost there were plenty of them at Horsey, and one day when I landed among reeds from a boat there were five corpses or remains of corpses of coots within a few yards, all freshly killed by otters.

Despite these instances of change of habit and of ground by birds and beasts of prey, it is true, generally speaking, that they suffer less than other creatures and in some cases find an easier living during hard weather. Otters love snow because, apart from questions of rations, they enjoy playing in it and sliding on ice. During the war I saw a mass of otter tracks on a frozen dyke, and six consecutive slides with one set of pad-marks between each, made by an otter apparently playing ducks and drakes with himself round a reedy promontory. Foxes, stoats and weasels can get a living although a frozen surface makes tricky stalking, so that they are apt to hunt more by day when the sun softens the snow and makes a silent approach possible.

I have on three occasions seen grouse in the act of migrating. Once from the high ground above Loch Killin in Inverness-shire, owing to snow at the beginning of October. They were passing high in large numbers. Once in Kirkcudbright, in September, when I saw a large pack of grouse come over a skyline, fly the whole length of a ridge, turn back along the same ridge and finally settle. They were, I think, changing ground in order to be within reach of ripe oats, or possibly to feed on bilberry on the ridge. The last occasion was the most interesting. On March 14, 1947, at 9 a.m., a pack of grouse flew just over my head at Netherwood, near Ilkley. They were coming from the direction of the Bolton moors and were making for Ilkley Moor. They must have flown at least four miles before I saw them and come right down or over the valley of the Wharfe. Soon afterwards more grouse took the same route and some of them looked tired, one landing under a bush in a hedge and others alighting in Fish Wood, which is well below the level of Ilkley Moor. There had been hard frost at night after a slight thaw and the snow was crusted, which no doubt made them change their ground. There was an average depth of two feet of snow at the time. Grouse are good burrowers and scratchers in snow and can stand hard weather much better than most birds.

When I first wrote this chapter in February I made various shots at what the result of the hard weather would be on wild creatures. The result has since become obvious, and the best plan seems to be to scrap the prophecies and give the facts. The crow family have come through almost intact. My garden pair of jays has survived and there seem to be at least the usual number of rooks and jackdaws, together with a superabundance of carrion crows. Pheasants have got through the frost practically intact for they are great walkers and great scratchers; indeed the numbers nesting in the parish are surprisingly large. The meagre stock of partridges seems about stationary and a starved bird was found dead.

Of the rest of the bird population, hedge-sparrows, meek and feeble though they look, seem to have been quite unaffected, and greenfinches and chaffinches appear to be in normal numbers.

We have got some goldfinches but nothing like the enormous quantity that bred in Norfolk in the summer of 1946. Normally in April great flocks of redwings and fieldfares take off from our bit of coast on their journey to Scandinavia. This year I saw one flock of eight fieldfares and two or three small flocks of redwings. The destruction among these two birds in England must have been terrible, and yet in the Sundal valley in June 1947 nesting fieldfares swarmed. Our song thrushes are reduced to far below a quarter, but blackbirds, although they have been hit, have stood it much better than thrushes.

Early in May I said to the keeper, "I heard a wren singing this morning at the back door." "Did you see it?" he said. "I should like that confirmed." I did not see another wren at Horsey until the autumn, and imagine that this was a cock searching for a hen, and that he searched in vain at Horsey and passed on. A few gold-crests passed through in March and April, probably birds about to brave the North Sea passage. Tits are supposed to be hardy, but one marsh tit that visited the bird table disappeared, great and blue tits were decimated and woodpeckers knocked clean out. I saw the first, a greater-spotted, in October 1947.

One bittern at least showed amazingly good sense. At some distance from the normal haunts of a bittern there lives a man who in the spring and summer has been invaluable to me as a watcher to preserve from human enemies rare birds that nest on my property. He keeps fowls and ducks and for their benefit he sees that a ditch which runs through his fowl-run is open every day. A bittern discovered the place and spent his days there; in the whole of Norfolk that bittern could not have made a better choice of host.

Both bitterns and herons seem to me extraordinarily stupid about hard weather. The distance they have to go on the advent of frost, in order to find open tidal water, is small. They could cover it by flight in under an hour and yet many of them put off the move, hang about getting thinner and hungrier until they die in the frozen ditch they have become too weak to leave. Our breeding stock of bitterns has been reduced to about one-quarter of last year's birds. Coots are equally stupid—a few of them have the sense to go, while the going is good, but most either take to grazing on marshes from which the snow has blown, but where grass is frozen and cannot be suitable for them, or just give it up and die one after the other. During the frost some open water appeared mysteriously in Horsey Mere and then suddenly froze up again. To one such temporary sheet of water many of the coots resorted. There was a sudden night frost and in the morning forty-eight corpses lay frozen in on the ice.

Mr. Crees saw, in the middle of April, a large flight of herons coming in from the south-east, and when they saw the marshes below them they all started to talk and to alight. They were, I presume, birds that had had the sense to go south in the hard weather, and were returning. Our residue of bitterns probably did the same thing.

Bearded tits rely in hard weather on getting grubs from freshly-cut reed bundles, and for this purpose flock to the reed-cutters while they are at work. In the last winter, snow and ice made reed-cutting impossible before about the end of March, and this has, alas, knocked the bearded tits practically out. Not one have we seen at Horsey and only a single cock has been seen at Hickling. In another county I have heard of one pair that had hatched a brood in May. Despite their remarkable powers of recovery and their normal habit of producing three broods a year, it is difficult to see how the meagre stock can repeople East Anglia. I believe there to be one pair of coots and one pair of water-hens in the parish, and water-rails have survived in just sufficient numbers to keep the stock going.

The few mallard which were foolish enough to remain in the neighbourhood eked out a precarious existence round the garden, in which the corpses of several were found. Sometimes part of a sewerage ditch at the back of the garden held a yard or two of open water, and this was presumably the attraction. When the thaw came however there appeared to be about the normal number of breeding duck, and in April for a few days large numbers of unpaired mallard wigeon and teal collected on a sheltered piece of shallow water.

The first birds seen to return were green plover; in fact they arrived a day or two before the thaw began. They certainly came from overseas and, remembering the annual migration of these birds from south-west to north-east across France in mid-March, I have little doubt that these plovers, which at once settled down on their breeding ground, were part of this migratory stream. In normal years there are plover in East Norfolk throughout the winter, which makes the advent of new arrivals difficult to spot, but at the end of this spell of hard weather there were none and the newcomers were at once obvious.

All this record of the result of the frost makes unpleasant reading and I do not like ending on a sad note what is meant to be a happy book. Two little creatures that entered this world a few weeks ago and are housed in the room where I am now writing supply a happier motif. They are even at this moment asking me to let them out of their cage to have a game. Two baby red squirrels were found lying in the snow at the bottom of a tree with a hole in it bored previously by a green wood-pecker. What had happened nobody knows, but there they lay, one of them apparently half-dead, his nose buried in the snow. They were taken into the house by Colonel and Mrs. Harry Bridgeman, and the house was Falloden, the home of historic squirrels tamed by Lord Grey.

These two little balls of fur were fed on milk sucked out of a glass tube and then on dry biscuit and a few nuts. They thrived and when I came to stay at Falloden about ten days later they were just beginning to play. That was three or four days ago; now play is hardly the word. After each of their three feeds a day they are allowed out of their cage in the drawing-room for about twenty minutes and that period of liberty is one continuous scuttling, bouncing romp.

Fear of human beings, or apparently of anything else, has not entered their heads; man or woman is a glorious plaything. From foot to knee, from knee to elbow, elbow to shoulder, shoulder to head and back again (I can't write fast enough to give it): round your neck, over your ears, into your pocket, up your sleeve: out again. Over the back of the chair, down the

leg, up again, with a ridiculous chortling ' hullo ': a peep at
you round the corner and then a leap on to the bookcase with a
violent scramble: another chortle (half grunt, half croak and
not unlike the sound of one of them landing after a leap), meaning, I suppose, "That was a bit of a jump: did you see?" When
angry, for instance at being caught and put to bed, they make
a noise rather like a sitting hen slightly disturbed. Then a battle
between the two of them on your knee or on whatever part of
your anatomy they happen to meet, suddenly interrupted for a
fit of ridiculous scratching done at amazing pace and usually at
parts of their bodies that no other animal could hope to reach.
Then off they go again, right way up and upside down, in a
fury of fun; playing hide-and-seek, scramble and jump, peep-bo,
king of the castle, and all the other games that we and other
animals know so well.

One day I tried the experiment of leaving the arm-chair in
which I had been sitting with the squirrels romping all over me
and it. They looked puzzled and annoyed. The great long, odd,
warm object with its funny angles and different surfaces of
cloth and skin, made for scrambling and jumping, was gone.
There were no hands to tickle them, no nails to bite at, no
glistening wrist-watch to play with; the familiar cliffs, abysses
and pockets were gone. It was not half the fun on an empty
chair. I returned at once and took my seat, when the games
began again with renewed abandon. The chair was not enough;
they wanted me as well.

Perched on a child's shoulder, one of the squirrels puts out
an inquiring fingered thumbless hand to test the feel of a mop
of hair. The little nails get entangled, the hand is withdrawn,
the squirrel sneezes violently, everybody titters and there is a
series of cascades as he races down and bounces across to me:
a bald head may be slippery but it is better than that tangle.
The squirrel perches on the arm of the chair, looks at my face
bending down to meet him, stretches up and examines my nose,
touching it with his own, his long soft whiskers questing and
tickling; then bounce and he is off again on a new voyage of
discovery and a romp with his brother. And so finally to bed;

curled up in their own tails, two little balls of fluff, wrapped in flannel in a box. The photograph on Plate 22 shows the squirrels (and the mop of hair) just before my visit. Plate 23 shows them about two months later.

What is going to happen to these red-brown imps? Already I hear that they are all over the place, up the curtains right to the ceiling, perched on a high picture-frame and demanding with a sharp tap of the foot to their human friends below, "Catch me, I'm going to jump." Their hostess writes, "I have become nothing but a nursery maid to squirrels." Soon they will be out of the room and out of the house; and they do not know what the word fear means. That is the danger. If a stoat or a cat or a hawk or a dog appears, they will probably want to play with it: they want to play with everything and everybody. I wonder whether they will ever learn that there are dangers in the world even for squirrels, and even at Falloden, where Lord Grey wrote *The Charm of Birds* and wild squirrels took nuts off his desk.

THE END